PRAISE FOR *BOTHEREDNESS*

Ripping read, cracking book. Full of fun and bursting with brilliant ideas. Every page fizzes with the same energy and inspiration I got from Hywel as a pupil twenty-five years ago. It is personally nostalgic because it's so recognisable and yet it is so timeless, and so vital for breathing life into lessons today. Makes me want to go back to school in the hope that every class buzzes like this. Read it, absorb it, live it, teach it. Top stuff.

Dan Johnson, BBC Reporter

Hywel takes being bothered about teaching to a whole new level in this wonderful book. It is brilliantly unique – it's neither a guide nor a 'normal' educational publication. Then what is it? In his own words it is a 'reverie' and he is right. Read it and you will be absorbed into a world where hilarious and often moving stories intertwine with educational research, where anecdotes and personal reflection will make you laugh out loud, where you will be inspired and motivated. You won't want to put this down, and you will find yourself being more bothered about teaching than you ever thought possible.

David Whitaker, Director of Learning, Wellspring Academy Trust, former Executive Principal, author of *The Kindness Principle*, Independent Thinking Associate

Botheredness could not be timelier in education! Weaving together pedagogy, philosophy, theory and creative curriculum, the book provides a critical space to reflect on teacher identity and the importance of the professional imagination. The book foregrounds authentic care, ethical and relational learning, articulating pedagogy in new ways which empower both teacher and learner. Grounded in years of professional expertise, Hywel provides powerful anecdotes of creative practice alongside versatile examples of curriculum design through story and drama. It is essential reading for any teacher in education who wishes to expand their pedagogical repertoire. Written with heart and wit – it is also an utter joy to read! Absolutely brilliant!

Lisa Stephenson, Senior Lecturer, Leeds Beckett University, Director, The Story Makers Company

Let's say ... as a teacher you only get out as much as you are prepared to put in. It is a truism: children work out what we are bothered about and how much we can be bothered about them. Hywel's book gets to the heart of good teaching as the right combination of method and warmth and the stories he tells will resonate. As you read the book, you will be reminded of the power of good teaching and will feel glad that Hywel has bothered to write it.

Mick Waters, educationalist and author

Talk about somebody who is 'bothered' about how children learn – Hywel Roberts! This is not a book about individual 'whistles-and-bells' lessons; this is a book about a whole school strategy that gets children invested in their learning and the curriculum.

Hywel has worked alongside Queens Church of England Academy for over twelve months, and this book epitomises the importance of using stories as an educational hook and stimulus. The pupils at Queens relish their learning and are able to make valuable links across the curriculum simply by embracing their imagination.

What more could a head teacher ask for than for her teachers to be 'bothered' about their teaching, and the children to be 'bothered' about their learning?

Thank you, Hywel.

Hannah Carvell, Head Teacher, Queens Church of England Academy

Botheredness is an illuminative, practical and uplifting book. In it Hywel describes how – through high expectations – children and young people can be 'protected into learning' so that they can become invested in what they learn and succeed relative to their individual starting point. Leaders of learning can enable this to happen by being warm, principled, alert, optimistic, authentic and compassionate.

Let's say you want to develop your art and craft and have some laughs along the way. Let's say you want to feed your soul and, maybe, feed Colin the lion too. Let's say you want to open a treasure chest that contains the experiences, stories and creative ideas of a travelling teacher. Then *Botheredness* is the book for you. Read it and you will be a better botheredness builder.

Professor Tim O'Brien, Professor of Psychology and Human Development, UCL, Institute of Education, London

This book places teaching where it should be: at the centre of a nexus of art and science and thoughtfulness and resourcefulness and practicality and dreaming and love. This is a book for all teachers and, let's face it, all human beings. Read it and grow.

Ian McMillan, writer and broadcaster

Botheredness is a remarkable book and one that only Hywel Roberts could have written. It is a brilliant combination of academia and anecdote, of evidence and experience, and is studded with cultural references.

It absolutely gets to the heart of what really matters if we want to enrich the lives of learners. It is warm, practical, entertaining, helpful and brave; all the things that mark Hywel out in all that he does.

And I am not just saying this because I get some nice mentions in the book, but I am honoured that I do.

David Cameron, The Real David Cameron Ltd

Botheredness is a book about rethinking how we teach children but will appeal to anyone that has ever taught, trained an apprentice, led a cookery class, etc. – the content has far broader applications.

In part a critique of the educational status quo, *Botheredness* is littered with engaging reminiscences of life on the educational coalface, simple tips to inspire young people and a healthy dose of pop culture. Hywel speaks with the authority of experience and the warmth of a veteran educator that never fell out of love with the romance of the profession. Like Hywel's lessons, *Botheredness* strikes the perfect balance between describing in detail a new path for teachers and keeping the reader (professional or otherwise) engaged and entertained at all times.

This book feels like sitting in a warm and welcoming hostelry with friends and colleagues, setting the world to rights and landing upon an exciting new idea. Hywel has given a lot to the teaching world and *Botheredness* sings with hope and aspiration throughout. A must for anyone who works or dabbles in education.

Arran Johnson, archaeologist and Training Excavation Director, York (GCSE English, Wackford Squeers, *Smike* (1998), Nick Piazza, *Fame* (2000))

Botheredness is a fantastic read not just for its content but Hywel's natural storytelling style which leads you through the book, keeping you fully engaged and unwilling to put it down. If you've worked in education or been educated to any level, you will enjoy this book.

Dan Sykes, principal villain in Hywel's first major musical production
(1998), now Asset Compliance Contracts Manager

I find it hard to write down the impact Hywel had on my life since being a very lost teenage soul in high school.

This book says it all though; the stories he writes down resonate with me and how my time went with him as a teacher too. I was somewhat lost throughout my last few years at school, and Hywel and another few teachers were really the main ones who rooted for me, took their time to understand me and pushed me to do better and never give up.

I have two children of my own now and still see what a profound effect having great teachers in your life can do and what course they can send you on.

This book isn't just for teachers, it's definitely food for thought for a lot of people.

Kate Sargent, Photographer (C in GCSE drama, Kingstone Secondary School)

I have just finished the book today and it has given me that energised feeling that brand-new teachers get when you first step into a classroom. Hywel was the reason I became a teacher. His enthusiasm shone through in everything he did. He told stories, he listened to our stories and most of all he was bothered by what we had to say. I wanted to be like that. I wanted to be bothered.

This book is brilliant for any teacher. New, old, inexperienced or near retirement. It's also very useful for others in education, from teaching assistants to further up the management scale.

If anything, it shows the reader that the most important element of working with young people is that to get the most out of them, you need to show that you are actually bothered. Bothered about what you are doing, bothered about why you are doing it, but most importantly you need to show that you are bothered about them.

Vikki O'Malley (GCSE drama), Head of Performing Arts,
The Market Weighton School

BOTHEREDNESS®

STORIES – STANCE – PEDAGOGY

HYWEL ROBERTS

independent thinking press

First published by

Independent Thinking Press
Crown Buildings, Bancyfelin, Carmarthen, Wales, SA33 5ND, UK
www.independentthinkingpress.com

and

Independent Thinking Press
PO Box 2223, Williston, VT 05495, USA
www.crownhousepublishing.com

Independent Thinking Press is an imprint of Crown House Publishing Ltd.

EU GPSR Authorised Representative
Appointed EU Representative: Easy Access System Europe Oü, 16879218
Address: Mustamäe tee 50, 10621, Tallinn, Estonia
Contact Details: gpsr.requests@easproject.com, +358 40 500 3575

Edited by Ian Gilbert.

British Library Cataloguing-in-Publication Data
A catalogue entry for this book is available from the British Library.

Print ISBN 978-178135409-4
Mobi ISBN 978-178135421-6
ePub ISBN 978-178135422-3
ePDF ISBN 978-178135423-0

LCCN 2022943038

Printed and bound in the UK by
Halstan, Amersham, Buckinghamshire

This book is dedicated to Maria and Tom Roberts, my loves.

And to my mum, Dorothy Anne, for whom every day is still an adventure.

And my late dad, who took me to see *Jaws* when I was 5 and my life changed forever.

The past always seems better when you look back on it than it did at the time. And the present never looks as good as it will in the future.

Jaws, **Peter Benchley (1974, 109)**

FOREWARNING

Before reading this book:

1 Brush up on your Northern dialects. You're about to be immersed in the best blend of Lancastrian and Yorkshire – a peace treaty of an accent. An audio book without the audio.

2 Don't drink hot drinks while reading. You'll spit them out.

3 Have all those old, nostalgic DVDs, CDs – dare I say it – cassette tapes and vinyl handy. This book is going to make you want to watch and listen to them all again. Which brings me to …

4 Take your time. This is a reverie with many digressions. Wallow in them.

5 Have a box of tissues handy. There are stories in this book – ones that make you feel like you have something in your eye.

6 Smile. You're about to be reminded of the good things in life. And God knows – we all need that right now.

Most of all, enjoy. I did.

Debra Kidd
(the one lucky enough to work with this wonderful human being)

PREFACE

Just so you know: this is a book for teachers. All teachers.

Hello. Before we get going, I just need to share with you two things. The first is a quick story about a little boy called Maxwell.

I'm working closely with a special school supporting children with their behaviour. It's a social, emotional and mental health setting, and it's trying to get a handle on its curriculum. I find young Maxwell sitting on the floor outside his classroom. He's booting his ankles against the floor, annoyed and wound up by something. He clocks me and moans, rolling his head skyward.

'Are the pedagogical approaches of the class teacher not to your liking, young man?' I don't ask. Instead, I say, 'Ay up, Maxwell! What's to do?'[1] It's a more human approach, I have found.

'I'm sick of them,' says Maxwell.

'Who? The class?' I motion to the closed door of his classroom.

'No! I'm sick of *them*!' And he points to the wall opposite us.

As I follow his finger, I see what he's pointing at: a beautiful display about the Romans.

'Are you sick of Romans, Maxwell?' I ask, smiling inside.

'Yeah. Sick of them.' He boots his ankles again.

Trying to avoid navigating some obvious Monty Python schtick, I ask, 'What have they done to you?'

Maxwell looks at me. 'Mr Roberts,' he says quietly, 'they're ages ago.'

---

1 We are in the North of England, UK.

And he's right. They are. The teacher can tick that one off when I tell her. So, the challenge is this. How do we get Maxwell *bothered* about the Romans? How do we build 'botheredness' across a curriculum, across a classroom, across a school?

And that is the point of this book.

Now for the second thing. When asked what they want it to be like to be taught by them, a group of novice teachers responded:[2]

I want it to be engaging and fun

Fun, exciting, varied and engaging

Inspiring a desire to explore and to ask questions

I would like to be remembered and stand out for the right reasons

I want to be seen as fun, but also taken seriously

Approachable

Fun, insightful, thought-provoking and inspiring

Memorable and inspiring

I want people to be able to talk to me positively and be encouraging

Engaging but focused

Inspiring and creative

Creative and fair

Inspiring, fun, exciting … not shouty or intimidating

I want my teaching to be meaningful

I want students to be excited to come to my lessons. I don't want my lesson to be the one they dread!

Open, engaging and child-focused

---

2   This was during an online 'new teacher' event where delegates were invited to respond to the question 'What do you want it to be like to be taught by you?' It's a good session starter. It's my first gift to you. ☺ Please get used to reading the footnotes. There are tons of them.

I would like my lessons to be interesting and fun and the kids to see me as someone who can help

I want to be approachable, engaging and know my subject inside and out

NOT boring or toxic

Engaging, memorable and thought-provoking

Inspiring, approachable, has empathy and understanding

Interactive and promoting further interest

Inspiring and reflective

Engaging, fun, inspiring, creative – but approachable and serious when needed

Fun, to bring out their inquisitive side and be memorable

I want to be the reason my class enjoys my lessons

Steady and humorous

Memorable

Challenging and enjoyable

Relatable

Produce a fun and engaging environment for learning

I want it to be a safe place to ask questions

Encouraging self-development

I want to be interesting but also effective at ensuring learning takes place

Interesting – not dull

Relationships are key

Engaging

Allow pupils to feel confident, both in their learning and in themselves

If you're reading this as a hugely experienced teacher or leader, these statements may smack of naivety. When we're seeking new teachers, however, it's interesting that these are exactly the sorts of things we're looking for in new professionals, aren't they? We want colleagues to be excitable puppies. We want them to be bothered. We want them in our own image. We want them to be bothered because we are.

Cheers,
Hywel

ACKNOWLEDGEMENTS

A cast of heroes in no particular order:

The Real David Cameron, Catherine Sanders, Dave Whitaker, Professor Rachel Lofthouse, Dr Lisa Stephenson, Phil Beadle, Laura Boyd Jones, Professor Tim O'Brien, Bandwagon, Martin Illingworth, King Creosote, Tim Taylor, Karen Ardley, Ed Southall, Tom Wallace, Kathryn Dunne, Professor Mick Waters, Ross Williams, Sir Tim Brighouse, Shonette Bason Wood, Simon Barber, Jaimie Holbrook, Richard Gerver, Darren Holmes, Paul Bateson, Richard Kieran, Michelle Storer, Andy Moor, Emily Reid, Hannah Carvell, Lisa Hinton, Paul Dix, Karen Burrows, Sarah Mitchell, Craig Clarkson, Dr Hereward Brown, Manic Street Preachers, Andrea Taylor, Ed Dorrell, Sarah Smith, Mandy Roberts, Sam Bailey, Hans Zimmer, Tina Farr, Keziah Featherstone, Vest and Pants, Sian Rowles, Will Wareing, Tom Sherrington, Jane Hewitt, Becky Carlzon, Matthew Milburn, Mary Myatt, Steven Spielberg, The Jolly Boys, Sir Elton John, Sir Ken Robinson, Daryn-Egan Simon, Ed Finch, Alan Brown, Pep Diiasio, The Maddens, The Rookes, The Beagles, R Daz and Stewart Lee. Hi to Jason Isaacs!

A shout-out to the alumni of Bretton Hall College, Wakefield, West Yorkshire. A place of dreams. A time gone.

With much affection to my pal and fellow pedagogical nomad, Dr Debra Kidd. I really appreciate her great company, kindness, knowledge, laughter and all-round botheredness about the stuff that happens in our schools. She also gets a round in.

Thanks to the crew at Crown House: David Bowman, Amy Heighton, Tom Fitton, Beverley Randell and Jonathan Richards. Also, my brilliant copy-editor Catherine Gregg.

Finally, my friends at Independent Thinking, particularly Ian Gilbert, Dave Harris, Rachel Davies and Nina Jackson.

CONTENTS

CARPE DIEM

CUE MUSIC: Hans Zimmer's *Interstellar* should do it.

CAPTION:

A reverie

It's got great crescendos and plenty of drama.

A CAPTION ABOUT THE CAPTION:

Reverie: to be pleasantly lost in one's thoughts – a daydream;

an instrumental piece suggesting a dreamy or musing state

The year blazes across the screen like it's
Lethal Weapon 2 or something:

~~1989~~ *1989*

(You can stop all this now, Hywel. Thanks – Ed.)

INTRODUCTION

1989

I went to the cinema with my pal Craig to see the new Robin Williams movie *Dead Poets Society*, which we expected to be a laugh-riot; a hoped-for echo of Williams' previous tour-de-force, *Good Morning Vietnam!* As soon as the director's name flashed up on the screen, and being a bit of a film nerd, I realised we were going to be offered something very different to what we'd expected. Peter Weir, an Aussie movie director, had previously served up such delicious cinematic treats as *Witness*, *The Last Wave* and *Picnic at Hanging Rock*, which I'd devoured courtesy of BBC2 and its late-night Alex Cox-helmed *Moviedrome* series. Look it up.[1]

When I stepped out of the cinema, I turned to Craig and said, 'I know what I want to do with my life' – dramatic pause – 'I want to be a teacher of literature in a 1950s American private school.'[2]

My pal looked at me and grinned, munching the last of the Wheat Crunchies from a crumpled-up bag he'd retrieved from his deep pocket.[3]

'The children are going to carry me on their shoulders as we run through the golden fields to the soundtrack of Beethoven,' I continued, 'and I'm going to laugh and hold my hands up to a sun-drenched Heaven.'

'Captain, my Captain,' sighed Craig, quoting a memorable line from the movie we'd just watched. He then pointed at a rusty-coloured car pulling up. 'Lift's here.'

....

1   The *Moviedrome* series was on BBC2 in the late 1980s with Alex Cox and, later, the great Mark Cousins. Both experts, they took your hand, Sherpa-like, and guided you through the dark and less-trodden paths of cinema. For each film they did an introduction that would, for me, absolutely suck me in. Cox, a lanky, awkward-looking fella, was brilliant. He introduced me to *The Wicker Man* and *Witchfinder General*, and I never looked back. He's basically the reason this book on teaching is dripping with movies. Cox built my botheredness like no tomorrow. He was inspiring, knowledgeable and loved his subject. Like what all good teachers should do and no mistake, yeah? See https://www.youtube.com/watch?v=K8IGJjukTzc.
2   See Ohio State University (2021) for a scientific reflection on the impact of moving and emotional films.
3   Wheat Crunchies are a brilliant food that bridges the texture gap between a Wotsit and a bog-standard crisp.

I looked and there was my dad behind the wheel of the Allegro,[4] pipe in mouth, sucking on St. Bruno Ready Rubbed pipe tobacco. Old school. He tipped a nod, and I couldn't wait to tell him about the film. He was a teacher, after all. Old school. He was buzzing, my dad. Other than Alex Cox, he was the most important man in my life at this point.[5] He, too, was really good at botheredness. Good adults are.

. . . .

CUT TO:

1992

Via a life-changing and wonderful English degree, I found myself staying on a year at Bretton Hall College in Wakefield, West Yorkshire, to do a postgraduate certificate in education (PGCE) so that I could be a secondary English and drama teacher.[6] My roots were down, and I was committed to a classroom career. I also didn't want to go back to Manchester and be a burden on my parents – today I know many teacher trainees and early career teachers don't have this luxury of choice, but I did.

As we went through the training year, I realised that actually it was all _very hard indeed_. I'd put a postcard depicting the film poster for *Dead Poets Society* on the front of my training journal (remember, this is the early 1990s, so no memory sticks, Facebook or email – they were things of the future. A twinkle in someone else's eye). The training journal was a sort of professional diary chronicling the teacher/writer's reflections on all things teaching and learning. The first time I was required to hand the journal in was midway through my first teaching placement. I handed it in to my tutor, hoping he'd see the movie postcard glued to the front and peg me down as a liberal, passionate educator who wanted the best for the children in his care. I wanted

---

4   The Austin Allegro. A car for the discerning motorist.
5   He would go on to assert his status as number one fella later.
6   Bretton Hall College: past students include Sir Ken Robinson, The League of Gentleman, Kay Mellor, David Rappaport, Gillian Wright, John Godber, Mark Thomas, Colin Welland, Louisa Leaman, amongst many others. The place amalgamated with the University of Leeds whilst I was mid-degree and eventually closed down in 2007. Going there changed the course of my life. There's a good radio documentary here with John Godber about the wonderful place: https://www.youtube.com/watch?v=zgvkM3YxAZ0&t=45s.

him to know that I was bothered. And also, that I'd be very happy to have kids carry me through orange fields to the stirring soundtrack of Beethoven.[7] When the tutor handed me the journal back, he'd torn the postcard in half, leaving one limp half glue-sticked to the cover. Robin Williams had been vandalised. I found the other half inside my journal. On the back of the abused scrap, the tutor scribbled

Like I needed telling. I was on teaching practice in Dewsbury,[8] teaching poetry to teenagers who stood on chairs for all the wrong reasons. I realised very quickly that teaching was nothing like it was depicted in *Dead Poets Society*. It wasn't genteel, well photographed or poetic; it was dark mornings, poor planning and, occasionally, cruelly dispiriting. Like space exploration, mistakes came thick and fast, but the journal writing helped. I started to see some themes emerge – things that would help me navigate a lesson, a hard day, a pressured week, a long placement.

I was learning a craft. An art. A profession. And I liked it.

---

7 I'm very keen on this visual from *Dead Poets Society*. Just go with it.
8 Birthplace of Bartholomew Binns – hangman for the City of London and Middlesex, 1883–1901.

. . . .

CUT TO:

Now (aka The Present)

This is an education book, but not one that's going to tell you what to do minute by minute, lesson to lesson. There are no silver bullets. Anyone who tells you there are is lying. You won't even find a scheme of work in here – some planning ideas for sure, even a template or two, but there's no spoon-feeding. There are no curriculum rules to follow or new acronyms to get stressed out about. It's just a book that's inviting you to consider and reflect on where you're up to in your own educational journey, be you a parent, a teacher or a student. Or, indeed, all three. You might be thinking the teaching profession is for you or you might be working with children or young people in a context other than a school. I want to help you texture your understanding of what it is to lead learning and thinking – to develop knowledge acquisition with warmth and optimism. With botheredness.

When I wrote my first book for teachers back in 2012, I didn't realise how much it was going to resonate with the classroom practitioner. And so, years later, here I am writing another. It's not a sequel to *Oops! Helping Children Learn Accidentally* (2012); rather a next step. Some more provocation and optimism for the professional constantly being told they're in crisis.

Crisis?

Yep, there's a crisis. A crisis of faith in learning, children and curriculum. I think so anyway. Especially when I've a harried Year 7 science teacher sitting in front of me telling me that, as an area of potential study, 'virus' is dull to deliver. It's like COVID-19, *World War Z*, *Resident Evil*, *Night of the Living Dead* and *Plants vs. Zombies* have never happened, right?[9] Something's gone wrong, and whilst it's nobody's fault, we're all to blame. We're all carrying the can for the erosion of the professional imagination.

If the *Oops!* book cleared back the nettles from the path for some, this book is intended to take things further; to offer opportunities to think beyond a path laid out by scripted lessons, downloadable schemes and slavish quick-fix fads, and perhaps

. . . .

9   I just couldn't ignore the pandemic that shook the world in 2020. It seems stupid to pretend it
    doesn't exist.

move into more uncharted territories (which is, incidentally, the title of the book I wrote with Dr Debra Kidd in 2018). It's a search and examination of the road less travelled, backed up with my own experiences and research down the rabbit hole of contemporary education. And films. There's mention of them as well. They're cultural touchstones, aren't they? Like music.

I do want to get children and young people ready for jobs that haven't been invented yet, but I also need someone to service my car, fix my boiler and give me advice on soft furnishings. I want to be reassured, humoured and supported by people; people who are good.[10]

I hope I'm clear enough when I say that I'm no longer a full-time teacher. I do, however, teach. For a long time, I was a secondary teacher (for ages 11–16) delivering English language, literature, drama, media studies and, for one year, due to an unfixable timetabling error, German. I didn't know what pressure really was until that latter incident. The only German language I knew had been gleaned from *The Eagle Has Landed* and *Kelly's Heroes*, and that, to be fair, was pretty limiting and probably another story for another day. All this unfolded in the flippin' fine town of Barnsley, South Yorkshire.[11]

I resisted the temptation to go into senior leadership but retain much admiration for those that do. I was an untrained middle leader for a number of years. I enjoyed the role but probably didn't realise how important the middle-leader role was going to become in schools today. I thought I just needed to spend the meagre budget on pens, paper and, if we were feeling flush, a new hole punch. My heart belonged to the classroom, however, and, in the spirit of Dweck's (2017) growth mindset (but probably not what she means), I eventually resigned my post and left my school. I think many of my friends and colleagues thought I was having some sort of breakdown, but, in reality, I just had lots of questions and was curious for answers. Sometimes, in order to grow, I suppose we have to take some risks and stick our heads above the parapet. This is what I felt I did. I was brave, took a risk, and my family egged me on.

I now teach in a variety of settings, practising what I preach. I model the approaches outlined in this book. Not *model* in the Vivienne Westwood sense of the word but in

10 People like The Real David Cameron, from whom I've shamelessly borrowed this sentence.

11 My spiritual home and site of my professional upbringing. Also birthplace of Brian Glover, a great actor, teacher and one-time wrestler (Leon 'Arris, the Man from Paris), famous for roles such as Chess Player in the mint *An American Werewolf in London*, the Armourer in *Jabberwocky*, and, of course, Mr Sugden, the cruel physical education (PE) teacher in *Kes*. I'd suggest the latter is one of the greatest films about childhood and school ever made. More on that later. Shaun Dooley is also from Barnsley and he's really good 'n' all.

the continuing professional development (CPD) sense, where I'll teach a room full of children I've never met before with professional adults watching and participating; CPD on steroids, I call it.

The examples in this book will draw from all settings – primary, special and, of course, secondary, as I'm still a secondary teacher at heart. The only thing you'll have to do, dear reader, is think and reflect. By that, I mean put all of it through your filter. An example of working with children in a behavioural school context should still have resonance to the mainstream teacher, unless, of course, we're totally institutionalised and can't see the wood for the trees. As a secondary teacher, I've found much to learn in the primary and special settings. This will be clear as I take you through some of the strategies that I've discovered to be, well, universally successful across the stages of learning (in my universe, at least) with children in their classrooms.

I mention middle leadership and I don't do it lightly. Middle leadership has become _the_ tier that actually makes things happen in any school that act. I say to school leaders, look after the middle leaders and your school will become the place you desire it to be. I ask middle leaders not just to swallow the spoon-fed instructions of their leaders but to offer developing wisdom and insight into classroom practice through a filter that places school values before structures. Middle leaders are the people who make things happen. They quality-control, give permission and set the tone. They're also under enormous pressure from everyone else. If you're a middle leader, I hope this book helps you and reminds you why you took the role on in the first place.[12]

School leaders set the tone of their school. They also give permission to their staff to deliver the most appropriate lessons to their pupils. If you're a school leader, I hope this book helps with continual innovation and improvement in your setting.[13]

If you're a teaching assistant, this book will support you with strategies and ideas to employ appropriately with the children who need the nettles clearing back more than others. I hope it'll also give you the genuine confidence to support the colleagues you're working alongside.[14]

....

12 I see middle leaders as the Keanu Reeves (circa _John Wick_) of the pack. Don't mess with his dog or he'll kick your ass. Try not to see yourself as either Bill or Ted and definitely don't project these latter personas to your pupils.

13 You're basically Sigourney Weaver in _Aliens_.

14 Teaching assistants need botheredness and many of them are the real deal, but we know there are those, like in leadership and in the classroom, who just don't get it. If you're a teaching assistant and you're reading this book, you already get it. You're basically Clint and make my chuffin' day.

And then there's the classroom teacher – who may also be a school leader. Or a middle leader. Or the acting special educational needs coordinator. Or in charge of literacy across the curriculum. You're the adult in the room who's constantly developing their repertoire to meet the ever-changing sea of faces in front of them. I hope this book liberates your thinking and returns to you the excitement that you felt when you decided to enter the profession in the first place. I want to help you reclaim your professional imagination.[15]

This book isn't like other education books out there. Don't get me wrong, there are a huge number I admire and won't be without – I'll provide some recommended reading later – it's just that I want this book to capture the essence of the approaches I'm sharing.[16] To this end, I've punctuated the book with a number of stories from my #TravellingTeacher column in the *Times Educational Supplement* (*TES*).[17] They're short snapshots of teacher life and reminders to us, I think, of what is important in teacher-to-teacher and teacher-to-pupil dynamics, amongst other things. I've put them in for you to enjoy, but don't interpret that as a direct instruction. The stories bring life to the ideas I'm sharing here.

I'm not trying to be either contentious or polarising with this book – I just want to report back to you and show what I've found out teaching in classrooms of all shapes and sizes all around the world, and the pedagogy that underpins the work.[18] I hope it resonates with you and perhaps reminds you of why you went into the job in the first place.

Dig in.

---

15 Just like little Billy Casper not wanting to go down no pit, I didn't want to leave the classroom. It's where it's at. Whenever I speak with great leaders, they tell me they miss the classroom. We all do, those of us who bailed. That's how important it is. Folk may be being paid more than you, but you're **doing the teaching**. Everyone else is there to supposedly make it easier for you. I know! I know! To me, you're Morgan Freeman in everything. A sage. Crack on!

16 You could do worse than check out what Independent Thinking Press offer if you need a reading list.

17 All the stories were originally commissioned for *TES* by the lovely Brian Blessed-like Ed Dorrell (@Ed_Dorrell). An archive can be found here: https://www.tes.com/magazine/author/hywel-roberts.

18 Interestingly, and tellingly, a review of this book in an earlier form appeared on Amazon whilst it was still in my head. That is before it was published! The damning sentence accused the unwritten book of being 'boring' and 'dated'; two words that are banned in my house, never mind the schools I work in and with. What the review demonstrated wonderfully was that education is, and always will be, a polarising and contentious world of debate and disagreement, where some prefer to snipe rather than show. It basically attracts nutters.

CHAPTER 1

CONCERNING BOTHEREDNESS

1 ....
....

2 ....
....

3 ....
....

If you stand for nothing, you'll fall for anything.

Anonymous proverb[1]

Okay. _Three words that sum up education for you. Go!_ In order to unpick any approach to education – dry, normal, greasy, traditional, progressive, Jedi, old skool – one must settle on some unshakeables, some non-negotiables. Some values we can hang on to. These are the agreements we have with ourselves in our own heads – principles that inform our own practice. When crazy Uncle Pete,[2] who likes Stella Artois and can't hold down a relationship, corners you again at the family event – the wedding, the funeral – and challenges you again on the ins and outs, ups and downs of state education, these are the words you may stutter back at him as he suggests being hit across the arse by a sweaty 50-something male as it never did him any harm.

He's an expert.

Because he went to school.

Uncle Pete's argument is solid in his head and your words back to him might sound like jazz-hands fluff, but don't worry about it. He'll call you a 'snowflake' or 'woke' and then moan that he wasn't allowed to go to university. Uncover them, your three words, and use them to arm yourself against the uninformed, the ignorant and the powerful. Fight on the bridge of educational misinformation for these words. They're yours. They're what make you bothered.

----

1 A number of potential sources have been suggested for this proverb; see O'Toole (2014).
2 This is a real person in real life and everything. If he were in a movie he'd be played by Steven Berkoff. He's a baddie.

I'll tell you my three words in a moment. But first I should explain the title of the book: *Botheredness*. Let's say that in your class sits Maisie and she's a real sweetheart. You're starting a topic on Ancient Greece and Maise's so excited because that's where she's going on holiday in the summer. And when you did Romans, it was cool because her family piled into their Volkswagen camper van and off they went to Hadrian's Wall for the whole weekend. It's splendid for lovely Maisie. She's buzzing and bothered. Her parents are ace and fair play to them for being bothered.

Amber isn't that bothered though. Amber hasn't got a bed or a mum. She hasn't really got headspace for Hadrian, walls or Romans. She's got enough on. Besides, these walls and ancients are just _so_ long ago. They tell her nothing about her life. They're a mirror that reflects nothing. A challenge for you then, as Amber's teacher, is: how are you going to get her bothered? How are you going to make it all matter?

'Botheredness' is a word I wrote about in *Oops!* to sum up the levels of authentic care and 'unconditional positive regard'[3] I witnessed whilst working at a social, emotional and mental health (SEMH) school in Barnsley, South Yorkshire. It's classroom/institution-level monkey-giving. And it's instilling it in the children. Giving it to them. Wrapping it up as a gift. It's real, deliberate and on the money. What it isn't is soft. To exude botheredness, you have to be an authentic professional. Basically, it's ensuring schooling is about children. That shouldn't sound weird, but as I write this, I feel it might come across as strange to some. I think it's strange I'm having to write it down.

Also, file botheredness under modelling interest, enthusiasm, optimism, values and manners. It's seeing the whole child. If you've got botheredness then you're a teacher who will have impact beyond the subject coverage. You'll be the role model for the child, a significant adult, a carrier of warmth. It's the opposite of cold survivalist and defensive classroom approaches – more on that later.

It's also about _you_.

And it's the title of this book. It's that important.

Again I'll say it: it's why you became a teacher in the first place.

---

3   Carl Rogers, the eminent humanistic psychologist, coined this beauty. Not to be confused with the other Carl Rogers who produced the movie *Blade Runner 2049*. For more information on unconditional positive regard, see Gobir (2021) and for a good article on its application in a school context, see Halliday (2018).

So, _three words_ to offer to Uncle Pete. Well, here are mine; experience distilled, like fine whiskey, into three cool words:

Stories

Stance

Pedagogy

Whilst you're thinking of your key three words, I'll explain these. Put some flesh on the bones, if you like. My uncle Pete won't tolerate their lightness or, indeed, their weight. That's because, like many secretaries of state for education, he's never stood where we've stood. He's never felt the rush of joy at getting a decent set of results or, indeed, the despair of finding the computer suite double-booked. He hasn't, to paraphrase Brené Brown, stood in the arena (think _classroom_) getting his arse kicked. Therefore, whilst being totally entitled to it, his point of view is basically _void_.

Word 1: Stories

Here's a tale.

In 2014, I set up a brewery with three other like-minded pals. We weren't setting out to rival Guinness or BrewDog. We were simply responding to one of our mates and the story he'd told us. Picture the scene: four happy blokes sitting in a pub by the sea; the Golden Ball in Scarborough, to be precise. It was one of those lads' weekends – a 'Jolly Boys' outing' if you're an _Only Fools and Horses_ fan[4] – and whilst the younger members of the party were drinking cheap lager in one of the

4 See https://www.youtube.com/watch?v=ay5eug0XfIU.

less salubrious haunts, the four of us reflected on how far we'd come. Everyone on the outing had worked at the same Barnsley secondary school and now, in 2014, we were all ploughing different furrows. I was a 'travelling teacher' working for myself, Paul was now a finance director for a large trust of schools, Dave was leading several successful special schools and Ondrie was teaching geography in a different school and doing very well. We were all very jolly indeed.

As the banter levels increased, Ondrie announced that he was going to have to leave teaching and become a full-time carer for his autistic son. Circumstances had led to Ondrie being the principal carer for the lad who was looking at having to leave full-time education soon and be 'cared for' full-time at home. This news broke the levity of the moment, to be honest. It didn't bring anyone down; it just made us all stop and think. Ondrie's a great teacher. What a loss that would be. We sat and ruminated, watching the Samuel Smith's hand-pulled beer leave its reassuring tidemarks on the insides of our glasses. I didn't know what to say but one of the other lads did:

'What do you want to do Ondrie? What's your perfect job?'

Ondrie took a breath and pondered a little. Eventually he responded, 'Lads. All I want to do is brew.' Somewhere in the universe a starter pistol rang out its deafening shot. 'Mi brother, mi Dad and me. It's all we've ever done. Brew our own. Shed brewing. It's science that you can drink. We love it. If I could just brew, my young 'un could knock around with me. He could be a real help.'

Nobody remembers who said it first, but somebody did: 'Let's set up a brewery. Let's make it happen.' So, we did. Within 10 minutes we'd registered at Companies House, purchased a web domain and costed out a very rough budget based on some internet research. The Jolly Boys' Brewery – tagline: 'Extraordinary beer brewed by four ordinary Yorkshire lads' – was born.[5]

The story could go on, but I'll leave it there for now. Suffice it to say we employ family as well as ex-pupils at our pubs. It's a lovely story and reflects the values we wanted to weave into the tapestry of the brewery – warmth, intimacy, banter and trust; a sort of manifesto of friendship, learning and, er, botheredness. Just so you know, the four of us who sat around that table in 2014 haven't taken a penny from the business; rather,

---

5   See https://jollyboysbrewery.co.uk/.

we've just kept on building it. So, the story doesn't have to end just now. It's going on whilst you're reading this.

When you think about it, we're bombarded by stories all the time. They're an essential part of who we are. Stories, according to Daniel Willingham (2004), are 'psychologically privileged', meaning that they help us retain information. I saw *Jaws* at the cinema when I was 5, going on 6, but grew up remembering the story until I got to see it again on the TV a few years later, and any memory blanks were filled in.[6] I also vividly remember *Aesop's Fables* as I had one of those card-backed Ladybird books telling me the tales, and I can picture the accompanying illustrations right now as I write this.[7] I also remember stories of my own schooling, stories Nainy would whisper me to sleep with,[8] and the stories my dad would tell about his time doing National Service. And that time he borrowed a horse on his way home from the pub.

Stories are useful for us as educators. They can be our stimulus, our hook, our case study, our design brief as well as being our way of 'protecting' our pupils into complex thinking and learning.[9] Stories essentially *build botheredness*. And they have the simplest of recipes: People + Place + Problem = Story. More on this later.

Word 2: Stance

Stance is where you stand as a teacher – both physically and mentally. It's how you *are* in a classroom. We know, don't we, that you can have two degrees, a doctorate and a book deal, but if you cannot find a way to communicate all your hard-won knowledge to children, as a teacher, you're screwed. Well, maybe that's a bit strong. Essentially, you've a struggle on. If you can't protect yourself into working with children, the job becomes much harder. If you cannot muster some rapport with an individual or a class, it's all uphill. This is why stance is so important. Where do you stand? What are your values? How do you demonstrate your authentic professional care? And how would you sum up your teacher presence? Who do you model yourself on? I had

---

6   On ITV, 8 October 1981. I'd just turned 11.
7   Now selling for a mint on eBay! For many, Ladybird Books are a nostalgic reminder of childhood. Do you remember them?
8   'Nainy' is the Welsh version of a grandmother.
9   The idea of protecting children into learning and thinking is explored in my *Oops!* book. Basically, it's about the ways in which a teacher can support a child (and a class) into caring about the topic being studied and, in a way, seeing themselves in it. If that makes sense?

aspirations of being John Keating from *Dead Poets Society*, but I also wanted to be Dave Matthews, Marc Doyle, Elizabeth Gaughan, Russ Thornton and Allan Horne and those other ace teachers who helped shape my 'new teacher' years.[10] I also wanted to be that teacher that children might remember fondly, in the same way I remember John Booth, Theresa Crowsdale, Chris Idle and Mrs Greenhalgh: teachers who supported me when I was a kid.[11] Real people with names and everything. Stance is botheredness, humanely and professionally enacted.

Word 3: Pedagogy

I couldn't say this word for a long time. It'd come out of my mouth as 'pedagorry' and would get quieter as I made my way through its sound. One day, after a high-powered senior leadership team meeting that I'd been seconded to, I asked the head how to say it and what it actually meant. Frankly, I had enough on with planning lessons and all that without having to namby-pamby about with academic words I couldn't pronounce. My boss set me straight on the pronunciation and neatly summed up its meaning: it's how we teach. It's the human delivery of stuff that's been written down. I love this. It's the human delivery of agreed content. It's the *how* of curriculum, the implementation of the *should*, coupled with the protection of children into learning. It's the holding back of the nettles on the footpath so the children don't get stung. It's not dumbing stuff down; it's making it accessible. It's making the world of challenging content inductive, wonderful and necessary. It's the building of botheredness.

There we are. The three elements of botheredness: stories, stance and pedagogy.

---

10 This is a list of teachers who taught me when I was a probationary teacher. They taught me more than teaching. They were mighty oaks. Not weeping willows. They were radiators. Not drains. As a new teacher, it's a good idea to spot these winners in your school and learn from them.

11 This is a list of teachers who taught me at Bury Church of England High School back in the 1980s. They left their fingerprints on my brain and my heart.

More of a good thing ...

Can you have too much of a good thing? I'm not so sure. I really like horror movies and I can't get too much of them. Same with Warren Zevon.[12] I can't get too much of him either. So, here's another couple of words I'm going to return to again in this book. They're part of the tapestry of botheredness as well. The first is this lovely word:

Imagineering

'Imagineering is letting your imagination soar and then engineering it down to earth.'

Promotional material, The Aluminum Company of America, 1942

'Imagineering' is the sort of word that brings out the eye-roller in you, for sure.[13] It's a fusion of the words 'imagination' and 'engineering'. I could explain more, but I'm hoping you can already feel the resonance for us as educators. We're the original campfire storytellers, the public intellectuals, the learning leaders in our communities – unless, of course, our fires have been snuffed out, and we're left scrabbling around in the dark.

'Imagineering' is a word first used amongst engineers around the start of the twentieth century.[14] It became embedded in parlance when Walt Disney adopted it as a way of expressing the creative approaches to the design and development of storytelling and filmmaking within its organisation. If you search for the word online, Disney dominates the results. For the engineers back in the day, imagineering was the visioning and thinking they did before they picked up their tools or operated their machinery to fashion new things that would help everyone move forward. It was the consideration and exposing of purpose, possibilities and opportunities.

---

12 Just an unsung musical genius. Really, do check him out.

13 Dear Disney, please don't take me to court over the use of this here word. It's been around for years. It's great you use it to describe your creative process. Honest, I'm a big fan. Just stop killing parents in your movies! Give them a break! Use some imagination! Oh (etc., etc., etc.).

14 For more on the history of the word 'imagineering', see Smith (2022).

As teachers, I feel we should consider the same. It's our pre-planning. It's our thinking. And it's our delivery. Delivery. Even the act of knowledge delivery takes imagination. And that's why we can't be replaced by robots.[15] And it's why 'virus' in high school science should _never_ be dull.

When you're driving in your car and you're thinking, *Tomorrow, I need to introduce my class to 'Ancient Egyptians'. What the hell?*, you usually sort it out in your own head and are able to rationalise it in terms of desirable outcomes whilst keeping in mind the characters you deal with on a daily basis in your classroom – and I'm not just talking about your teaching assistant, if you're lucky enough to have one knocking around. Planning for the children in the room takes us beyond any curriculum document or intention – it personalises, whilst bringing to the fore the need for in-the-moment changes to said intentions and plans. As well as providers and facilitators of classroom learning, we're reactors – our agility makes us human. And humanity is key to teaching. Isn't it?

'Imagination is more important than knowledge. For knowledge is limited, whereas imagination embraces the entire world, stimulating progress, giving birth to evolution'

said Albert Einstein on a meme I found on the internet. So no one knows if he said it, but the point stands.

'Imagination, could make a man of you'[16]

crooned 1980s sophist-pop-poser-hero Belouis Some (real name Neville Keighley, pop fans).

---

15 If you do want teachers replaced by robots, check out the ace and bonkers *Class of 1999* with Stacy Keach and Malcolm McDowell. It features a really weird scene where John P. Ryan as the Terminator-style history teacher spanks some classroom hoodlums across his knee. Yes, you read that right. You don't get that on a consequences policy. Yet!
16 Belouis Some, 'Imagination', *Some People* [song] (Parlophone, 1985).

> 'Stories of imagination tend to upset those without one'

– a neat line often attributed to Sir Terry Pratchett, my brother-in-law's favourite writer.

... and nearly finally:

> 'Children see magic because they look for it'

– words apparently whispered by Christopher Moore, writer of the absurd. I particularly love this one.

Print them all off, stick them up on your wall. Or on the cover of your planner as a reminder of what could drive you, other than the next curriculum book scrutiny. I'd like to think that none of your superiors would tear the quote from the front of your planner, but I'm not so sure. Is there a war against professional imagination, do you think?

Oh, and this:

> 'My imagination makes me human and makes me a fool'

wrote Ursula K. Le Guin (1996). Make of that what you will.

The application of professional imagination should be the thing that makes any educator buzz with their job. It *should* be. I'll return to this theme in more detail later, but our Professional Imagination (I've given it capitals now so you can see I really mean business with this) is something we should position ourselves to elucidate on. It is a great power we have in the classroom and one that can support the planning and execution of fantastic learning experiences for children and young people. Professional Imagination is what equips teachers with the tools to direct a class that is tough, that is hard to reach or that is consumed with distraction. Without Professional Imagination and the capacity to be an active imagineer, a teacher is de-professionalised to the point of being a simple content provider. A knowledge deliverer. A cheat-sheet machine who could easily be replaced by a robot. And one day, probably will be, if we take that course.

And very finally, this beautiful word:

Phronesis

Phronesis is Ancient Greek for 'practical wisdom'. In other spheres, it's simply 'living well' and 'knowing what you want and what you don't want'. It could be classed as the know-how you collect as you get better at something. The knack. The toolkit. When Indiana Jones knows exactly what to do: that's *phronesis.*

I've been looking for the word for years. A word that describes that professional growth we experience as we move through our jobs and careers. We grow our layers of experience, like skins – our first difficult class, our first inspection, our first professional reprimand (is that just me?), our first parents' meeting, our first school trip, our first form group, our first child bereavement, our first child suicide. Each skin makes us tougher, fairer, more empathetic and hopefully creative, imaginative and optimistic professionals, seeking the good. It's the knowing what to do or what to say when you don't know what to do or say. And that happens in our trade *a lot.*

Professional vocabulary grows over time, and we grow our wisdom, often by cocking it right up. 'I didn't learn this on teacher training!' is a familiar cry of the new early years teacher faced with their first 'brown alert'. The simple response to that is 'No, you didn't, now fetch the kitchen roll!' Professional wisdom is something you gather, like nuts in May. It's being able to read between the lines, being agile and having wisdom that underpins decision-making at work, at home and in the world.

All a teacher training course – and I should know because I've taught on some – can hope to do is get you ready for working with children, offer you the theory, the research, the warmup. Much like a behaviour management day at a soulless city-centre hotel, promising you the dreams of a hitlist of approaches that will cure you of your most fragile classroom-based traumas, led by people who couldn't hack it in front of kids, nothing is better than *live* (rhymes with *thrive*) *professional learning*. That is, in-the-moment experience. It is praxis. The growing of another skin.

If you want to have great behaviour management skills, then teach a challenging class. But don't just metaphorically fight them every lesson – grow your wisdom; build your *phronesis*. If for nothing else, do it so you can see the wood for the trees.

Phronesis doesn't just emerge from nowhere. It's something that's cultivated by a regular walk through the ethical dimensions of classroom reality.[17] Domènec Melé (2005) sets the scene: '*Phronesis* demands ethical character or personality characterised by virtues and values. Right action demands keen perception of particular situations rather than mere knowledge of general principles which are applicable everywhere.' It's the collision of understanding, experience, virtue and sharp perception built upon on a shifting foundation of knowledge and theory. It's what D. A. Schön (1983, 62) called 'reflection in action and reflection on action'. So, it isn't enough to just read the book or quote the research, it's actively reacting to it.

Anyway, enough academic name-dropping. There are too many education books written by people who have simply read a book. They're even writing books about books they've read, these days. Like pop, we're in danger of eating ourselves.[18]

This is something I read somewhere that takes us close to the point:

	Teachable knowledge	**Unteachable knowledge**
Necessary truths	*Episteme*	*Nous*
Contingent truths	*Techne*	*Phronesis*

(Harfield, 2014)

Or put another way:

	Teachable knowledge	**Unteachable knowledge**
Necessary truths	How it is	Common sense
Contingent truths	Skills	Wisdom

(adapted from Harfield, 2014)

17 I'm particularly proud of that sentence.
18 Pop Will Eat Itself are a band from the West Midlands. They're great.

None of this is new. It's not a shocker. It's as old as the hills. It goes back to Aristotle. This is the basis of principled action. And it goes way beyond schooling. Let me explain Harfield's table above. In fact, I'll just define the words, because, God knows, I needed definitions as well. I've got enough on without having to go back to the Ancients.

Episteme (aka 'How it is'; the stuff everyone knows)

The theory of everything. The universally understood. The rational and agreed. Basically, someone telling you how best to manage the administration of an examination group.

Techne (aka 'Skills'; you doing your bit well)

The reality existing beyond and despite theory. The craft. The skill. Basically, you're managing the administration of an examination group and reflecting as you go.

Nous (aka 'Common chuffing sense'; gumption)

The capacity to understand what is true and real. And to do so intelligently. Basically, you have a coherent understanding of what is expected of you and your pupils when you're responsible for the administration of an examination group. Incidentally, my dad used to use the word *nous* all the time when complaining that people lacked it. Because of him, until recently, I thought it was a word with its origins in the foothills of Snowdonia, not ancient Greece.

Phronesis (aka 'Wisdom'; knowing what yer doing)

What I'm on about. Basically, you're in charge of the administration of an examination group. You crack on with it. And when someone tells you Lilibeth can't be entered into the exam because her predicted result will adversely affect the overall results of the school, you enter her anyway. Because you're in touch with your values and your wisdom tells you it's the right thing to do. Because you're bothered. The senior cohort during COVID-19 in 2020 had their exam results based on teacher assessments – this was *phronesis* unbound and trust in teachers was restored. For a short while, anyway.

Episteme and *techne* are there to be learned and understood; to be handed down or shared across by those already in the know. They're to be found in journals, instruction manuals and blogs. *Nous* and *phronesis*, however, are unteachable. They need to be grown and nurtured. They're found in the secret stories of teachers' successes in their own classrooms and in the quiet words of encouragement whispered into the ear of a tearful child. There isn't a cheat sheet for that.

And combined, they're the essence of botheredness – principled thought and action, all for the greater good.

Who's in?

THE WARM AND THE COLD

The most beloved and widely read Pulitzer Prize Winner now comes vividly alive on the screen!
To kill a Mockingbird
starring
GREGORY PECK
WITH MARY BADHAM · PHILLIP ALFORD · JOHN MEGNA · RUTH WHITE · PAUL FIX
BROCK PETERS · FRANK OVERTON · ROSEMARY MURPHY · COLLIN WILCOX
Screenplay by HORTON FOOTE · Based upon Harper Lee's novel "To Kill a Mockingbird" · Music by ELMER BERNSTEIN
Directed by ROBERT MULLIGAN · Produced by ALAN PAKULA · A Pakula-Mulligan, Brentwood Productions Picture · A UNIVERSAL RELEASE

Only a jive-ass fool would pop a cap in a mockingbird

Wisecrack (2013)[1]

There are two primary schools outside one of our major Northern cities. Both schools are full of people who are bothered about their children and the challenges they face. They're practically next door to one another. There's a massive, busy main road running past both. There's one of those signs on it with the number of casualties last year due to road accidents.

One school I'd describe as a Warm School. When you go there, you're greeted by an enthusiastic caretaker who watches your parking in a very non-judgemental way.[2] Which is really good for a caretaker, to be fair. When you go through to the reception area, it's like you've been offered a bowl of really chunky hot soup.[3] With warmed crusty bread. With butter melted in. It's really homely and comforting. The adults in this place are kind, hard-working and committed. The children are characterful, joyful and in your face. It's boisterous in a purposeful way.

---

1   This is chuffing brilliant: Wisecrack, To Kill a Mockingbird – Thug Notes and Analysis [video] (18 June 2013). Available at: https://www.youtube.com/watch?v=IntI62LWSJA.

2   Caretakers. An interesting bunch. The two who stick fast in my head are Les and Phil, who sound like a double act from Blackpool's end-of-the-pier heyday. They were great blokes, sadly no longer with us. Phil always looked as though he was in cigarette mid-roll and Les had the kindest of faces with an enviable perpetual twinkle in his eye. Both were bothered. I know because I bothered them *a lot*: 'Les, can you build me a man-eating plant for our next musical?'; 'Phil, are you able to open the school up for the next six Saturdays?' Like a lot of caretakers at the time, they'd had lives in other industries. A lot of wisdom. A lot they'd witnessed over the years. They were sages holding onto broom handles. Caretakers in movies are given a bad rap, to be honest. You've got Jack Nicholson as Jack Torrance in *The Shining* and David Bradley as Argus Filch in the *Harry Potter* films. They're a grim couple, to be sure. I guess we have Sally Hawkins as Elisa Esposito in *The Shape of Water* to balance things up a bit. Oh, and *Hong Kong Phooey*

3   Think Heinz Big Soup.

The school down the busy road is serving exactly the same community. I'd describe it as a Cold School. When you arrive, you're greeted by a lady named Joy who sadly does not live up to her name. She needs to be sent on a course. Any course. The soup being served on arrival is tepid and thin, like Dickensian gruel. Or what you might have had when you were a pupil. In fact, it's an own-brand Cup-a-Soup still in its packet. After negotiating Joy (great album title right there), the teachers are found to be hard working, kind and committed, just like in the Warm School. Here, though, they're harried and cowed. The children, of course, are characterful, full o' beans and in your face, just like the kids up the road.

The Cold School has reached out to the Warm School and asked for help. The former are aware that things need to evolve in their setting and aren't afraid of asking the latter for help. This is an institutionally courageous act. The Warm School want to support because, hey, they're all serving the same community, right?

So, the best CPD in the world kicks in. Professional educators sitting in rooms talking together about Special Educational Needs and Disability (SEND) provision, literacy and effective use of teaching assistants. The very experienced special educational needs coordinator from the Warm School spends precious time with the inexperienced, recently qualified teacher in the Cold School and wisdom is shared. It's a good thing. Well done, everyone.

As part of this process, I'm asked to go and spend some time in the Cold School and take the temperature of classroom practice there. Like reading the meter. I've worked with colleagues at the Warm School for a while and so it seems a natural thing to do.

I find myself in a classroom and the kids have been doing _'Vikings'_. Now, if you teach older kids and are thinking none of this will apply to you, stay with me. In primary schools, they don't mess about. They _do_ stuff. They _do_ 'Vikings', they _do_ 'Mayans' and _do_ 'chocolate'. Then they cut it short because they have to _do_ a nativity. As I say, they don't mess about.

As I look to the walls, I see a lot of Viking-related paraphernalia. Images downloaded, websites scoured and resource sites plundered. The teacher has greeted me, and I try and stay out of the way. She's got enough on. The children are ordered, and routines are clearly established. I'm eyed with suspicion but not by the children, just by the assistant teacher who has emerged from a stock cupboard – God knows how long she's been in there – pushing a resource trolley.

A boy with blonde tram-lined hair is showing me his topic book. He's made a beeline for me because he's assuming, as I'm visiting and wearing a suit, I must be doing a book scrutiny. He's proud of one drawing in particular: his sketch of a Viking longhouse. It's labelled up:

- Fireplace

- Chairs

- Bed

- Chill area

- Animal area

- Hot tub

- Pizza oven

- Xbox

- TV

I smile at him. The teacher is settling the class. As she does so, she approaches me, and I see the absolute 'as if I need this' in her eyes. I do my best to be bright and breezy.

'What are we doing?' I ask, knowing the answer.

'It's Vikings today!' she musters, and I gently muster surprise. I say *gently* because I'm more than aware that I'm the guest here. I'm treading on sensitive ice.

'And what's the focus?' I ask, my eyes drawn back to the well-stocked trolley the teaching assistant has wheeled out. I'm distracted by what's on there. There's a pile of quality card – not the budget stuff you get from the stationery catalogue – I'm talking *quality* card. The sort that brings your weird stationery envy to the surface. There's also a lovely collection of scissors all standing to attention in a wooden block; sharpened coloured pencils, present and correct; and glue sticks, all with lids. They look new. It all looks new. It's like someone blew the pupil premium budget at WHSmith. And then there's something really incongruous sitting on the end of the trolley, dominating it. A huge bowl, of the Tupperware variety, filled to the brim with glitter. A billion colourful particles sitting, awaiting action.

It's like watching the opening minutes of an archive episode of *Casualty* when there's a man supping from a can of lager with one hand whilst operating a chainsaw with the other – you're predicting the accident about to happen.[4]

'We're making Viking shields,' says the teacher. Look, I'm going to call her Helen. It makes it easier. So, Helen looks at me awaiting my response to the shield revelation. She knows what I'm going to say because she's been around the block.

'Why?' I ask. And it's a fair question.[5]

And Helen knows that I know.

And I know that she knows.

And we both stand for a moment.

She sighs and says, 'Because it's *Week Three.*'

The needle skips off the record. And I *definitely* know that she knows that I know. This is that moment when, as teachers, we realise that we've unwittingly become slaves to a curriculum that's been written down, unwilling sacrificial lambs at the altar of mediocrity. Zombie-pursued survivalists searching for anything useful at the abandoned store.

Shields.

Well-resourced cardboard shields at that. With glitter on them.

'And we need to tick off art,' Helen offers as a throwaway. Try as I might, I can't help my face. I smile and nod.

'Buzzing,' I say. And I know she knows because her eyebrows arch a little and there's definite evidence of a smirk at the sides of her mouth.

---

4   The stalwart Saturday-night misery fest disguising itself as light entertainment, *Casualty*, particularly back in the 1980s and 1990s, always opened with the *accident* set-up that would essentially dictate the unravelling of the drama. Formulaic and simple in its execution, it was (and perhaps still is) compelling with its story structure. Much like the Irwin Allen disaster movies of the past – *The Poseidon Adventure* (1972), *The Towering Inferno* (1974), *When Time Ran Out* (1980) and *The Swarm* (1978) – the audience are introduced to characters to root for, dislike, love and despise, all in a short space of time. Low-budget horror movies such as the *Friday 13th* franchise (1980–2009) sought to emulate this model in the 1980s where character development was replaced by splatter and tension (not a bad thing). What the original *Halloween* (1978) managed to do was get the audience to genuinely care about its lead character *and* do the splatter and tension thing. In this class, I'm feeling the tension from the teaching assistant and her trolley of September stationery. It's palpable.
5   Whenever we plan *anything*, we should always ask its purpose.

. . . .

CUT TO:

The Warm School

Back in time a few weeks from the *Casualty* set-up in the Cold School. This is <u>Week Zero</u>. Essentially, the last week of the previous topic. The school's trying to do a couple of things:

1   Tap into the flipped-learning approach where children research a topic away from the classroom prior to the beginning of study.

2   They're trying to increase the engagement of parents and carers with children's learning so are attempting to encourage home-based conversations – build the botheredness, if you like – through low-level activities which are delivered via the school's texting system.

In this case, Week Zero could essentially be summed up as: 'When you're at home, talk to someone about what they know about Vikings. If you've access to books or the internet, use them!' Something along those lines. So, Week One begins with the kids piling in and sharing their stuff. Frankly, not every kid has got something, but at least there's a whole-group interest in what's happening. This is what we reap from the Week Zero home-based activities:

1   A DVD of the movie *How to Train Your Dragon*.[6]

2   A Viking picture book, which is cool.

3   A few printed-off resources from the internet showing Viking buildings and clothing.

4   A dad's pencil sketch of a Viking (fair play!).

5   A massive pile of A4 paper where a child has printed everything under the 'Vikings' entry on Wikipedia.

----

6   *How to Train Your Dragon* (2010–2019) is a brilliant franchise of three top-quality movies and some mint TV shows based on the ace books by Cressida Cowell. The voice artists are fab and the animation, particularly in the movies, is breathtaking. I'm no expert on animated movies but I know there are some corkers out there.

6   Darryl. Yep, we get Darryl. He's a kid who <u>knows everything</u> about Viking longships. I'm talking <u>EVERYTHING</u> and that's why I'm putting it in capitals. He's a mine of information and knowledge. We get to a point when Aidy, the class teacher, and I are frankly out of our depth. The kid could be saying anything, but we're sucking it in like sponges. If we threw a paper and pen at Darryl, I reckon he could knock out a decent project just based on his new Week Zero knowledge. Longships are his <u>new thing</u>. He's buzzing with them. During a pause in his lecture, I ask him where he's gained all this info? 'YouTubes,' he says, unintentionally deadpan. I love that extra 's' kids can put on things that don't need them. He's bothered, interested, excited and obsessed.

That's about it. Like I say, at least the school is trying, and Rome wasn't built in a day. Aidy begins constructing a working wall and the tangible stuff gets stuck up whilst Darryl is on standby for the provision of longship information.

A place

I point to the clock high on the wall at the back of the classroom and ask the children to look. They do and spin their heads back round to me. I ask them to keep looking and begin my narrative concerning 'place'. For the sharp-eyed amongst you, I'm establishing a setting.

This is what I say as I point:

```
Look. Up there. The clock. I know it's a clock, but let's say it's a cave.
No, I know it isn't. But let's say it is. A cave, high in the mountains but
visible with the naked eye. A cave, seemingly large and deep. Two days
hike, I reckon. It's got a name. Let's say it's called DRAGON CAVE.
```

During all of this, I've been pointing and 'scene painting' the place; basically, describing it to the children as if it were in the distance. They respond positively with huge grins on their faces as if they were in a game. Which they are, kind of. The thing is, when I'm talking, I absolutely *mean it*. I continue:

And closer to us are the forests and treelines. And rivers and streams that flow to the flatlands where we stand. And behind us is a mighty river where we have moored our longships.

Now, I'm not writing you a script here for the next time you're _doing_ 'Vikings', I'm just showing you that there's another way. All the time I'm speaking, I'm also gesturing and pointing, describing this place, because …

We are Vikings. And this will be our home. A new settlement for us by this mighty river.

And here comes a *pearler* of a question. A question that can contribute to children thinking beyond their life experience, into the past:

If we're living in the time of Vikings, what don't we have?

And when I ask that question, I'm not all 'giddy *Glee Club*', I'm the straight man – the Syd Little, Tommy Cannon, Bud Abbott – face blank, yet inquisitive … *I mean it.* Because in the classroom, I mean business.

I mean business.[7] Do you? If I walked into your classroom on some ill-thought-out learning walk, how would I know that you mean business in terms of your teaching and their learning? More of this later, perhaps. Remind me to tell you about the piano in my classroom. The one they were chucking out.

---

7   This is about keeping your face straight, both metaphorically and really. To show we're bothered about something, we avoid taking the piss out of it. When John Landis decided to make a beautiful pastiche of the old black-and-white Universal Studio horrors of the 1930s and 1940s, he did so with a reverence and honesty that produced an unforgettable classic – *An American Werewolf in London*. If teaching and moviemaking can be considered art, then we need to recognise the botheredness in both. You only need to look at the sequel to Landis' classic – *An American Werewolf in Paris* – to see a paint-by-numbers, cold, dead offering. It has its moments for sure, but doesn't mean business. Its British director, Anthony Waller, had cut his teeth on a self-financed gem, *Mute Witness*, a movie that was dripping in botheredness and creativity. Check it out if you can find it. Meaning business in a classroom is made of the same *Mute Witness/ Werewolf in London* stuff.

Back to *doing* 'Vikings' and the class are hushed as I survey them. Then the hands start going up with suggestions of what we didn't have in the time of Vikings. I nod at a kid seriously, and he seriously responds, 'Greggs'. I nod, sagely and then manage a smile whilst a genuine healthy tension is broken. I still mean business. Some hearts may sink at the mention of a town-centre favourite like Greggs – it's a sharp contribution for sure, but we can gently smooth it out if we choose to. We often get pointy, sharp contributions, don't we? Sometimes we need to find the energy to do the donkeywork of fashioning the piercingly jagged ideas of children into something useful and purposeful. We might find ourselves crafting responses *in the moment*. It can sometimes feel like the kids are throwing eggs, but they just need help making the omelette.

In the spirit of the national curriculum in England, I write the word *diet* on the whiteboard. We all agree that there would be no Greggs, but there would be an obvious need for food and the means to plant it, grow it and harvest it. But what food will it be? What climate do we need? What is the staple diet of our community? Are we farmers or Vikings? Can we be both?

I hope, as you're reading this, you're seeing the curriculum bubbling under the surface. The tasks, the potential for enquiry, for deeper understanding, for writing and, perhaps, during the planning of sowing the crops, grid referencing. Okay, that last bit might be a little tenuous, but you'll have to admit that it has potential. Might take a bit of professional imagination or maybe just use the creation of a Viking community as a way of practising the grid referencing work being explored during numeracy time. That's a bit of 'looking across the curriculum' right there. It's a bit of creativity.

So, there's no Greggs.

Or technology.

Or internet.

Or football.

Or space travel.

Or [*insert contemporary C-grade reality show's D-list celebrity*].

Nowt like that.

A blacksmith?[8] Yep, I reckon they had to fashion their metals somewhere. I wonder what metals they fashioned? And for what purpose? What skills were needed to be a great blacksmith?

A hospital? They probably didn't call it a hospital, but there's evidence to suggest that Vikings cared well for their elderly and that they were good at resetting broken bones. They also had excellent teeth!

Then Zac, a kid with form, raises his hand. He's a mini-Gallagher,[9] and speaks as if listing a series of cold-hearted demands: 'I would have thought there's a school.'

I nod. 'I'm not sure there's a school like the one we're sitting in, but I do know that the Viking women held the stories – the sagas, as they were known – and they'd pass them down to the generations coming up. Stories of battles, family arguments, elves and dragons make up these sagas. What do you think a Viking child in our community would need to learn?'

There's a beat, and Zac raises his hand again. 'Bear Grylls,' he says, bless him. Now, at this point I could smirk gently and nod. In fact, that's exactly what I do. That's because I know exactly what he means. My *phronesis* tells me it's all good.[10] Bear Grylls. International survival expert and world chief scout ambassador. And definitely not around in the time of the Vikings. A couple of colleagues eye me like hawks from the back of the room.[11] 'So, if we're *learning* Bear Grylls, Zac, what are we learning about?' In teacher-speak, that's basically, 'Describe the Bear Grylls curriculum'.

---

8   In movies, blacksmiths only usually appear in montages about swords being made. There's Will Turner (Orlando Bloom) in those overly complicated *Pirates of the Caribbean* films. He was a blacksmith.

9   Bit of a lazy Manc touchstone here. I should probably think of a better example – John Cooper Clarke, perhaps? The thing that bothers me about Oasis is that they revelled in laddish ignorance. Noel bemoaned fiction as 'a waste of fucking time' (Bury, 2013), whilst at the height of so-called Britpop, the band revelled in what they thought was entitled ignorance. Compare them to Manic Street Preachers, a proper working-class band who practically imbued their fans with a reading list; 'Libraries gave us power' – Manic Street Preachers, 'A Design for Life', *Everything Must Go* [song] (Epic, 1996). When it comes to Oasis, I lack botheredness. ☺

10 My teacher choice here is simple: take it or leave it. This one of those 'pivot' moments in a classroom where the teacher needs to respond in the moment; react productively.

11 Observations can be the bane of a professional's life. Not just teachers. Everyone who has a job to do and someone looking over their shoulder: the new mum doing her best in full view of the busy café; the bus driver doing an emergency stop, simultaneously saving the cyclist's life and pissing off the passengers; the politician struggling to put party before people; the child judged by the cleanliness of their clothes. As teachers, we've grown a culture of observations. If ever there was a time when you can demonstrate your botheredness, it's in an observation. And as an observer, you can do the same. Unless you're some sort of useless power-nut who finds great joy in leaning on classroom folk as a way of feeling good about yourself.

'Fishing,' he replies after a couple of easy moments. It's a good response considering our closeness to the imagined river. Now, there's a crossroads for me as a teacher in this moment. I can either nod, praise and move on, or push Zac a little more. A bit of 'kind relentless challenge',[12] if you like. Kind relentless challenge. All it means is that I'm not letting anyone off the hook. When a pupil offers a response, it's always worth giving them another crack; an opportunity to deepen their initial response. Too often, we might simply take the first response and then move on. All that does is keep thinking on the surface. And we want to get some depth, don't we? So, after Zac has offered 'fishing' as a key curriculum area for Viking children, I respond with this:

'Fishing? Where do we get fishhooks from?'

I don't smirk or get a twinkle in my eye. The question is serious and yet kind. I'm not intending to humiliate Zac, of course; I just want a bit more from him. In my head, I'm expecting him to either shrug off my question or to suggest the blacksmith in the village. He says and does neither. Instead, he offers this, eyes unblinking (remember this is in answer to 'Where do we get fishhooks from?'):

'From the claws of lions.'[13]

Okay, so no one in the room expects this. The observing colleagues are a mixture of smiles and raised eyebrows, with one looking at me as if to say, 'Deal with that!' I look at Zac as words start to form into some sort of sentence on my tongue. But before I can say anything, he follows up his lion comment with 'Do you want me to show you?'

Now, here's the thing. I've always been a _yes_ kind of person. You're either a _yes_ person or a _no_ person as far as I'm concerned. I guess if we're talking about the concept of botheredness here, then it could be argued that you've _got_ to be a _yes_ person. So now there's this kid asking me if I need a visual representation of some fishhook reaping.

And I say _yes_.

---

12 This is you modelling keen listening, curiosity and enquiry through questioning. For an example of unkind relentless challenge, watch any movie with a torture scene. Or that delicious and sad sequence between Dennis Hopper and Christopher Walken in _True Romance_.

13 Now, if this was a Hollywood blockbuster, say of the late 1990s, this would be the moment Hayley Joel Osment (the kid from _The Sixth Sense_) would whisper this line and the whole packed cinema audience would gasp in amazement. The camera would pan across the assembled class, all wide-eyed, and come to rest on the teacher (I'm going for the casting of a 50-something-year-old Donald Sutherland or, if he's not available, Emily Watson), nodding gently whilst wondering what the hell to say in response.

(An observing teacher's eyes widen out of their sockets as the head, who's dropped by, smiles as if fearing the worst. A fixed grin sensing an approaching doom.)

Stories and anecdotes are evidence that just hasn't been written up yet.[14] 'Anecdata', if you like. This is what happened, and this is all I've got. Zac stood and did what I can only describe as a piece of dramatic movement that clearly depicted the capture and strangulation of a potentially geographically inaccurate lion, the withdrawal of its claw from its paw, and him falling to his knees whilst holding the bloody claw aloft, like Russell Crowe in *Gladiator*.

We're all pretty much aghast as the class clap Zac's performance. I think the head is chuffed that no one is injured. As the clapping subsides, Zac walks past me and says, in his warm Madchester twang, 'That's how you get a fishhook.'

Buzzing.

Now we can all agree that Zac is engaged in this stuff, and I'd like to suggest that he's upgraded that engagement to INVESTMENT. He's 'inside' the work. He's committed. He's not just doing it to get points. He's *in it*. He's bothered.

. . . .

CUT TO:

Week Three … Back in the Cold School

If anyone wandered in on a learning walk,[15] they'd now see around twenty-five children busily making Viking shields with all that lovely stationery. This is following a fifteen-slide PowerPoint and there's even a cheat sheet of instructions that some of the class are using. I guess that's differentiation ticked off. A visiting observer would notice three boys standing around the resource trolley, talking.

---

14 This is true, right? Have you got any stories of happenings in your classroom? I'm not asking for a thesis. Just a story! I write mine here: https://www.tes.com/magazine/author/hywel-roberts. You can send me yours to hywel@teacherhug.co.uk and I'll read them out on the wireless. ☺
15 Learning walks had their origins in good intentions but quickly became a tool of hierarchical misery in some institutions. Exercises in compliance, conformity and crushingness, administered by people who couldn't wait to get out of the classroom and away from the kids. The original *self-preservation society* celebrated by Michael Caine and his gang in *The Italian Job*.

All engaged.

Well done, everyone.

And that right there is the problem with the word *engagement,* which I'll come back to shortly. I mean, they're engaged, but who's learning?

I'm not on a learning walk so I'm seeing the whole thing like one of those fixed observation cameras favoured by some schools. I can see the twenty-five kids busy being engaged but not really learning anything. And I've clocked the lads at the trolley. They're egging each other on with their eyes. Each has a glue stick in their hands, and I can see that one of them has screwed a good 10 cm wodge of glue out. All three keep glancing at the ceiling.

Oh, I know what this is. *Glue stick rockets.* That's what this is. Get the wodges lengthy and shoot 'em up to the ceiling. They're ready to launch when they're brave enough, just like the astronauts of old. They're the definition of furtiveness. They're not evil.[16] Just distracted.

But we're all distracted by another. A boy. A small boy for his age. He's wandering the class and bothering the others who are busy at their tables. And then I see his face. This lad has obviously had a glue stick to his face. He's coated his eyebrows and all around his mouth. And then he's chucked his face into that massive bowl of glitter. So, now he looks like Roy Wood singing 'I Wish It Could Be Christmas Everyday' on *Top of the Pops* in 1973. Some of you might have to google that.

He floats to me whilst Helen and the teaching assistant tactically ignore him. They must've been on a behaviour management course. He's another proper little Manc. A weird fusion of Gollum, the actor Stephen Graham and Bod.[17] 'Alright mate, have you checked out my beard? It's a glitter goatee'. He strokes his glitter chin and coloured specks fall to the floor like mutant snow. I do wonder if this happens to Inspectorate

---

16 Oh, what a time to be alive! Some young people these days are painted like the cast of *Children of the Corn* or *Village of the Damned.* The former is a classic for me. When I see its lurid movie poster featuring the silhouette of a scythe against a blood-red background, I'm catapulted back to being an adolescent in 1985, staring desperately at the video art and wishing I could watch the movie. No chance. That's what got me into reading. Reading horror fiction was a good way of getting closer to the movie adaptation. I did this A LOT. When it comes to horror, I'm bothered up to my neck.

17 *Bod* was a frightening kids' show that was first broadcast in 1975. Featured a bald bloke in a yellow dress and charted his adventures navigating his own environment. Difficult to explain the plot when reminiscing with friends. Conversation usually ends up with said friends staring into middle distance. *Bod.* Check it out. Then have a drink.

much when they visit classes? I reply simply, and unintentionally curtly, 'Back off'. He does. He's dancing around like that ex-leper from Monty Python's *Life of Brian*. Glitter beard aside, it must be normal, as no one is really paying him any mind. Eventually, the teaching assistant notices him, double-takes and suddenly loses it like an exploding volcano:

'GARY!!!'

. . . .

CUT TO:

Ice shelf sliding into the ocean

She rushes to him whilst eyeing me and grabs his wrist, moving him to a table. I notice Helen has the look of someone who has just watched their house collapse, or their mother kissing Hitler; a kind of 'Christ, not now Sandra!' as the teaching assistant goes loco.[18] It's all professionally desperate and, strangely, I think we can all relate to that. This kid is a challenge and I reckon, just based on what I'm seeing here, his needs aren't being met but that everyone is doing their best. His beard's good though. Proper shiny.

I can rationalise it now, no worries, but in the moment, standing in a corner in that classroom during Week Three of 'Vikings', all I'm actually thinking is:

Gary.

Gary Glitter.

Chuff me. Is that wrong? I'll leave that with you.

. . . .

18 It's not that Sandra isn't bothered. She is. She's a teaching assistant. She knows her role. My concern, on behalf of teaching assistants, is that they don't often get the professional development or access to the toolkits that will empower them to deal with a boy with a glitter beard appropriately, fairly and with compassion. They also don't get paid enough.

The bottom line is that the lesson is frayed at the edges. It's lacking purpose and Helen knows it and is powerless, I think. She's got herself stuck in a rut. She never wanted this, but this is now how it is. And she hasn't got time to think about airy-fairy nonsense like botheredness. She just needs to get to playtime. And prevent Sandra from killing anyone. After that, it starts again, unless she's gone and gotten herself some planning, preparation and assessment time, but you never have it when you really need it, do you?

. . . .

CUT TO:

The Warm School

It's Week Three and the kids enter the classroom all excited. The school (like the Cold School) is located on a very busy road artery to the city centre. So, this morning, the cherubs are getting a special Road Safety Talk and they cannot wait. The main reason they can't wait is that they've been told by older siblings and peers that they get to watch a short film where someone gets run over by a truck. Apparently, there are blood and guts. They're buzzing. I can confirm that this _does not happen_ in the film.[19]

As the special talk is cutting into our 'Vikings' time, the class teacher, Aidy, gets stuck in with our plan. He points to the huge map that has formed on the working wall at the back of the class and the kids turn to it as he speaks:

Look. There is smoke coming from Dragon Cave. And look behind me
– the river has run dry. Our longships lie on the riverbed, our shields
washed away. All our water has gone. What could have happened?

That, right there, is the task getting set. Did you hear it?

19 There was that public safety film from 1977 made by British Transport Films called _The Finishing Line_. It's the most gruelling shockumentary ever made for kids. It's like someone decided to do a mash up of Lionel Jeffries' _The Railway Children_ and Eli Roth's _Hostel_. It's a mad, trippy 1970s _The Hunger Games_ that is easily tracked down online ☺. If you can be bothered. Okay, it's here: https://player.bfi.org.uk/free/film/watch-the-finishing-line-1977-online.

The children speculate with one another, and hands start to go up in the air with theories about our mountain water. The first theory, from a girl called Sunny, is that another community has blocked the river and that we should prepare for war. Spoken like a true Viking. Sasha offers a second theory: there's a dragon in the cave that is drinking all the mountain water at source.

I join in: *(seriously)* 'A dragon?'

Zac offers to slay it and wear its skin as a trophy, bless him. Darryl says that we wouldn't slay a dragon – look at our longships![20]

> If we are going to hike for two days to Dragon Cave, what do we need to think about? What do we need to take with us? Who do we leave behind? Will our community be safe without us?[21] Any other questions?

Sasha doesn't have a question. She says, 'We just need to show the dragon that we mean business.'

Mean business. I love that.

So: *(meaning business)* 'How do we show a dragon that we mean business?'

All the hands go up. We're all truly *invested* whilst simultaneously looking forward to seeing someone hit by a truck.

Not a full stop. It doesn't end there, of course. It goes on. But here are some points I want to make about the story of the Warm and Cold Schools in Manchester:

- In terms of curriculum coverage, and to use a good old Lancashire expression, they're the *'same dog, only washed'*.

---

20 Viking iconography is awash with dragon and serpent imagery. These mythical creatures represented the Viking's power, cunning and strength. The three most famous Viking dragons were Nidhogg, Jörmungandr and Fáfnir, and they'd be represented in stories and jewellery, and at the fronts of dragonships (longships).

21 Can you hear the potential for taskwork in these questions? Because they're questions coming from the teacher, the children are being invited to draw on all their rich knowledge and put it into action, thus investing them more in the topic. In a sense, the children are being 'lifted' to the Viking curriculum.

In both classrooms the children were engaging in thinking and learning about Vikings.

Helen, the teacher in the Cold School, was doing what she was doing even though what she was doing shamed her a little. That's dreadful for a teacher to be feeling that, but you know what? Like the school, she's got herself stuck in a rut. I really want Helen to be okay. She's trapped in a 'pedagogy of poverty' (Haberman, 1991) and it may drive her into a position where the part-time job at the accountancy firm her pal offered her, to utilise her brilliant maths skills, might seem a more attractive option than teaching.

The children in the Cold School are cracking on and simply slotting into the expectations they have of themselves and others have of them. If they were in the Warm School, their reaction to what was on offer would be different. The warm invitation from the teacher coupled with curriculum delivery (the implementation and humanising of a paper document, the enaction rather than inaction of a pedagogy) encourage investment – what we could call 'enhanced engagement' … botheredness. If Helen worked at the Warm School, she wouldn't be seeing accountancy as the green grass of the other side. Everyone would just be a shade more content, happier in their day-to-day, I'm venturing.

Week Six of the 'Vikings' plan essentially invites the children to write a Viking saga in their topic books. This is envisaged as a culmination of the previous five weeks' study. An opportunity for the children to capture everything they've navigated – all the rich knowledge, the immersion, the surprises, the enquiry, the difficulties, the people, the setting, the dilemmas – everything. All wrapped in a narrative.[22] Where do you think the best pieces of writing came from? Yep, you're right.

We're *doing* the English national curriculum, covering the curriculum, but in the Warm School, we're nailing it.

It's distinguished academic Martin Haberman that kickstarted my thinking around this idea of the *warm* and the *cold*. Haberman's (1991) piece 'The pedagogy of poverty versus good teaching' focuses on how schools under pressure (his focus is urban

---

22 Just to finish the narrative unfolding in the Warm School, the children ventured into the mountains and encountered the dragon – a huge beast lolling in the darkness of Dragon Cave. She spoke to the children and told them she needed all the mountain water to quench the burning throats of her young. All sixty of them. Using teacher-in-role, I was the dragon. I asked the Vikings for their help and told them I was happy to share the water in exchange. I could see they meant business.

schools) can de-professionalise teaching as an act, and this in turn can lead to a poor experience for everyone, child an adult alike. If you're a teacher, write a list of the professional pressures you're currently operating under – go on, write a list in the margin. For those of you who just want to write the word _everything_, it's a fairly good sign that things are pretty cold where you are. I've no idea what pressures you're under, and I guess it could depend on your role. One thing that might appear on your list is the word _curriculum_ which is what we talked about when I shared the _'Vikings'_ story: two schools both delivering a curriculum around Vikings; two schools where the very curriculum itself might appear similar when written down and yet, when delivered, it's totally different. That's because – just like you writing your 'pressure list'; me writing this book, you reading it – everything is open to interpretation.

A pedagogy of richness can come down to the human adult in the room and their response to the material they've been given. These curriculum interpretations can/will cause a tension for those humans delivering it.[23] As Daskalovska et al. (2012) point out, 'Even though teachers cannot control all aspects of motivation, they can do a lot to help these learners develop motivation for learning the language by creating a positive atmosphere in the classroom'. So much can be dependent on leadership, permissions and community pressures, as well as access to quality CPD, that it's little wonder colleagues can sometime feel like they're wandering in a swamp.

---

23 I'd like to offer some movie analogies here in my brand-new game, Warm or Cold! (CUE FANFARE) I'll name a film and you respond with 'warm' or 'cold' in your head (or out loud, if you want to freak out those you're with). Here we go:
The original _Robocop_ (1987).
The remake of _Robocop_ (2014).
Jaws (1975).
Jaws 3-D (1983).
A Shot in the Dark (1968) with Peter Sellers.
The Pink Panther 2 (2009) with Steve Martin. Steve Martin. I love Steve Martin, but jeez.
Star Wars (1977).
The Phantom Menace (1999).
See what I mean? Why settle for less when you can have something really good? Something you're really bothered about. That's the whole problem with failed reboots of great movies as well. Remember the daft remake of _The Wicker Man_? We all knew it was going to be pants, didn't we? And we all love Nic Cage but this was awful. And there was that _Fantastic Four_ that nobody saw with Billy Elliot in it. Then, conversely, you get the ace _Dredd_ with Karl Urban that blows the Sly Stallone one out of the water. Absolutely mint and ace. Maybe what I'm talking about is the school curriculum equivalent of a masterful movie reboot, but instead of Daniel Craig storming onto screen in _Casino Royale_ or Christian Bale batting it in _Batman Begins_, we've just got Egyptians to matter to 8-year-olds in Stoke and data handling to be relevant to the burgeoning mathematicians of Monmouth.

An assertion could be made that any curriculum that is written down or stored electronically is, for all intents and purposes, _dead_. It has no life. It has ceased to be. Life is breathed into the curriculum by the teacher delivering it. There are also variables that need to be considered; for example, could a lesson planned for a class of 13-year-olds in an independent school in rural Surrey be replicated for a class of 13-year-olds in challenging urban school in Yorkshire? Maybe not. And yet, the concept of a national curriculum does not appear to differentiate for this. Nor does the growing industry in online downloadable resources that, although a boon to some, erode the thinking and reflecting space existing within the teacher's own creative mindset. Teachers have been robbed of an understanding of pedagogy, finding themselves instead with tick boxes, pen drive-reliant curriculum content, acronyms like WALT (we are learning to) and WILF (what I'm looking for) and a fear of not covering everything that's been outlined in a scheme of work or syllabus.[24] This cold approach to the delivery of learning opportunities sits at odds with the productive pedagogies, so, as highlighted by Haberman, 'teachers are accountable only for engaging in the limited set of behaviours commonly regarded as acts of teaching in urban schools – that is, the pedagogy of poverty' (1991, 35). Or, the creative practice of teaching has been allowed to slip down the drain.

Concerns around curriculum have been a perennial issue in education, and the debate is reignited every few years. Dorothy Heathcote (1978), Leonard Marsh (1970) and others called for an experiential and immersive model of content delivery where teachers shifted their position from the front of the classroom to working alongside children – to me, Heathcote's Mantle of the Expert approach,[25] itself rooted in narrative and imaginative enquiry, is a good example of what could be described as a warm approach to curriculum and at the opposite end of the spectrum to what Haberman (1991) described later as the 'pedagogy of poverty'.

Haberman offers a checklist of what 'specific teacher acts' constitute this pedagogy of poverty and they draw in things like:

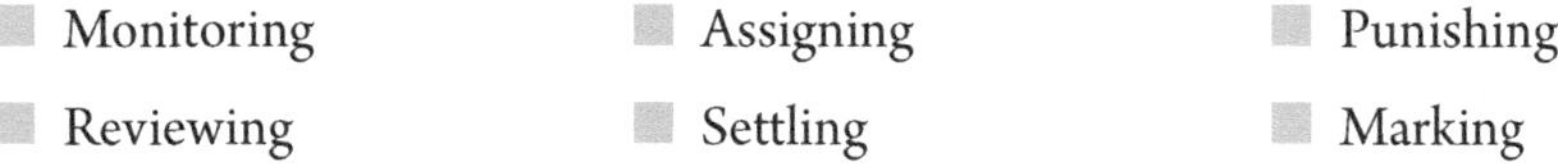

| Monitoring | Assigning | Punishing |
| Reviewing | Settling | Marking |

----

24 WALT and WILF sound like two very disappointed middle-aged men pulling golf carts on a course in the West Midlands. And it's raining.

25 Tim Taylor's (2016) *A Beginner's Guide to Mantle of the Expert: A Transformative Approach to Education* is the go-to text for the busy teacher. Tim is one of the greatest teachers I've ever met.

These are all very teacher-led and are, as Haberman notes, what children, 'their parents, the community and the general public assume teaching to be' (1991, 3). The tension that has emerged recently is complex. I do think that we have many teachers entering the profession believing that the pedagogy of poverty is what teaching actually is.[26] This loss of curriculum richness is where Helen and her class rest as they wrestle with their Viking shields. To me, they're victims of geography, circumstance and the pressures felt by some schools.

A beautiful risk

The greatest risk a teacher can take is to look at the children in their class, professionally reflect on what needs covering and then decide on pedagogical approaches that will work with those particular children at that given time, in their school and community context.[27] This risk transcends those public expectations of what teachers actually do and brings the ownership of the curriculum back into teachers' hands – a *notional* curriculum fuelled by professional imagination – informed and transformative, operating inside the national curriculum: the content and coverage operating within the context. That's what builds botheredness. This idea of professional imagination is something I explored in the writing of my own book *Oops!* (Roberts, 2012) and in my collaborative book with Dr Debra Kidd, *Uncharted Territories* (Roberts and Kidd, 2018). Rather than being mouthpieces for a prescribed and rigid *cold* curriculum, teachers are invited to unshackle themselves and do so within the genuine constraints of the current English curriculum, one which is viewed as the gold standard internationally.

So, to humanise Haberman's (1991) list, perhaps the specific teacher acts we should be looking for include:

- Laughter with children
- Time with children
- Encouragement of children
- Smiling before Christmas
- Praise for children

26 See my chapter 'The soundtrack of the pedagogy of poverty' in Gilbert (2018) for more of this.
27 For more on curriculum and community (and a whole load besides), you should check out Dr Debra Kidd's (2020) *A Curriculum of Hope*. It's a spectacular book from another great teacher.

I understand that, to a weary class teacher who lost their prep time today, this list is all a bit 'jazz hands'. But look beyond that if you will, and you will perhaps see:

1   The teacher who always crops in government teacher recruitment ads.

2   You, when you signed up to become a teacher.

The people I've quoted so far – Heathcote, Haberman – are great academics writing, well, not recently. So, where are we now? Well, to me, that's the thing. The nub of it, if you like. We're in the middle of a research-led renaissance in teaching at the time of writing, no question about it. There's a nagging feeling for me though that, while we are told to be active researchers, there are some voices in education – many of whom have fled the classroom, if they were ever there in the first place – who would slap your own lived experience down with a rolled-up copy of their desired reading list. This is what led me to do my own research; I wanted to immerse myself in the academic literature around my own focus, which was education, poverty and engagement.[28] It's like whilst trying to keep up with the latest obscure research offered to us by a supply teacher from Suffolk, we've forgotten what humanity-informed teaching looks like. That's what Haberman's pedagogy of poverty reminds us of. It's a warning. Don't lose your art. When you lose your art, you lose your soul.

A big bloke came up to me at the end of a conference where I'd shared the anecdote of Zac and the Viking dragon. I was grabbing a brew and he made a beeline for me, unsmiling. He pointed at me as he got closer and did that thing where he started talking *at* me as he walked. Not being used to this sort of reaction to my work, I did my best Roger Moore eyebrow raise, and steeled myself. It went like this:

---

28 *Engagement*. There's a word that can wind folk up. I'll come back to it later.

MAN: (*pointing, talking and walking*) 'So you think it's okay for children
     to believe there were dragons alive in the time of Vikings then,
     do you?'

ME: (*maintaining eyebrow raise*) 'Do you need a cuddle?'[29]

Whilst we're on this sort of thing, what about the member of the Inspectorate who wrote a report on a school after asking a child what they'd enjoyed learning the most during their study of Vikings?[30]

BOY: 'They invented dragons.'

The child's response apparently demonstrated misconceptions in his understanding of Vikings. This quick-fire response was cited three times in the school's report and given as a reason for their overall 'requires improvement' judgement. The member of the Inspectorate greenlighting the report clearly didn't know their Viking sagas for toffee. Just wait until they come across a school studying Greek myths: 'Too much emphasis on monsters'.

Some might say we're chuffing doomed.

The Inspectorate responses neatly reflect the stealth-like erosion of the professional imagination mentioned earlier. They sum it up, in fact. How on earth are we going to develop a responsive and creative teaching workforce when there's such

---

29 I didn't say this, of course, as I didn't want my head kicking in in the car park. I didn't know what to say. It's like the time some fella in Norfolk got shirty because I told a story about lions in Kenya – that's Year 1 Kenya, not the real Kenya in the real world. He was fuming because his daughter was in real Kenya. And he thought I was making light of the terrible state of real Kenya. I wasn't, I was making light of the Year 1 study of Kenya, where we look at it through apparently well-meant, but misguided, colonial goggles. He definitely couldn't see the wood for the trees. He was holding me responsible for his daughter's difficult experiences in real Kenya. She'd been shot at apparently. I was sorry about that but didn't know how I could change things for her in a conference hall in Norfolk. If I was him, I'd have suggested she come home.

30 See Lightfoot (2020). For fuck's sake. The opening paragraphs. See also:
'What did you learn about the Egyptians?'
'We wrapped Oliver up in toilet roll!'
'Is that all?'
'I'm 7 years old mate. Back off.'

mouth-breathing blandness and lack of vision in the organisations monitoring us? I don't have the silver bullets – and would be no good in a werewolf smackdown because of it – but we need all Inspectorate, all consultants, all observers, our colleagues, to invigorate us and show us the possibilities beyond our own grasp in that place and time. We need them to support us; to hold our hands and point the way. Many do, I'm sure, it's just that they don't appear to have the monopoly of airtime.

One thing we should and can do, however, is keep our classrooms shining by embracing fresh teacher acts; reflecting on the new whilst respecting the old. We need to push back against cold mediocrity and embrace warmth, imagination, transformative practice and botheredness.

[T]heir persistence, their physical and emotional stamina, their caring relationships with students, their commitment to acknowledging and appreciating student effort, their willingness to admit mistakes, their focus on deep learning, their commitment to inclusion, and their organization skills. (Haberman, 2004)

A word about warm demanders

Don't get confused like I did. I thought this was another version of that awful *warm strict* ideology. It isn't.[31] It's rooted in the work of Professor of Psychology Judith Kleinfeld (1975) from the University of Alaska. She manages to comfortably place the concept of being *a teacher exuding warmth* in a realm of high expectation and challenge. Kleinfeld demonstrates this by placing the warm teacher – she calls them 'warm demanders' – alongside other teacher types. I recognise these as I'm pretty sure I've been all of them.

---

31 *Warm strict* has a real sense of powerplay to it. The problem isn't the word 'warm', it's the word 'strict'. It connotes unreasonableness, humourlessness and having the agility of a boulder. A bit like Darth Vader. *Warm demander* on the other hand offers us high expectations with integrity and decency. A bit like Princess Leia.

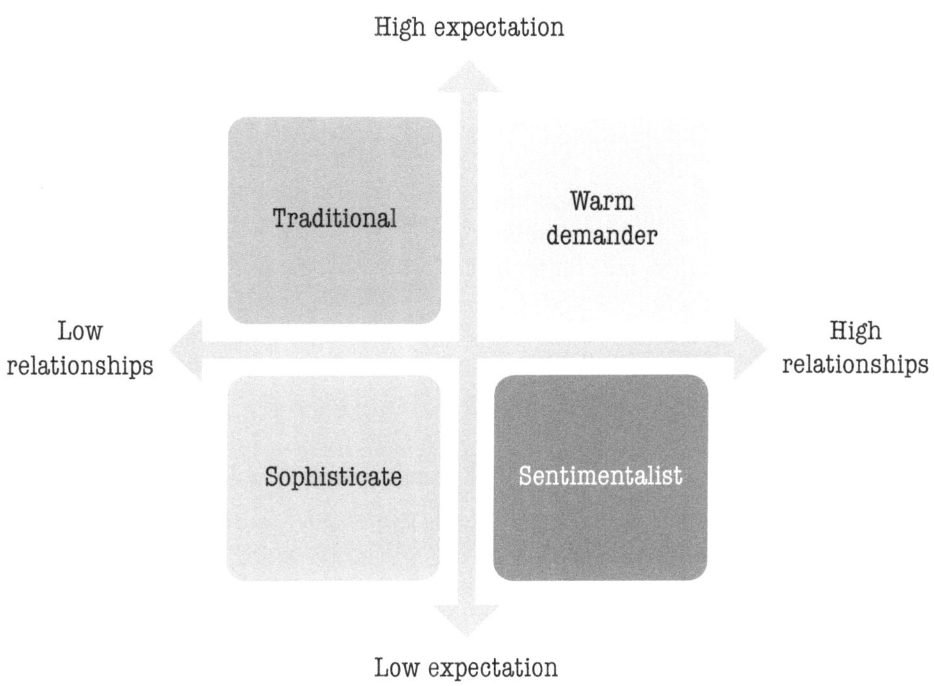

based on Kleinfeld (1975)

Sophisticates

These are teachers with <u>*low expectations and low relationships*</u>. They're not demanding and can be aloof and 'cold'. Their approach is very flaky, and they appear unconcerned by progress: *You either learn it or you don't, I've already passed my Year 1 exams.*

Traditionalists

These are teacher folk with <u>*high expectations and low relationships*</u>. These are teachers who set high expectations for pupils but view developing personal relationships with them as outside their professional remit: *This is absolutely vital to your understanding of my subject. Stop crying.*

Sentimentalists

Teachers with <u>low expectations and high relationships</u>. These are teachers who are genuinely kind and interested in their pupils; they may even have sympathy for them and will go the extra mile for them. Unfortunately, the sentimentalist drops the ball with low expectations: *Forget it. There's more to life than homework. Have a chocolate.*

Warm demanders

This is the sweet spot. Transformative teachers with <u>high expectations and high relationships</u> who can combine high levels of personal warmth with supportive demandingness. Or botheredness.

As I say, I've been all four of these over the years. Where do you see yourself?

Meanwhile ...

Bill and Ted are working on their history report:

> BILL:
> Okay, Ted, George Washington. One: the father of our country.
>
> TED:
> Two: born on President's Day.
>
> BILL:
> Three: the dollar-bill guy.
>
> TED:
> Bill, you ever made a mushroom out of his head? It's like, just like ...

BILL:

Ted. Alaska.

TED:

Okay. Um … Had wooden teeth, chased Moby Dick.

BILL:

That's Captain Ahab, dude.

Bill & Ted's Excellent Adventure[32]

Let's stop going around in circles.

CAPTION:

INTERMISSION #1[33]

Tales of a Travelling Teacher

A reverie of professional learning misadventures

Voluntary trumpet

The fog clears and here we are.[34] We're in Year 4 and it's all kicking off. You see, the children have created their own island, named it Fortune and essentially decided they are going to live in a utopian vision of peace and harmony with each other. All the laws are fair, and people who are naughty will be sent to the volcano in the centre of Fortune and lobbed in. So, that's all ace.

32 *Bill & Ted's Excellent Adventure*, dir. Stephen Herek [film] (Nelson Entertainment, 1989).
33 So, you're really enjoying the movie and then suddenly it comes to an abrupt halt and the lights go up. It's the 1970s and you can now get an ice cream. Or you can read this quick story about a lad and his imaginary trumpet.
34 This section was first published in Roberts (2017a).

Then, after playtime, it emerges (via an overheard conversation I've made up) that the ruthless king of a neighbouring island has decided to invade Fortune and claim it as his own. Authentic footage of the king announcing the decision is played to the people of Fortune.

And that's when it kicks right off.

Oliver suggests a covert assassination attempt which I 'value' by nodding my head whilst pointing at Darcy, desperately hoping for a more reasoned response to the news from her. She doesn't disappoint:

'We need to travel to their island and see if we can sort it out.'

Good girl.

Brandon, an epiphany child if ever there was one, launches his hand in the air and chunters, as epiphany children do, and offers his services. He's more than happy to travel to the island, which we name Moist – their idea, not mine (apparently it rains a lot which is why the king is a grumpy git – my idea, not theirs) – and so preparations for Brandon to travel are made. We are all satisfied that Brandon's spontaneous and often unexpected enthusiasm will be enough to win the nasty king over.

Hang on. What's he going to say to the king? What is the right thing to say to a difficult king? How should we approach such a tyrant? The class decide on taking along a variety of things to the audience with the king – an inventory of diplomacy. We reject Oliver's suggestion of poison but take on board Darcy's suggestion that Brandon shouldn't go on his own. We're all going. And we're all wrapped up in this playful fiction that is the avenue we're running up to get to some quality writing. Well, I think we all are.

I can see there's a boy who's not really joining in. He's a quiet one. A shadow kid. A ghost child. The kid who comes along and does everything right but stays in the shadows. In the tumult of what we're doing I quickly ask his name.

'Ben,' he whispers.

'Ben,' I whisper back, 'would you be able to announce us all to the king in his chamber?'

'I don't really want to say anything,' he responds.

'That's okay. Just announce us without saying anything. I'll be the king. Just do what you want to get my attention to tell me they are all here.'

The children are now gathered in one corner of the classroom. They have safely arrived on Moist. They struggle carrying the imaginary diplomatic gifts and their mouths are full of arguments yet to be heard. Ben stands next to me. I can sense his uncertainty. I can hear him thinking about how to announce Fortune's arrival without using words. I play with my cruel nails, plotting an invasion.

Without warning, yet wholly appropriately, Ben raises an invisible trumpet to his lips and sings a piercing yet flourishing fanfare. He sings it. It's spot on and ace in equal measure. Everyone, including twelve observing adults and Ben himself, crack up laughing. The fanfare is so brilliant, we make him sing it three times.

The fog descends. The quiet little boy found his voice and it was truly fit for a king. The spotlight-avoider had his moment, and it was beautiful.

THE MIDDLE GROUND

STEPHEN KING
CARRIE
CARRIE
STEPHEN KING
A MAJOR MOTION PICTURE
FROM UNITED ARTISTS

Y'all know me. Know how I make a livin'.

Quint, *Jaws*[1]

My work is a mish mash. I'm a travelling teacher, salaried by no one. I'm a speaker, writer and, according to my website biography, a humorist – but I'll leave that one with you. I'm also an anecdote collector and storyteller. I like to keep hold of stories, and teachers have loads of them. They don't even mind sharing them with me, the generous lot.[2] In a research context, anecdotes and stories are often viewed as flimsy and shallow, but what they are is evidence of one's own experience. It could be said that experience is research that hasn't been written up yet. It hasn't been cooled by cold, detached academia. _Research, it could be said, is just someone else's story. A remake of reality._

The last chapter suggested that many teachers entering the profession believe that the pedagogy of poverty is what teaching actually is. But as Oxford University and edu-legend (in my house, anyway) Professor Ian Menter points out, the twenty-first-century teacher needs to be something *more* than what the public expects. Menter offers four paradigms of teacher types, and I like 'em and that's why they're written here:

- **The effective teacher:** Skilled, content-confident whilst being effective in measurement and performance. They do the teaching business.

---

1   *Jaws*, dir. Steven Spielberg [film] (Zanuck/Brown Productions, 1975). The greatest film ever made.

2   Find my #TeacherStories show every Saturday morning at 9 a.m. on https://teacherhug.co.uk/.

- **The reflective teacher:** Incorporates the approach of the effective teacher, along with a clear ethos and values as well as a thorough knowledge of the children in front of them.

- **The enquiring teacher**: Incorporates the approaches of both the effective and reflective teacher, but includes a research-informed stance. They're hungry to know the *why* of teaching, as well as the *how*.

- **The transformative teacher:** Looks beyond the classroom, understands social context, moral and ethical stance, has useful alliances and networks whilst holding a holistic view of what education is. They *get* teaching. And they go for it.[3]

As a collective, they butter the parsnips, don't they? They do a good job of defining *stance*. Menter's four paradigms build on and usefully redefine what Haberman offered back in 1991 and later in 2004.[4] They're useful as they challenge what the public perceptions of teaching might be, and, in my experience, *beyond* what some teachers expect their own job to be. This is not meant to sound disrespectful to fellow colleagues. In fact, any sense of disrespect lies in the hands of uninformed policy-makers and leaders who put their teachers through burn-out processes and *un*intelligent accountability measures to simply survive as bureaucrats. This defensive approach to pedagogy – how we teach, our stance – flies in the face of what Menter and Haberman offer.

Teachers should be viewed as public intellectuals. But, in many ways, we've cast ourselves as curriculum deliverers, and if that curriculum is served cold, it's the children who are short-changed. We become the disappointing remake of *Robocop*. Cold soup lobbed in the face of innocent children.

I really like Menter's four stages. They're helpful in defining the teachers we want to be – that we signed up to be; the growing of each skin reflecting a developing ownership of what it is to teach. The stages sum up *phronesis* in action. Another reason they work is that they assume a teacher can do their job.

---

3 Ian Menter's lecture outlining this work can be found at Leeds Beckett (2016).
4 Haberman's (2004) attributes of star teachers used in the US: persistence; organisation and planning; beliefs about the value of students learning; approach to students; approach to at-risk students; ability to connect theory to practice; ability to survive in a bureaucracy; fallibility; explanation of students' success; explanation of teacher success. This is further explained by Nicolas Hartlep and Sara McCubbins (n.d.).

Read that last sentence again.

It's a useful professionally respecting starting point, which is welcome in the world where the 'inadequate' label essentially means 'chuffing shite'. What a terrible label to give a public intellectual.

This upward trajectory from the effective teacher to the transformative teacher is one of professional revival. The transformative teacher sees the school and its children in and beyond their context; they see the child in the world. Our issue is the fact that the effective teacher has become the gold standard in our schools. If you look back on my definitions, you'll see that to be such a teacher is still pretty good! And yet, there's that sense of being kept in a box; a place where creativity, risk and innovation are dispensed with in favour of conformity, middle-of-the-road-ness and unquestioning professional compliance rewarded with well-being events, a staffroom coffee machine and a stationery allowance. The status of 'public intellectual' is eroded to one of 'public servant': a sheep rather than a Sherpa.

This isn't an appeal to the maverick or the subversive. It's an appeal for professional imagination.[5]

A Shakespearean case study

Professional imagination and an agility of stance is prolific in all good classrooms. Menter's transformative teachers are alive and kicking in many of our schools. I'm a visiting teacher to a SEMH school where we understand that some of the children in class have had awful starts to life, but also we have the agreed curriculum stance that the bairns should be exposed to the works of Shakespeare.

Now the underskilled, cold-curriculum-serving teacher may walk into a challenging classroom like this one – with Max, Dom, Charlie, Seth and Rango sitting on separate desks – with downloaded worksheets explaining 'Why we have to learn about Shakespeare'. The skilled teacher who I find myself working with in this setting protects the children into a Shakespeare play by introducing them to themes first. In this case study example, I work alongside this ace teacher with this aforementioned group

____

5   Do you want to be the teaching equivalent of *Jaws* (1975) or *Sharknado 5: Global Swarming* (2017)? ☺

of Key Stage 3 boys. As teachers, we're metaphorically holding the nettles back that are wrapped around the Shakespeare curriculum by discussing the following two real-world characters:

Sepp Blatter (well-known, disgraced and recently forgiven footballing impresario)

Lance Armstrong (conflicted charity-supporting hero, public confuser and self-confessed cheat)[6]

A couple of boys know the two men and they immediately begin conversations, make judgements and offer responses to us about them. The rest listen and take on board the stories of the boys in the know. The class teacher nudges and 'tucks in' misconceptions and misunderstandings. A kid they all seem to call Rango (he's got big glasses, bless him) runs to Google, researching these dubious role models. We then all migrate from desks to desktops, trying to find out what we can about these men. It's a no-great-shakes research task but does the trick. The middle ground that can be a bit

6   See https://www.youtube.com/watch?v=N_OPSZ59Aws.

of a no man's land in a classroom between the teacher and their charges is safely traversed and the kids are *doing*.

On flip-chart sheets, we begin to capture words that are cropping up in the stories of these two men. For us as teachers, we know what they are, we're seeing themes emerge which are built upon in the ongoing task narration; that is, the teacher and I chipping in, describing and capturing what we, as the class, are finding out. We talk about:

- Greed
- Money
- Dishonesty
- Determination
- Corruption
- Power
- Lying
- Leadership
- Blood

The last bullet comes from a conversation around what we've found out about the cyclist Lance Armstrong; how he faked blood tests and influenced a bunch of top riders. We know this is an English lesson, right? Feasibly, at this point, it could be a lesson on ethics in sport, the science behind doping or an examination on tricking global audiences. So, PE, science, with a bit of media study thrown in, perhaps.

An introduction to Shakespeare is the actual focus and we're protecting the children in this SEMH setting into themes we may encounter in one Shakespeare play in particular: *Macbeth*. If we'd simply presented the boys with some original text, we'd have been doomed. Hey, along with the support teachers, we could have dressed as witches and re-enacted Act 1 Scene 1, and they'd have loved it initially, but that would have eventually moved past 'novelty', and we know what lies beyond novelty, don't we? Yep: chaos.[7]

---

7 This is why drama and drama strategies have disappeared from our schools and from the strategic toolkit of teachers: the fear of a loss of control that drama is perceived as inviting. The treatment of drama as a novelty approach in the classroom has deskilled us as transformative teachers. Inside drama lies the power of storytelling, and storytelling lies in the power of drama. Without it, teachers remain simply *effective*: deliverers of knowledge without context, purpose or perspective.

The child they called Rango[8] (real name, Ben) offered *power* as his thematic contribution. We talked about the nature of power – how it can be shared, abused, bought, given – and it made sense through the lens of the 'settling' images of the two men, up there on the whiteboard. This 'pulling in' of relevant and contemporary real-world examples is not a model for a curriculum but is perhaps a feature of what teachers need the capacity to be able to do – the taking of curriculum coverage and *re*-presenting it to children in a way that may resonate with them – an application of *phronesis* and professional imagination.

Power was also a good focus of chat for this setting, where classroom power struggles are a real thing. Thematic study of a Shakespeare classic being the kickstart for a reflection on one's own life is probably why he's still revered as an English literary great and why he features on our curriculum in this particular school.

Heathcote referred to this as 'bringing the out there into here';[9] the real world into the classroom, the unfamiliar made familiar. The sense of difficulty and perceived threat that the study of Shakespeare can present is kept low whilst the challenge of negotiating the text is kept high. The boys greet the arrival of Shakespeare with more warmth now, and for this to happen there has had to be some risk-taking from the teacher. And none of it can be achieved through dumbing down. In his book *The Beautiful Risk of Education*, Biesta (2016, 1) offers many descriptions of risk, including this one in his prologue:

> The risk is there because education is not an interaction between robots but an encounter between human beings … if we take the risk out of education, there is a real chance that we take out education altogether … Yet taking the risk out of education is exactly what teachers are increasingly being asked to do.

Blatter and Armstrong are not there to dumb down the study of *Macbeth*, but present to hook the children in; to build the botheredness. They're there to emotionally engage and provoke the children – their stories of infamy provide, as Curran (2008, 17) notes, 'large emotional content [that] may be learned very effectively. Your emotional brain is centrally involved in the vast majority of things you learn'. This emotional transaction cannot be found in the pedagogy of poverty, other than arguably in the emotion of fear, where negative emotions pervade.

8   Great film title right there. Oh, wait.
9   Personal correspondence.

We'll leave Splatter (as the kids called him) and Armstrong to drift back into the mists of a case study example, as we consider this assertion:

In the pedagogy of poverty, there is no middle ground.

The teacher stands at the front of the class and delivers the knowledge they know the children need in order to successfully navigate an imposed hurdle, like a test or exam. Occasionally, the teacher will shift to the side of the room, and then to the back to see what it looks like. Their stance is stilted and cold.

I remember standing on a chair, channelling *Dead Poets Society* again, whilst delivering some information about Seamus Heaney's beautiful poetry about his father to a biddable senior class. I'm proper going for it. Nobody could accuse me of a lack of passion. I'm practically performing the stuff like Brendan Gleeson on crack.[10] At times I'm thinking, *How would Gabriel Byrne read this?*[11] Then Callum puts his hand up. I pause and he speaks.[12]

'Sir. Get down from the chair. Just tell me what I need to know.'

(beat)

'If I get a grade C, mi mam says I can have a tattoo.'[13]

I get off the chair and metaphorically push Callum back in his chair, force his head back, dentist-like, and pour knowledge down his willing throat. Repeat ad nauseum. As I recite this memory right now, and at conferences worldwide, I get that feeling that we're all getting it, understanding it. And we're collectively shrugging our shoulders and saying to ourselves, 'Well, buddy, that's just the way it is'. It's like we've had *our*

---

10 Gleeson is a mint actor and one-time teacher.

11 Ah, Gabriel Byrne. Another mint actor and one-time teacher. The thing is, when I grow up, I want to be Gabriel Byrne. I mean, what a presence. What an actor. Look at his movies. Go on, just take a handful: *Miller's Crossing, Into the West, Wah-Wah, Excalibur, The Usual Suspects, The Courier, Gothic, Defence of the Realm.* Classics. And what about his turn in *Hereditary?* Just wow. Okay, enough fanboying. I recently listened to the audiobook of his autobiography, *Walking with Ghosts,* and I can confidently report that it is without doubt one of the most beautiful listens I've ever had. You must seek it out.

12 What is worse, he says it *sympathetically*. I'm mesmerised in the moment by the bleakness of my role as an *effective* teacher, *doing it* rather than *getting it*.

13 Grade C was a decent pass in England back in the day.

heads tilted back and *our* throats filled with gunk that sums up all Menter's effective teacher actually is: an articulation of the teacher lacking *phronesis*; the teacher who is doing what is expected of them by people who have forgotten what it is to teach; or have never taught a lesson in their lives. And their kids are *engaged*, so that's all brilliant then. The pedagogy of poverty is alive and kicking, and the effective teacher, the foundation point in Menter's list (and I know I'm repeating myself), is the *gold standard* of teaching; something to aspire to, and not to be built from. I'm trying my best to pull back from a full-blown rant, but let me put it like this:

> There is nothing wrong with being an effective teacher. Of course there isn't. It's just that this shouldn't be the end of the teacher story and yet, for some, it is. The job is done when the books are marked, the sanctions recorded and the parents informed.

Teaching is so much more though. *It's a social, academic and human endeavour.* Put it like this:

Social	Academic	Human
Relationships	Knowledge	Warmth
Circles of influence	Skill	Optimism
Collegiality	Understanding	Creativity
Family	Research	Trust
Community	Application	Communication

Three strands. Three pillars. The social, academic and human considerations around teaching could be expanded on further than I've done here. You hopefully get the drift, though. When I look at this framework I've concocted for you, I see an attempt to entice the most naive of teachers alongside the most worn down, into a space where great things can happen. This place, good people, is *the middle ground*.

The middle ground between teacher and class has become a no man's land for some: teachers don't want to go there and the class aren't bothered – they're too busy tracking the teacher's movement at the front of the classroom, like drones programmed to watch, observe and engage with their eyes but not their hearts.

In some classrooms we've lost this middle ground, but it's not so difficult to open it back up. Working in the middle ground is where the interesting stuff can happen, as I'll outline in later chapters. It's the place where the *us and them* becomes the *we*. And don't misread this as an invitation to a softening of the teacher's role or status in the classroom; it's actually an open invitation to offer complexity to children's understanding and processing of knowledge. It all happens in the safe space of the middle ground. And it's where botheredness is manufactured, built, developed, established and cultivated. Look at it like this:

Here's a little story about this so-called *middle ground*. When I was a 14-year-old clumsy, crash-helmet-haircut-adorned Specials fan back in the 1980s, I had a penchant for lurid horror fiction. By lurid, I mean the covers of these pulp gore-rippers caught my eye and I was fascinated by them.[14] I devoured novels by Guy N. Smith, James Herbert and Stephen King. King was a particular favourite. He still is. When I was 14, all I wanted to do was watch horror movies, but often they were difficult to track down. The films I wanted to see didn't always get a cinema release and if they did, there was no way I was going to get in to see them. I had the face of a small child. The alternative was to get stuck into some VHS tapes – themselves a dandy vehicle for shocking art[15] – but they'd be hard to rent without a false beard.[16] So, I read books.

---

14 A forgotten art form. See https://www.pinterest.com/jonnothin/the-best-horror-paperback-art/.

15 Ah, the mighty big-box VHS horror movie art is a thing of collective beauty. Some great examples at Mulcahey (2013). Or in my attic.

16 At Bury Market there were two stalls I loved. One sold books. The other sold VHS movies. This is in the 1980s. *Jerry's Vids*. It's where I picked up my first copy of Tobe Hooper's *Texas Chainsaw Massacre* and a big-box widescreen copy of *Monty Python and the Holy Grail*. They're on a shelf close by as I type this. Yep, I'm a right geek. I paid for them by being the youngest pit orchestra double bassist in Lancashire. It was a lucrative cash-only pursuit. I was minted and it was a great alternative to getting piss-wet through doing a paper round.

Horror novels. The more unsettling, the better. One of my favourites was the novel *Carrie* by Stephen King.[17] The cover echoes Sissy Spacek's portrayal of the doomed titular character. I loved the book, longed to see the movie but had no chance because it was hard to track down. *Carrie* would be part of a collection carried around school in the depths of my Head sports bag, alongside my stained homework diary (complete with forged parental signatures[18]), my blue Yoda flask, schoolbooks and pencil case. My very own mobile library had the aforementioned *Carrie*, who was joined by William Peter Blatty's *The Exorcist*, David Seltzer's *The Omen* and another of King's – the mighty *Salem's Lot*.[19] All crushed into the bottom of the bag and my source of company for the long bus rides to and from school. Every Friday afternoon of my fourth year held a particular treat for me as this was the time that I'd be able to read one of my library *in class*.[20] Buzzing! This was because the English teacher had deemed this particular lesson a *silent reading lesson*, which meant I could whip *Carrie* out of my bag and continue to devour it ahead of my bus journey home.[21] Next to me is Phil and he's reading one of Enid Blyton's The Faraway Tree books. He loves them with the same fervour as I have for my treasures. The teacher – we'll call him Mr Wilson (because that was his name) – is sitting at his desk at the front of the class. He's been our teacher for a couple of months. One of those men who can't understand how he's ended up teaching, when the world had promised him so much in his younger years. I've never seen him stand. Until today.

'What on earth is that?' Mr Wilson asks, using his red biro as a pointer.

I let the Carrie drift up to cover my face, showing Mr Wilson the book, its title and image.

He blows his top. And stands. 'What a disgusting thing!'

I think he means the book. He tells me to stand, and I do. I can feel my legs beginning to quake a little. I'm not a bad lad. I'm getting done for reading. Everyone else has buried their faces in their own silent reading books. Mr Wilson is now in front of me. He's not a big man but has a red beard that makes his head look unfeasibly large. His

---

17 This one: https://www.pinterest.com/pin/380906080954273378/.
18 Sorry Mum.
19 At this time, the movie of *The Exorcist* was banned on VHS and impossible to track down. Apart from *Jerry's Vids* on Bury Market but it'd set you back 50 quid and might be a bit shaky.
20 'Fourth year' would be Year 10 to you young 'uns.
21 Silent reading lessons are essentially a hangover-shifter for hard-drinking teachers. Well, they were when I was at school.

eyes are bulging out of his head. He has the reaction of someone who is genuinely angry. I mean, really angry. Like, grown-up angry. Proper pissed off. I find it discombobulating to say the least. It's also a little upsetting and I'm trying to control my tear ducts. It's not good to be reduced to tears in front of your peers because of a book. No one cries over books, do they?

Mr Wilson, who I've stopped listening to, snatches the book from my limp grip, turns on his heel and lobs it into the 1980s classroom waste bin overflowing with pencil sharpenings and discarded curled-edged sandwich crusts. It's a good shot, to be fair. He feels it. He spins around and points again with his finger extension.

'Share with him.'

I drop to my seat and Phil moves himself across the desk and I jump into the middle of some Faraway Tree adventure. He knocks my knee with his in solidarity. I compose myself and the room is silent again. Every so often I look to the bin at the front of the room.

When the lesson finishes, we all leg it. I forget to check the bin straightaway but at the end of the day I return to Mr Wilson's class. He's a proper 3 o'clock merchant, so there's no sign of him. I've missed my bus but want my book back. When I get to the bin, the cleaner hasn't done their rounds yet. The bin is still full, but I have to get my hands in as the book isn't on the top where I thought it'd be. It must have slid in due to its weight. Pulling back stale food, chewing gum and debris, I see there's no sign of it. It's gone. And I know where.

I picture Mr Wilson, sitting at the lights in his used Sierra, glancing at *Carrie* on his passenger seat and looking forward to devouring her that evening. I feel the injustice of it. Another kid might have run off with the book, sure. But that doesn't sit with my teenage brain jumping to conclusions.

The next day in assembly, our head teacher, Miss Smith, who I really liked, warns us not to bring inappropriate literature into school. It's nicely done, and all my pals know it's me she's talking about. I went to Bury Market that weekend and bought another copy of *Carrie*. It went back into my Head bag library. It just never came out in Mr Wilson's lesson again.

As I write this all these years later, I still feel a twinge of annoyance at the petty little man. I should get a grip but, frankly, I can't let it go. The man – my English teacher

– had no concept of what it meant to inspire. He could not find it in his professional oeuvre to meet me halfway. Me. Spotty me. Crash-helmet-head me. Literature-hungry me. Mr Wilson couldn't invite me to the middle ground.

Here's what he could have done on seeing my silent reading text of choice. This is the fantasy alternative I play out in my head:

WILSON:

What's that you're reading?

CRASH HELMET:

It's *Carrie* by Stephen King, sir.

(Wilson moves to Crash Helmet and kneels at his side to speak to him quietly. The class are oblivious.)

WILSON:

(gently) Put it away, Hywel. It's not really appropriate for this class.

(Crash Helmet puts the book away because he's a good lad.)

WILSON:

Look, have you heard of Edgar Alan Poe?

(Crash Helmet shrugs.)

WILSON:

H. P. Lovecraft?

CRASH HELMET:

I'm not sure, sir.

WILSON:

Look, my knees are killing.

(Wilson stands.)

WILSON:

Stephen King is very influenced by these writers from the nineteenth and early twentieth centuries. Poe. Lovecraft. If you go to the library, try them. Seek

them out. They'll challenge you and you'll see what an influence
they've been on the horror genre – films as well as books. Anyway, for
now, share with Phil.

If he'd done that … if it had played out like that, Mr Wilson would have been my hero. My inspiration. Instead, I did an English degree to spite him. I'm writing about him now because he never found the middle ground. That's how important it is. Mr Wilson never shared his passion for his subject. It was like he never wanted to be there. He was not bothered. And it showed. And that's why I carry him around with me to this day. His stance was mostly seated in a physical sense, but it was in a mental sense as well. Passive resignation.

The middle ground requires a shift of stance, where we respond rather than react to things. Reactions are knee-jerk and, although perhaps justifiable in the moment, are not great in the long run. Responding, as Leo Babauta (2013) notes, is 'taking the situation in, and deciding the best course of action based on values such as reason, compassion, cooperation, etc.'[22]

Stance is the way you shift yourself mentally (and perhaps physically) when you know a child in the class is anxious and you're worried about them. That is, you're shifting your stance from 'knowledge curator' to 'concerned adult'. It's the physical and mental agility I talked about earlier. Think of the teen always silent in your form time, or the small child in dirty uniform – they're invitations to the middle ground. In those situations, you take the pastoral lead because (hopefully) your values, your authentic care and your decency kick in. In a curriculum-delivery scenario, how do we get to the middle ground? We may well find it easy to step into, but what about the children in front of you? Why don't they just leap in with gusto? Well, dear reader, we're back with the idea of 'protecting children in'. Just like employing Lance Armstrong to prepare a navigation of _Macbeth_, we need to find a strategy, some way of inviting children to the middle ground; a building of botheredness. A hook, a lure, a stimulus, an enquiry. Something that celebrates curiosity and makes it enticing. Something that will encapsulate teaching as a social, academic and human endeavour.

That something, dear reader, is _story_.

....

22 It's a good piece by Leo Babauta. He notes the power of taking 'pause', which is very zen, but
   when you think about it, really true.

CHAPTER 4

LET'S SAY

Human minds yield helplessly to the suction of story. No matter how hard we concentrate, no matter how deep we dig in our heels, we just can't resist the gravity of alternate worlds.

Jonathan Gottschall (2012, 3)

Sometimes reality is too complex. Stories give it form.

Often attributed to film director, screenwriter and film critic Jean Luc Godard

Let's say ...

- We are the last of our tribe.
- We are on the ship trapped in ice.
- A disease has infiltrated our tight-knit community.
- The old, abandoned factory hides something magical.
- There are two lions in a zoo.
- We are taking our circus to town.
- The kebab shop is going to close down.
- The big bad wolf is frightened.
- The old man won't leave his house.
- The Vikings have lost their water supply.

The phrase 'Let's say' is a useful one. It acts as a contract between teacher and class. It's far preferable to 'Let's pretend' or 'Let's imagine', which can reduce teacher instruction to begging. This was a regular feature of a classroom in my early career. I'd ask the class to pretend, and they wouldn't see the point of it. I'd ask them to imagine, and some kids would opt out, saying they couldn't. Getting kids to join in often felt desperate. When I started using 'Let's say', things changed. It's hard for kids to fathom a negative response to the invitation and by the time they've thought of something, we've moved on.

'Let's say' is an invitation to the imaginative realm; a story world, if you like, that rests in the middle ground we've already talked about. As soon as the teacher says, 'Let's say …', we're shifting stance and opening possibility, using narrative and story as a washing line on which to hang key knowledge, learning, challenge, enquiry and curiosity.

A 'Let's say' leading to a story or narrative can build a sense of cohesion across a project where a body of knowledge needs to be learned, understood and applied. It also builds children's botheredness around a topic when they experience a narrative unfolding. The washing line analogy helps, as we can see a line on which to clip the key bits of knowledge and, in turn, cover the coverage, and thus, sleep well at night.

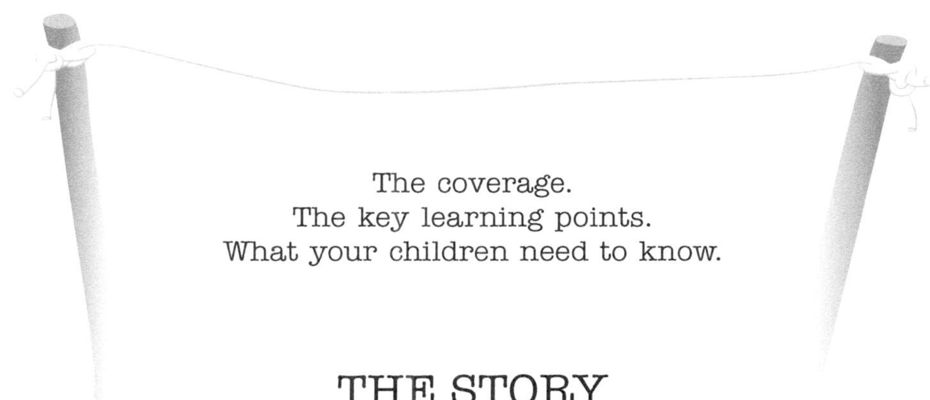

THE STORY

The story is the through-line and is there to help, not to hinder. Think of the Vikings project in the Warm School. The story helped, and the coverage was covered and then some. The story also helped the children remember and retain the learning; as Daniel Willingham (2004) reminds us, stories are 'psychologically privileged … there's something inherent in the story format that makes them easy to understand and remember'.

Storytelling could be regarded as a key teacher skill – the ability to communicate complexities and concepts in a way that doesn't dumb down; rather, it protects children into understanding and learning the knowledge, skills and ideas they're being presented with.

So, now I've burdened you with the transformative trait of being a storytelling teacher, we should perhaps look at how a story, or a 'Let's say', can be planned out for the classroom. All stories have familiar elements, from characters – heroes, villains, mentors – settings – future, present, past – themes – comedy, tragedy – and structure. You can look at Joseph Campbell's (2008) hero's journey for more on all of that. The good news is right here though: you're not creating a story that, finger's crossed, is going to be turned into a Hollywood movie. No. _This is teaching. This is still teaching._ And we're going to look at a simple structure that will support your planning of a teaching and learning experience.

Think about what all stories have. All of them. Here you go, check this out:

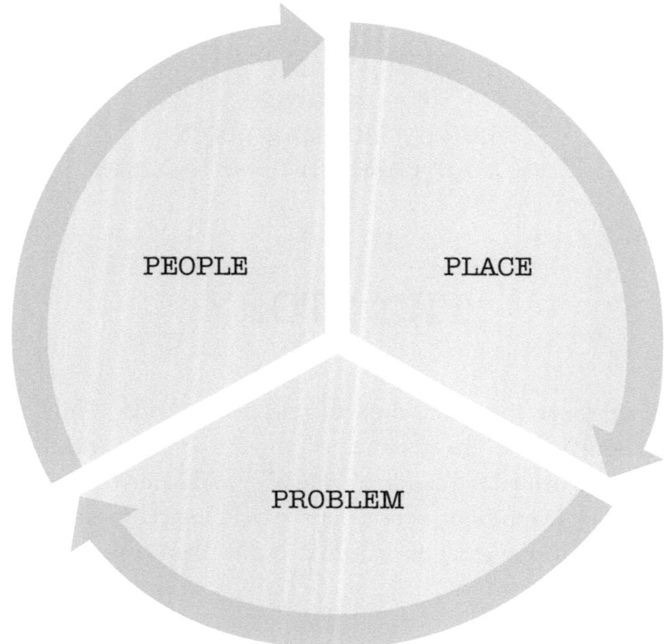

Story wheel 1 (created with Dr Debra Kidd)

There you go. That's _all stories_, right there. I've tried to nail down here that through-line of a story. ALL stories are here in these three elements:

- People

- Place

- Problem

Imagine an episode of your favourite TV show where there were no problems. _EastEnders_ where there's zero tension between characters, and everyone is happy to mind each other's stalls.

No.

Stories require people (or voices) in a place (and time) encountering bumps in the road – problems, dilemmas and predicaments. Have a play with the wheel. Maybe this can help:

- People:
  - Voices
  - Beliefs
  - Communities
  - Attitudes
  - Perspectives
  - Articulation
  - Standpoint
- Place:
  - Environment
  - Landscapes
  - Where are we? When are we?
  - Pressures
- Problem:
  - Challenges
  - Concerns
  - Dilemmas – how can our new knowledge help?

In the classroom setting, the story is a vehicle on which to hang the coverage, as mentioned earlier. In the story of the Vikings and the Warm School, the narrative came from this humble beginning:

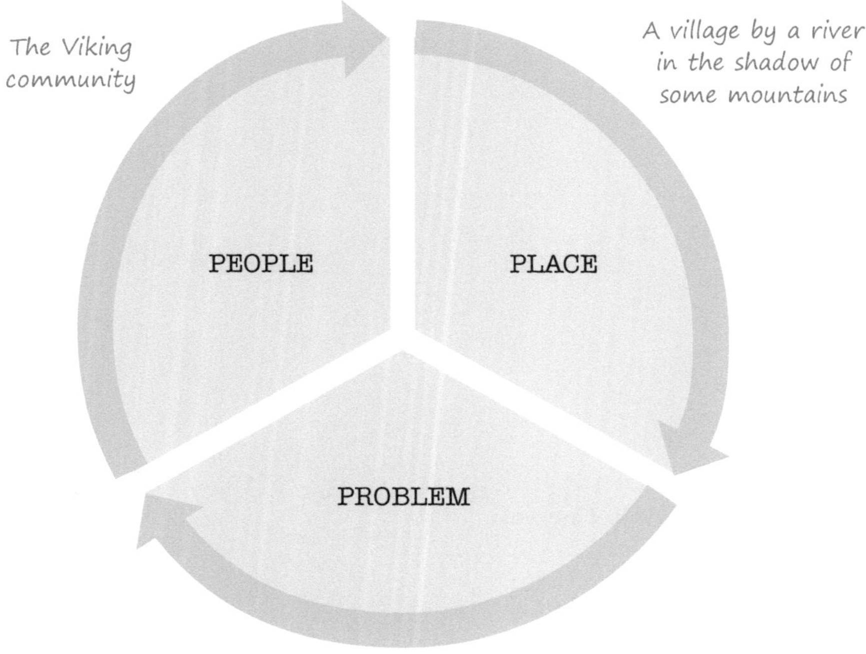

Prior to going to the school, that's all I had in my plan. Three snappy sentences that could get a narrative launched. Another way of looking at it is this:

Let's say there's a Viking village and the river that supports them runs dry.

That's not the whole story of course, but it's a decent springboard for the professional imagination to kick in.[1] It's the foundations to a project that can then be peppered with knowledge.

So, basically, via a '*Let's say*', we can take the children inside a story. It's a story that's set in the imaginative world but is one that crosses into the real world due to the nature of curriculum demands. If not, we are, if you like, remaining in the world of play. That's not to say that that doesn't have purpose, but we need to make sure that whatever strategies we're using to hook children into learning, there needs to be a value attached to them. Otherwise, there's a danger that what we're doing with the children is shallow. That takes us comfortably to my second set of P's:

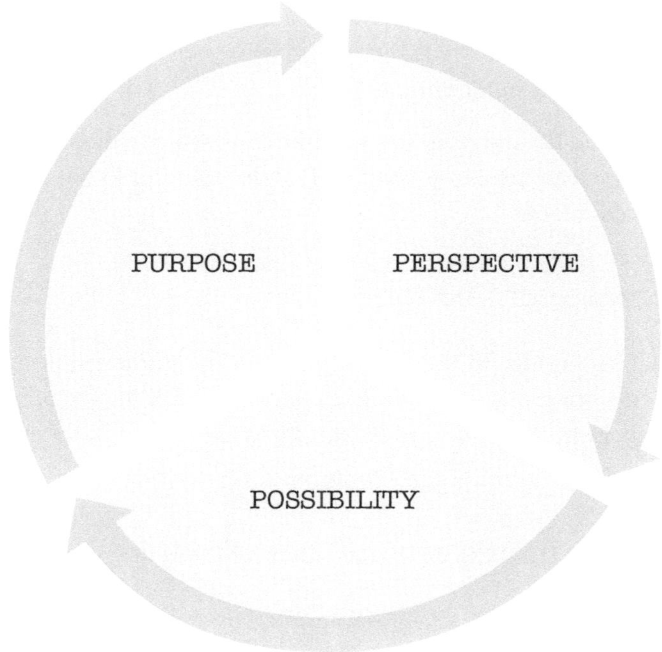

Story wheel 2 (created with Dr Debra Kidd)

1 You can find the complete narrative later in this book. ☺

As the research into how we learn has developed, it's become apparent that narratives and stories can be a real boon to supporting children in navigating complexity and challenge. In their article for Harvard Business Publishing, Vanessa Boris and Lani Peterson (2017), share their thoughts about how stories can be used to help learners. They offer these headlines for us to reflect on:

Stories can:

- Create connection.

- Develop investment.

- Align with purpose.

- Enable retrieval.

- Provide risk-free experimentation.

- Promote growth and an exchange of ideas.

This is a pretty good list and resonates with the aims and intentions of using story to support classroom learning. Stories help us find the emotional slam dunk in the curriculum. Let's take a look.

Stories create connection

Stories can act as a bridge to the middle ground. The introduction of human and societal elements can protect children into complexity. Finding the person in a mess who would benefit from our learned knowledge is the start of a story: a person, in a place with a problem.

Stories develop investment (botheredness)

Why on earth should kids care about Mayans? Not only are they ages ago, they're also miles away. You don't get much Mayan action in Bridlington. Except when a teacher builds a narrative around the key knowledge. The study of Mayans in upper primary school is long-established project, so what if we were the scientists behind the discovery of a long-lost city in Guatemala that revealed to us new information, not known before: huge wall defences and raised highways telling us that the Mayans feared invaders and that trade between cities was a big deal? How would we get this new information across to the world? How could we ensure the preservation of the ancient ruins, hidden for centuries under rainforest vegetation, that will become vulnerable when the discovery is shared? The science of a (real) story from 2018 suddenly has that emotional punch. Especially if the scientists are met with some resistance from groups hoping to protect the site and deny scientific access.

Stories help learning align with purpose

If children are required to write diary entries about what it's like to be a Victorian street urchin, the danger is that they and the teacher will go all Lionel Bart and produce something so far removed from reality, it'd belong in a musical. Using an image of a Victorian street child as a hook can get children focused in, aligned. Especially if they give the anonymous child in the old internet-sourced image a realistic name. Not Bilbo, SpongeBob or Dave.

Stories enable retrieval

Stories help children remember stuff. It's the emotional content that hits home. The little boy remembering the Viking dragon may also have been able to say where the Vikings came from. It's just that the dragon was more interesting to him. Because he was 8. Ask me about a story I can remember everything about: *Jaws*, the film about a shark chomping down on the residents of a holiday island. I saw it when I was 5 (it was classed as an A certificate – the old version of a PG) and I remember it because of its emotional impact on my young mind – John Williams' iconic music, the leg drifting to the bottom of the lagoon, Ben Gardner's head falling through the gap in the boat bottom, Quint getting bitten and gulped by the beast, my dad's pipe burning St Bruno Ready Rubbed, him holding my hand in the scary bits and my brother laughing quietly and nervously. Emotional stories enable retrieval. You'll have loads.

Stories provide risk-free experimentation

And this is why drama and enquiry pedagogy offer an ace vehicle where children can stand in the shoes of people living other histories than their own. During the study of Guy Fawkes, another mainstay of the English primary curriculum, what if the children were the Royal Guard responsible for the protection of King James I and his

Parliament? Or, another example, the children are the monks of Lindisfarne seeing the Norse invaders on the horizon in AD 792. Where is the curriculum in that?

Stories promote growth and an exchange of ideas

Using story, drama and acquired knowledge to navigate dilemma and desirable difficulty places children knee-deep in ideas. They're not just getting their toes wet with a PowerPoint and an accompanying worksheet. They're finding their words, their opinions, articulating their responses to material and developing ideas based on *their* learning. As edu-legend Dr Debra Kidd (2020) reminds us in her brilliant book *A Curriculum of Hope*, stories place children 'in' the learning, alongside the teacher, embedding not just key intended knowledge but also basic human values around compassion and kindness.

As I say, a pretty good list of why stories help from Boris and Peterson. Let's be clear on this, though, stories aren't there as a façade to lie to children. This isn't the realm of 'lying for learning', which, now I've written it down, looks like a potential money-spinner. I'll call it *#L4L* and do a few webinars. I'll be in clover …

Lying for Learning – A bluffer's guide

We should never lie to kids. Having written that now, I'm pretty sure I've lied to kids a few times. Like the hand-in date for the essential homework a week before the real deadline. Or the fact that I'm an ex-Olympic whistler. Or that I keep pigeons. According to research, 84% of parents lie to their children to get them to behave. I'm sure it's a lower percentage of teachers. Some of you reading this will be parents and you may have just done a little bit of reflection about whether you yell some lies to the small people in your house. That's okay. I did the same and I'm definitely in the 84%. Don't judge me. It works a treat.

And do you know what? When my own son was younger, I was quite happy for him to believe in unicorns and dragons. Now he's older, I want him to have the capacity to suspend his disbelief. When watching Peter Jackson's films of *The Hobbit*, I don't want him to deconstruct Andy Serkis' mo-cap suits, or sit there, aged 8, explaining to me how the filmmakers have achieved the visual feast we're eating up; I want him to be absorbed into it through the powerful story-telling, the tension and the visualisation of Tolkien's Middle Earth. Films, like books, aren't lies. They're fiction. Deconstruction of filmmaking technique can come later. For now, let's get stuck in it. As I write this at my tired and fragile age, I still want to believe in unicorns and dragons. Is that okay with the Professional Imagination police? Or the Inspectorate?

But in the classroom? There shouldn't be any peddling of genuine, dark-hearted lies? No. Absolutely not. It could be misconstrued that a lot of what I'm writing about here is tricking children into learning by telling lies wrapped in stories. It isn't. It's hooking them in and getting them emotionally involved within a context – the Mayans, the Vikings and so on. Tricking implies that there's a devious motive on the teacher's side; hooking and luring children has no malice but rather a real focus on participation, progress and botheredness. The teacher's desire and motive is to have investment and more from their children. With the classes I work with, I introduce the learning by explaining what we're going to be doing. These are learning scripts I have in my repertoire; they're good examples of inductive language:

> It's great to be with you today. Is it okay if you show me how good you are at listening? Good. Can you help me? Can you help me with a story?

Of course, that's fine for the younger children. What about the older ones? If I go in all children's-TV-presenter, they'll eat me alive (or phone Childline). I will, however, find the words and they'll have the same intention as the words I choose with the younger children. When getting to the heart of the context, this is a familiar exchange with older children:

> ME: 'We've had a letter from NASA.'
>
> YEAR 8: 'You wrote that.'
>
> ME: 'Yes, I did. Is that okay with you?'
>
> YEAR 8: *(shrugs shoulders in a knock-yourself-out-Sir kind of way)* 'Whatever.'

The direction for the children comes from my question 'Is that okay?' For such a brief question, it carries a lot of weight, especially when backed up with some excellent Obi-Wan/Johnny Rotten eye contact. The question 'Is that okay?' is not confrontational (as I may have just suggested it could be). Rather, it suggests that we're in it together and operating in the moment. It's seeking a consensus where, in order to move on, we all have to agree. Just like 'Let's say'.

Another example of this (and one we use a lot in the special setting) is the moment we need to speak to a witness or someone from within the learning context. We may call this 'hot seating' or 'teacher-in-role' but, certainly in these special educational settings, we don't name them. Instead, we may say:

We need to hear from her, don't we? I'll be her for now. Is that okay? I'll be her.

This, like a lot of what comes out of our mouths as teachers, is a script which is looking for agreement. Here are some others:

- Do we all agree with …?

- Can we assume that …?

- Thinking about what we've discovered, what is our priority action now?

- Could we find disagreement with this?

- Would it be okay if we …?

- Are we all happy with this?

These scripts can place the children firmly in the learning and, if nothing else, are a useful way of seeking participation from those who are reluctant – they drive for opinion and a reaction to the work, again, in the moment. They can support the filling of a gap in a child's confidence and nature.

So it's never lying. It's seeking an atmosphere and environment where we can step into the imaginative for a while – the middle ground of joint productive activity. If you fear the word *imaginative* (or it simply makes you cross), call it a fiction, a story, a context. When children work in this imaginative story frame, they are challenged, face setbacks, have to make difficult decisions and so on. And they get to do it within the security blanket you've created. We all know it's not real. And scripts like the ones above can help and support the suspension of disbelief.

Disclaimer

I do regularly hear about schools running theme days where an alien crash site has been set up on the school field, with the local community police officer standing around like an extra in a low-budget Z-grade sci-fi movie. If you've done one of these and it's worked brilliantly, well done. I'm a big fan of things that work well – when children are having a load of fun, are learning and are challenged by the context of the special event or curriculum drop-down day. These days aren't what I mean by hooks but, by all means, knock yourselves out – as long as:

- It has value.
- It has purpose.
- It offers possibility for future enquiry and study.
- We've got it all in perspective.

Health warning

I've also heard of days like this when things have gone wrong, however. And this makes me appeal to you in the strongest terms:

DON'T DO A BRADFORD.

I even used big letters here. And underlined it.

Bradford is a great city and down the road from where I live. It's a diverse city steeped in beauty and history. It has, like many cities, its fair share of challenges and areas of deprivation. I've worked in a few schools in Bradford and have written about one of them elsewhere in this book.

I heard recently of a Bradford school where the entire (primary phase) school were brought into the hall for some important news. There was a palpable air of tension dripping from the walls as the children waited for the head teacher to speak. The gym bars were secured to the wall, the battered CD/radio combo pumped out 'Incantation' and teachers sat on chairs flanking the quiet crowd of youngsters. A piano propped up a large wardrobe that could well house rows of CDs, song sheets and a miscellaneous haberdashery of forgotten shite. The wardrobe stood, keeping its secret.

A couple of weeks before, a really well-meaning gang of teachers were planning the school's first theme day where the whole timetable would be suspended, and all the children would be working to the same remit. In this case, the school were going to look at 'Monsters'. And one monster in particular: Gollum, from the aforementioned works of Tolkien. If you listen carefully, you can hear Tolkien spinning in his grave as I recount this tale.

I can picture it now. Can you? We've all been there. Excited teachers divvying up responsibility. Charlotte is a whiz with papier mâché and will make a Frank Sidebottom-style head mask for someone to wear. But who? Sam suggests the new, young teaching assistant, Mr Meek, who has the physique to pull Gollum off. Just get him dressed as Gollum and bung the head mask on.

(Dressed as Gollum???)

Can you see where this is going?

On the trigger word that fell from the head teacher's mouth, the wardrobe doors burst open and out jumped a homemade Gollum, who proceeded to leap around. To be fair, all accounts suggest Mr Meek was committed to the role, in his massively inappropriate Middle Earth loincloth and paper helmet head.

A hook?

A lure?

No.

A trauma.

Do you know that bit in 1970s disaster movies when the disaster is revealed and everyone legs it, panic-stricken, in loads of different directions? Well, that's what ensued.

Mr Meek running around the front of the hall was supposed to inspire the children in the hall. Instead, he horrified them. Realising it was all going Pete Tong, the head attempted to calm everyone down with: 'It's okay! It's just Mr Meek!'

Mr Meek, realising it had all gone a bit south, then committed an additional ill-judged act by ripping off the mix of papier mâché and latex that obscured his own face. Holding the remnants of his misguided face in his hands, the reassurance of 'Children! It's me! Mr Meek!' fell on deaf ears.

The children were bereft, traumatised and upset. So were the staff. So were the parents who came to collect their children. Then it got into the press.

Ouch.

Ten things for the school to consider here (and no, I haven't done *that* many lists so far):

- Children should be (and can be) protected into learning.
- Shock tactics, by their very nature, are shocking.
- Never allow anyone to rip their faces off in front of children.
- The proposal of Hunting Gollum (as I've called it) was flawed and lacked integrity.
- Gimmicks don't make for great learning.
- Someone willing to dress up, trigger words and all the adults playing along may make for an exciting atmosphere, but it excludes the children from the context and is, therefore, unfair and, in my opinion, doomed.
- Tricking children by leaving them out of the 'joke', is tight and, above all, humiliating.
- Getting children's attention shouldn't be an upsetting experience.
- The only learning is on the part of the adults ('Well, we won't be doing that again') and the danger is that any future creative risks will be lost.
- When you're 5, an adult pretending to be Gollum can shit you right up.

Clearly, none of the adults in this little vignette set out to upset the children. They didn't look at themselves in the mirror that morning thinking, *Today, I'm going to ruin everything*. No. They were misguided, and it all went very pear-shaped. But no one was intending that. Unfortunately, it did go wrong, and the results of that can be, in the cold light of day, demoralising, amongst other things. When things go wrong, as I'm sure we can all agree, our confidence is knocked and we take on a reluctant disposition so that any thoughts of risk-taking and innovation down the line are placed in the filing cabinet marked 'No thanks, not today. I think we'll stick with what's always worked. None of that New Age trendy stuff'. And I don't blame anyone for that. What went wrong here though was that from the outset, the whole thing was flawed because of its conceit: lie to the children and they'll play along.

Well, they won't. They'll find out and hate you for it.

CAPTION:

INTERMISSION #2

Tales of a Travelling Teacher

A reverie of professional learning misadventures

Don't Stop Us Nar

The fog clears and here we are.[2]

I have filled the request form in and submitted to the copyright owners everything they need to give my school and I permission to do four performances of the newly released schools version of the hit Queen musical *We Will Rock You*! Permission granted, rehearsal schedule published and our auditions-of-sorts complete. I say *auditions-of-sorts* because, basically, if the kids rock up to the auditions, they can be in it.

---

2   This section was first published in Roberts (2019a).

Big, small, old or young – if you wanna be in it, turn up when you're needed, then you are *in* and you will reap the glory and rewards of a showbiz lifestyle for three nights in February! You'll also be the envy of your peers and all those who sacked it off before opening night. Yep, we are cruising for greatness.

We aren't *Glee Club*, and we aren't in the West End. We are a proper town-centre high school in Barnsley, South Yorkshire. It's 2006 and the rights to put the show on haven't been available long. The great folk at Queen Limited, or whatever it might be called, have given it to schools and amateur societies to perform for a cheap fee – for a song, you might say. They are generous and we are buzzing.

When I announce it's to be our next production, the kids go bonkers and start the instantly recognisable *stamp stamp clap* that signals the title song. I'm bleary-eyed for the right reasons as I fondly remember an ancient Christmas as a kid, giving my dad the cassette of *Queen's Greatest Hits* – the one where they all wear leather jackets on the front. He loved that tape.

A week before curtain-up and the tickets have been sold, Mad Max-style costumes nailed and Elaine in reprographics is wearing out the photocopier doing the programmes. It's all systems go, and we are levitating with hard-won joy.

Then a letter arrives. It's from the copyright people. There is to be a Northern tour of *We Will Rock You* in a few months and one of the venues is Bradford, an hour's drive away. It's a professional production and our performances will apparently have a negative impact on ticket sales. I can hardly register what I'm reading. My first instinct is to ring them, and so I do. I'm greeted with an inhuman first responder who ignores my arsenal of human arguments:

'The cast are not professional … the cast are kids … the cast are kids in Barnsley … the cast are kids in Barnsley who have worked their socks off … the cast are kids in Barnsley who have worked their socks off and just want to show their folks. They love Queen'.

'It's all in the terms and conditions, Sir' is the response I get.

And then it hits me. I have an internal downward rush and feel sick. What do I tell the students? I'm thinking of Nathan in particular. He hasn't had any bother in school since he got to be in the show. His recent record is spotless. This news could ruin him.

He'll kick right off, bless him. Then I see all their faces in my mind's eye and my head starts melting.

I go to teach Year 7.

At home that night, I fire up the computer and hope the current internet provider we have will give me a break from their often-temperamental consistency. I google *BRIAN MAY*. I google *CONTACT BRIAN MAY*. It honestly takes me moments to find a 2006-equivalent of a 'Contact me' page. And I write. I try and maintain my dignity, but it's close to begging. Hopefully Brian will hear me. *HEAR ME, BRIAN!!!*

School the next day is tough and I'm keeping a low profile whilst the levels of excitement are hitting fever pitch. Oh cripes, it's going to be tragic, I fear. At the end of the day, I do my usual email check and there is one that sticks out. As I sit and write this, I can't remember the name of the sender, but it is someone close to Queen's stargazing guitarist. The gist of it is here:

> Thanks for your email. I showed it to Brian, and he is livid. He said you should crack on and not worry. He told me to tell you to have a great show!!!!

I could levitate again. All good. Panic over.

Later, I confided in Nathan as to what had happened, my panics and the eventual happy outcome. He smiled and said, in his beautiful South Yorkshire drawl, 'I would have said: Brian! Don't stop us nar!'

And the fog descends.

Giving permission, building bridges, being kind … it's not rocket science.

CHAPTER 5

CURRICULUM ADVENTURES

I found this story in an after-dinner speech given by Chief Education Officer of the West Riding of Yorkshire Sir Alec Clegg (1909–1986) on 3 August 1972, at the end of a vacation course for teachers at Bingley College of Education. Sir Alec retired 2 years later when the West Riding was abolished as part of the reorganisation of local government in England. I really encourage you to seek Sir Alec out. In his summation of what head teachers he worked alongside saw as all-important, he offers this:

> From what they have said to me and from the way they directed their schools, they hold the following beliefs. I apologise if this list seems trite but the items in it are in my view extremely important:
> - that there is good in every child, however damaged, repellent or ill-favoured he might be;
> - that success on which a teacher can build must somehow be found for every child;
> - that all children matter;
> - that happy relationships between head, teachers, and pupils are all-important;
> - that the life of the child can be enriched by the development of his creative powers;
> - that encouragement is far more important than punishment;
> - that teachers just as much as pupils need support and thrive on recognition.
>   (Clegg, 1972)

Great list, or what? Anyone who dismisses these voices of the past – and they do – run the risk of looking like plonkers.

Life moves pretty fast. If you don't stop and look around once in a while, you could miss it.

Ferris, *Ferris Bueller's Day Off*[1]

To see the world, things dangerous to come, to see behind walls, to draw closer, to find each other and to feel. That is the purpose of life.

***The Secret Life of Walter Mitty*[2]**

Everyone needs references when going for a new job. When Michelangelo was going to Rome to see the Pope prior to being employed to build the great dome of St Peter's and paint the Sistine Chapel, as well as taking with him the tools of his trade, he took a reference. This is what it said:

The bearer of these presents is Michelangelo the sculptor. His nature is such that he requires to be drawn out by kindness and encouragement. But if love be shown him and he be treated really well, he will accomplish things that will make the whole world wonder. (Clegg, 1972)[3]

He walked in and got the gig. Fair play to him. And fair play to the interview panel for seeing the human in front of them as well as the incredible artistic and technical achiever. They saw someone who needed encouragement and kindness. And this is a really good starting point when considering what we might want from the curriculum we offer in our schools. Or the curriculum we offer in *our* school.

1 *Ferris Bueller's Day Off*, dir. John Hughes [film] (Paramount Pictures, 1986).
2 *The Secret Life of Walter Mitty*, dir. Ben Stiller [film] (Twentieth Century Fox, 2013).
3 See page 96.

I'm writing this sitting in my attic in Yorkshire, England, and yet, when I think of the word *curriculum* at the moment, my attentions are drawn across the hills to the land of my fathers, Wales, and its brilliant Curriculum for Wales.[4] What Welsh schools have been offered are twelve pedagogical principles on which to design a purposeful curriculum for their children, building on the great stuff that's been established over time, whilst giving space for new creative and dynamic directions. All of this is planned and delivered through the lens of the 'four purposes'; an articulation of what the country feels it wants from its education system:

- Ambitious, capable learners, ready to learn throughout their lives.

- Enterprising, creative contributors, ready to play a full part in life and work.

- Ethical, informed citizens of Wales and the world.

- Healthy, confident individuals, ready to lead fulfilling lives as valued members of society. (Welsh Government, 2022a)

This is a cool set of four, right? It's a genuine attempt by a country to say 'this is what we need for the nation's children'. It also does that clever thing of putting out there unequivocally that Wales is a global player and seeks to support its children into becoming well-rounded humans – healthy, creative, ethical and ambitious citizens of the world. At no point does it state that its purpose is to ensure disenfranchisement, competition or petty flag-waving nationalism. Be proud of where you're from, sure, but make sure you experience the world as well. It's the 'curriculum as window' idea made real.

The twelve pedagogical principles offer a checklist for how the new curriculum in Wales can be delivered. They're a steer to teachers and curriculum planners and are, again, an articulation of how a country sees its educational provision for its children. It is, in a sense, a political affirmation of what teaching and learning could be. Should be. Here they are, in case you're wondering.

....

4 I've used the word *brilliant* here because that is essentially what the Curriculum for Wales could be. I think the Welsh Government have offered a gift for Welsh schools. Unfortunately, the gift isn't wrapped, and schools are having to find their own pathways through it. The principles on which it's built are magic, mind.

The Curriculum for Wales states that

good learning and teaching:

1 maintains a consistent focus on the overall purposes of the curriculum[5]

2 challenges all learners by encouraging them to recognise the importance of sustained effort in meeting expectations that are high but achievable for them

3 means employing a blend of approaches including direct teaching[6]

4 means employing a blend of approaches including those that promote problem-solving, creative and critical thinking

5 sets tasks and selects resources that build on previous knowledge and experience and engage interest

6 creates authentic contexts for learning

7 means employing assessment for learning principles

8 ranges within and across Areas[7]

9 regularly reinforces the cross-curricular skills of literacy, numeracy and digital competence, and provides opportunities to practise them

10 encourages learners to take increasing responsibility for their own learning

11 supports social and emotional development and positive relationships

12 encourages collaboration. (Welsh Government, 2022b)

When I first saw this list, I nodded my head. A lot. Then I had the realisation that all my talk of botheredness could be easily found resting within this checklist. If I think about the use of story and narrative as discussed in the previous chapter, I can see how it can support approaches in the classroom. Over the last few years, I've worked with Dr Debra Kidd supporting Welsh schools with their implementation of the

---

5 Purpose. It's all got to have purpose.
6 Although I might be often labelled as a tree-hugging drama *progressive*, I'm also a big fan of telling kids stuff they need to know. And that sometimes means standing at the front and banging on.
7 'Areas' refers to areas of learning and experience (AoLEs) – think faculties. The AoLEs are expressive arts, health and well-being (PE and personal, social, health and economic (PSHE) education), humanities, languages, literacy and communication, mathematics and numeracy, and science and technology.

government's vision. One thing that has come out of this work is the completely understandable unease that teachers have when having to change what they teach and how they teach. The thing is, that's not necessarily being asked of them. Rather, schools are being invited to create content that meets the needs of their children in their classrooms. It's *how* we're teaching, not just the *what*, that's being emphasised by this invitation to innovate. Teachers are being asked to transform what teaching looks like and are being asked to do it thoughtfully. In other words, teachers and schools are being placed in the driving seat of curriculum innovation. That's pretty scary, but preferable to being stuck in a rut. Stuck with a pedagogy of poverty. Stuck in a Cold School. As Wales-born Dylan Wiliam (2011, 20) puts it, 'Pedagogy trumps curriculum. Or more precisely, pedagogy is curriculum, because what matters is how things are taught, rather than what is taught.'

When I break down what I mean by classroom botheredness, I place pedagogy as a key foundation to its success. I think that's why the Curriculum for Wales is so attractive. There isn't one way to deliver knowledge, but many. And I suggest that using stories as a vehicle for discovering and embedding knowledge is one of these.

Many of the teachers that Debra and I have had the privilege of working alongside with their curriculum planning have realised the uniqueness of opportunities offered by the curriculum frameworks of purposes and principles and have demonstrated a genuine refreshed enthusiasm for the job.

Just when I thought I was out, they pull me back in![8]

Michael Corleone, *The Godfather Part III*, 1990

The first task we'd do with these teachers is to ask them to write a statement of intent. A mission statement for their AoLE or year group. Here's one the expressive arts AoLE team at Ysgol Harri Tudur (2019), Pembrokeshire, came up with:

Our curriculum for Expressive Arts encourages students to look inwards and outwards to recognise the similarities and differences between their own lives and those of others. Students will develop skills in a range of media and use

8   I'm not saying schools are like organised crime syndicates, by the way. ☺

those skills to express themselves and to better understand how others express their own experiences. Over the two years, students will explore Art as Identity, Art as Resistance and Art as Reflection. Year 7 links closely with the Humanities AoLE.

In the languages, literature and communication AoLE at Ysgol Bro Gwaun (2020a) in Fishguard, we get this:

Our curriculum for LLC aims to provide children with a window to the world, through which they can access and appreciate their cultural heritage and roots while recognising the interconnectedness of their language and lives with others'. We hope the curriculum will lift the children to use their communication skills to raise aspirations in writing and speech and to find joy and appreciation of language and literature. Wise roots, bright future – Anghori doeth, dyfodol disglair.

And a final example from science and technology, again at Ysgol Bro Gwaun (2020b):

In Science and Technology pupils will learn to work safely with their health and well-being in mind. They will develop an understanding of how to use equipment and be able to develop hypotheses while selecting appropriate materials and processes. They will work towards authentic outcomes so that they see Science and Technology as part of the real world they live in. They will develop a broader understanding of the role of science in society – that it can be both the problem and the solution to human difficulties and challenges. Within all of this will be a drive to incite curiosity, confidence, and the capacity to solve complex problems.[9]

I've taken these statements from the original documents Debra and I created alongside the teachers. What's lovely about them is that as well as being passionate and aspirant, they're also absolutely subject to redraft – the reason being that that the teachers own the curriculum. It's not being done to them. In a sense, the curriculum will serve them and their pupils. And if it needs a tweak, it can have one.

---

9   These statements remind me of the taglines you get with movies but with greater detail. Some great ones can be found at StudioBinder (2020). If your curriculum had a tagline, what would it say?

In Wales it appears that teachers have been given some autonomy in terms of how they deliver the curriculum and the content that sits within it. In England it feels less free, and yet there is give in the system. In my work over the last decade, I've been astounded at the creativity and innovation I have witnessed in English schools.[10] It's there in the leadership and the teaching staff. Just like the schools teaching 'Vikings' in the earlier chapter, it actually could come down to school culture. So, what is the curriculum culture of your school? Your classroom? We can assume the Welsh Government are seeking a warm culture with their aspirant curriculum, similar to the Curriculum for Excellence in Scotland. But what of England? What does the aspirant curriculum look like there?[11] What does England want for its children and young people?

It's fair to say that the idea of a national curriculum is a good one. With the rise of academies and free schools,[12] the English national curriculum has morphed into a notional curriculum where as long as we deliver English, maths and science, we should all be okay. This leads to a mixed bag of potential learning experiences for children across the country. Schools are asked to deliver a broad and balanced curriculum and do so even though they're not exactly clear what it means. It can mean that some schools have three theatres for the study of drama (not a national curriculum subject),[13] easy access to an on-site swimming pool and a helipad,[14] whilst others have questionable central heating, poor facilities and a demogorgon from *Stranger Things*. In other words, there's supposed to be an equity of curriculum experience, but it's not backed up by reality.

So, what the heck can we do about it? Well, the reality is that it's us, the adults in the classroom, who must dig for that equity. We need to sharpen our shovels and get chuffing digging. I'll park that metaphor there, but you get my point. The curriculum and its delivery should be an extension of us. The pedagogy is *our* pedagogy. How we deliver our curriculum is an articulation of our botheredness. Think about it like this:

---

10 In her book *Curriculum of Hope*, Debra Kidd gives a great account of our work with the Ignite group of schools and their collaboration with Chester Zoo. This work has been simply wonderful. Details here: https://www.chesterzoo.org/news/ignitezoo-project/ and https://vimeo.com/444496630.

11 Or *here*, as it's where I'm sitting writing this.

12 Don't make me explain these. I want to get to the good stuff.

13 I bang on about this relentlessly in my book *Oops! Helping Children Learn Accidentally* (Roberts, 2012).

14 I have no evidence of this but believe it to be a *fact*.

There are three strands to curriculum:

1 *Should*

2 *Could*

3 *Must*

Allow me to expand on this.

Should curriculum

This is what we're required to teach as part of a nationally agreed curriculum. In Wales, as I've said, this is open and subject to a framework. In England, we have the *national curriculum*, which offers us a list of things we need to cover; essentially, what you'll find in a decent knowledge organiser.[15] This is what you make sure you teach so you don't get done. Told off. It's the coverage we need to cover in order to sleep well at night. It's kids knowing the periodic table. It's them knowing the order of the planets. It's what Eric Gutstein (2012) calls our 'critical knowledge'; the knowledge the government want our schools to deliver to children.

Could curriculum

This is how we get children *bothered* about the above. This is our toolkit of techniques, approaches and strategies, coupled with our stance and humanity that make learning matter. In schools I've worked with recently, we've taken our keenly established knowledge organisers and placed over them a layer of narratives and stories to give the necessary knowledge room and space to be exercised; room to breathe, room to be practised by the children on the receiving end. The *could* curriculum is the professional articulation of *Botheredness*. It's what this book in your hands is all about. It's our stories, stance and pedagogy, formalised and made tangible.

---

15 Not a Dalek. Knowledge organisers did my head in when I first heard about them. I thought they were another storm to erode the cliffs of professional imagination. I was wrong. They're a decent basis on which to develop, cultivate and grow that professional imagination we should all hold dear. They're the *should* to the *could* of narratives, stories, play, spontaneity, excitement and investment. They're Sid Little to Eddie Large.

Must curriculum

And this is all the other stuff we do as schools. It's sometimes known as the *hidden* curriculum. It's where we place our values, as well as the aspirations we hold for our children. I found this area of the curriculum juggernaut very pronounced in the SEMH setting, where social learning was on a par with academic. This is where we'd place PSHE and well-being. It's where we teach children our values by living them. Again, the latter I saw constantly in the SEMH setting. The *must* curriculum is what right-thinking adults believe children need in order to navigate the world. Gutstein called this 'communal knowledge'. In theatre, books and movies, it's the subtext. The underlying key theme.

Now, the thing is, these aspects of curriculum do not need to operate in silos. They can be (naturally) intertwined. If you think of them as train tracks, then you can see that there are opportunities for touch points; for weaving and for crossover. It's possible to teach a Key Stage 4 history lesson about the rise of fascism in Spain whilst contextualising it with illustrations and examples from more recent times (the *should* weaved with the *could*). It's possible to teach the Industrial Revolution in Key Stage 2 whilst tipping a nod to child labour in the world today. It's possible to teach Key Stage 1 about the season of autumn whilst thinking about keeping hedgehogs safe. Another way of considering these three aspects is this:

Aspect	Realm
Should	**Academic:** how it is published
Could	**Social:** how it is presented
Must	**Human:** how lives are enhanced

Using the metaphor of the train tracks, the realms of academic, social and emotional learning are weaved together to make a coherent curriculum journey that has botheredness at its core. Look at it like this:

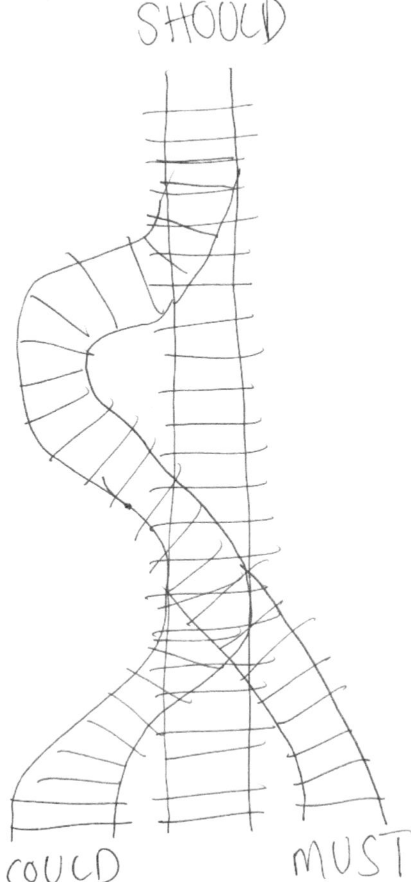

Three aspects of curriculum

We weave, blend and crisscross our curriculum whilst moving forward. The realms are all as important as each other whilst being mutually supportive. The _could_ and the _must_ provide the warmth and the _should_ ensures we're delivering the knowledge we need to deliver. The hard graft of cold knowledge is tempered by a comforting arm around the shoulder and a reassuring whisper. Think Mr Farthing – Billy Casper's English teacher in Ken Loach's movie *Kes*.[16]

Back in the day, a kid in a school would be labelled based on their social and academic qualities. Some kids would be labelled as *difficult, nutter, quiet, weird* and, maybe, *off his tits*. Those days are gone, thankfully, as our professional understanding of performance and ability has evolved.[17] Similarly, whole swathes of kids were written off by the very teachers paid to support them. Only a few years ago, I remember going into a school with Dr Debra Kidd where we did a staff training session. Okay, no one likes a twilight, but we do our best.[18] We genuinely do. We still see ourselves, as I've said a number of times so far in this book, as teachers. It's how we identify ourselves. And so, at this twilight we're sharing stuff we've found out about teaching. At the end of the session, which we both felt had pressed the right buttons, been useful and, most importantly, not been boring, a gent in a sharp suit, hipster beard and with the air of someone unimpressed with any articulation of experience and expertise, approached.[19] Now, don't get me wrong, I thrive on feedback, but I do carry a genuine air of fragility.

So be chuffing gentle.

Edu-Hipster comes up and tells us that although he'd found much of what we'd offered 'useful to some' and 'amusing', none of it'd work with the kids in this particular school.[20] Now at this point I can actually hear Debra's back going up like a hedgehog preparing for battle. Me? I'm just despondent and trying not to show it on my face. My despondency is rooted in the fact that this fella thinks it's okay to talk in such a

---

16 Such a great film. And essential viewing for anyone wanting to teach.

17 I say this with some confidence. Not complete confidence, but some. That's okay, right?

18 By *twilight*, I'm referring to those after-school staff meetings where everyone is knackered and expected to look enthusiastic about Mark, from the Trust, who's come to talk to us about teacher-assessed grades. It's like me binge-watching *Game of Thrones* and getting really pissed off with the bits where the young lass is being trained to be a ninja surrounded by all those wax-like masks. Went on for ages that, didn't it? By *twilight*, I'm **NOT** referring to those cuddly vampire/werewolf films – although I did like the bits where Michael Sheen rocks up. He's one mint actor and I loved him in *The Damned United* nailing Brian Clough. He's also really good on Welsh independence here: https://www.youtube.com/watch?v=bbVdA7zS8dE. #JustSayin'.

19 It gets on mi nerves when edu-folk slag off people who clearly have got a wealth of experience and expertise in what they do. The late, great Sir Ken Robinson got a lot of this. Fancy having to put up with that nonsense after a lifetime of contributing. I guess it's about having manners and grace, whilst behaving appropriately in the face of a monolithic knowledge machine. Or not.

20 An earlier incarnation of Edu-Hipster was Edu-Footballer, where male teachers dressed and groomed themselves as if they were going to appear on Sky Sports rather than in front of Year 9 on a wet Tuesday in March. Nothing wrong with being smart, mind. The particular Edu-Footballers I'm thinking of as I write this are lovely fellows and great teachers.

limiting, ceiling-reinforcing way about the children in his place of work. A freestyling dream-hobbler.[21] And that is all it is, maybe. A place of work. A place where time spent will equate to money received. That is okay for him, I guess, but to me, it's a waste of life. His choice appears to be not to have an impact on children's lives. To him, there's only the *should* aspect of curriculum. One high-speed track and you'd better keep up. Everything else is frivolity and distraction. His kids won't cope with warmth, humour and sensitivity because he himself sees no power in those things. There's no room here for *social* and *emotional* curricular. And he looks at me as if I'm robbing a living. Ironically, I look at him the same way. We pack up and clear off.

But it isn't a hit-and-run twilight, thankfully. Because even though Edu-Hipster had left me feeling a bit shite, we got an immediate invitation from the head teacher to return and work with the children in class.

And guess what? Yes, you're spot on. The kids and the staff loved it. The children loved the story aspect of the modelled practice whilst the staff appreciated observing the work and being able to debrief it afterwards. It was a shame our hipster mate did not get to experience seeing the children as he was not in school the day we were in. He was probably getting a chest wax.

A few words about knowledge

I'm a *big fan* of telling kids stuff. I'm also dead keen on them finding stuff out for themselves. Who is not? I'm well up for a knowledge-rich and experience-rich curriculum; one that puts the child at the centre of the action, ably managed by a knowledgeable, warm and bothered adult.

What the narratives and stories do through the *could* curriculum is offer context to the cold hard facts learned within the *should* aspect. It's why we use case studies, design briefs and real-world sources and data in our work. They offer a hook on which to hang learning. They also offer the space for children to play with, use, adapt, organise and apply knowledge.

---

21 I'm reminded of the Tom Waits lyric ''Cause the dreams ain't broken down here now, they're walking with a limp' – Tom Waits, 'Small Change', *Small Change* [song] (Asylum Records, 1976).

Eric Gutstein's (2012) social justice pedagogy is essentially interested in supporting children in becoming readers and writers of the world.[22] How nailed on is this? He's primarily interested in social justice in mathematics but I can see how his 'three C's' of knowledge, citied earlier in this chapter, can help us understand that there's more to knowledge than meets the eye.[23]

The three C's:

- Critical knowledge

- Classical knowledge

- Communal knowledge

Botheredness and knowledge go hand in hand, and this is echoed in this breakdown of what knowledge can be. So, anyone who might suggest they're not aligned is missing the point. Here's an expression of how the three C's can be interpreted by us:

Critical knowledge:

- The stuff we, as teachers, are required to teach children.

- The *should* curriculum without pedagogical direction.

- What the government dictate as knowledge.

- The lists you needed to revise at school in order to do well in a test.

Classical knowledge:

- What your grandad believes children should learn in school.

- The stuff we believe children need to know; for example, when someone says, 'They need to learn about the Battle of Waterloo!' when discussing how shite schools are. Like my uncle Pete after five pints of Stella.

---

22 When I'm writing stuff like this, I can't help making links to movies. In talking about the social justice pedagogy of Gutstein, and I'm drawn to thinking about social justice movies like Jean-Marc Vallee's *Dallas Buyers Club*, Spike Lee's *BlacKkKlansman* and Ken Loach's *I, Daniel Blake*. Movies are vehicles for messages. Curriculum is the same. Both vehicles need context and emotion.

23 See Tanko (2015) for an interesting interpretation of Gutstein's work.

The education that privately educated government ministers received that makes no sense to a 7-year-old in Leeds but said children are expected to learn via osmosis.[24] In later years, it's the knowledge that makes them feel stupid when they do not know it. Like me and post-war history. When, as an educator have you not known stuff you feel you should know?

There was that time when I was teaching Year 8 and Nicky pointed out of the window to a bird on a wall. 'Look,' Nicky proclaimed, 'a magpie!' We all looked. It was not a magpie. It was a robin. A lovely, tufty, red-breasted robin. 'It's a robin!' the class responded, with no malice, just incredulity. 'Well, I don't know, do I?' responded Nicky with a grin. And she was right. She didn't.

Communal knowledge:

In our case, this is the knowledge children come to school with. It's the stuff they've learned outside formal education. For the child brought up on a farm, or the child brought up living by the sea. Or the traveller child. Or the child from a very musical family. Or the child refugee. We sometimes refer to this aspect of knowing stuff as 'funds of knowledge'.[25]

Not all communal knowledge is great. It can be difficult, negative and need challenging.

You'll either embrace or challenge communal knowledge if you're bothered to do so. The alternative is to say you don't care about this aspect of knowledge. Are you going to do that? Didn't think so. ☺

---

24 Therefore, conceptually, some of our *critical* (or *should*) curriculum is so challenging for our children – and not in a good way. It's a million miles from their experience of the world. When we teach 'The Great Fire of London' to Year 1, we need to ensure we're protecting them into the learning. Let's face it, to some kids in England and the UK, London might as well be on Mars. The narratives and stories are part of this protective pedagogy.

25 Funds of knowledge can be broken down into geographical, practical, cultural and social types. They're that body of informal knowledge that can be brought into a formal classroom by a child or class. It's like me when I manage to drop *Jaws* references in when teaching an English class about tension. Or when the kid obsessed with dinosaurs manages to get them into EVERY PIECE OF CLASSWORK THEY CHUFFIN' DO!

Pull up a chair for this one, good people!

Here's a good example of how a young, professionally naive teacher uses the curriculum to challenge the difficult communal knowledge walking en masse into his prefab temporary classroom:

As we've established, my professional background is Barnsley in South Yorkshire. The town is famous for Michael Parkinson (who now lives in Maidenhead), whilst Kate Rusby, the folk singer, and Dickie Bird, the iconic cricket umpire, are local residents.[26] The town is also synonymous with the classic novel *A Kestrel for a Knave*, which you may have read at school. It was a mainstay of the secondary English curriculum for years, and rightly so. It's completely mint. I taught that book a lot because I'm in Barnsley and I've got Barnsley kids in the room, so I'm bound to teach a book that's set in Barnsley, aren't I? I'd be completely mad not to. So, in as many exam classes as I could, I'd make sure we'd read that book and, if you've never read it, it's worth revisiting because it's beautiful. The author, Barry Hines, knew what he was writing about as he too was a teacher.

I had my Year 10 bottom set, and they were an interesting group. They'd clearly been set by attitude rather than ability. They were a colourful group of children. They were children who had the attitude of pissed-off alcoholics being served water rather than whisky. They were like *The Dirty Dozen* (1967) – all lads, all rebels without a clue, save for one. A new kid on the block. A giant of a boy, silent and bright. He was called Robert.

They'd march in and usually they'd just start off by saying, 'We're not doing stories, are we? We're not doing English, are we?' And it was English. That was the class.

'Well, we are, Callum. We are doing English, 'cause it's English now. When you've got history, you do history, mate. It's how school works. Is that alright?'[27]

And Troy would stomp in and set my learning objective by proclaiming, 'This better be good'.

---

26 There's a statue of Dickie Bird in Barnsley. The statue has him doing the index finger *you're out* gesture. The council had to raise up the statue so it was higher off the ground because every Sunday morning there'd always be a kebab tray (or worse) on the end of his finger.
27 Some very high-calibre behaviour for learning, right there.

They'd moan a bit but quickly they'd strangely mutate into a state of being alright and this would be the point where I'd need to do some protecting in – protecting into what we were doing today. Our text is *A Kestrel for a Knave* and the lads have loved it. Troy is particularly buzzing about it and is desperate to watch the movie version as his auntie Val is in it. They also like the novel because it has swearing in it and they love hearing me chant, 'Pig. Hog. Sow. Drunken bastard!'[28] in a not-very-teacher-like manner. They also like my brave go at a decent Barnsley accent. If this class were a football team, it was like playing at home, you know? The crowd are behind you and have got your back. Now, I'm trying really hard to paint a positive picture of these young men. I have the benefit of some decent rose-tinted spectacles as I write this and there would be days prior to this class walking in where my belly would be doing flips and the nerves would kick in. I could never really predict how the class would be when they arrived. Behaviour across the school was challenging in the way that behaviour can be – low-level stuff mainly. The most visible manifestation of this would be when kids were sent out to corridors all the time.[29] It was a bit bleak at times.

Now, sometimes my class would be horrible. They'd be absolutely horrible. They'd say horrible things to each other, usually preceded by the term 'thi muther' as an insult to the mother of whoever they were talking to.

'Thi muther …'[30]

We'd often end up with a game of 'thi muther' tennis. One day I noticed that suddenly, out of nowhere, the vocal key insulters started using awful racist language. Out of the blue. Obviously, there was no excuse for it and completely no reason for it. We were in a mainly White working-class school and I didn't like that at all. Unfortunately, I had no real tools in my toolkit to help me. There was no button I could press as a call for help. I had just my own resilience and capacity to not lose it at the kids. I realised later that this horrible language was a result of the Tarantino classic *Pulp Fiction*

---

28 Billy Casper's chant to his inebriated bully brother, Jud. Young Billy is played by actor Dai Bradley, who also appeared in *Zulu Dawn*, *Absolution* and *Malachi's Cove*, alongside horror genius Donald Pleasence. These days, Mr Bradley can be found at https://www.kes-billycasper.co.uk/.

29 'Corridor learning', as it's known. As ridiculous as the rebranding of internal exclusion as *sanctuary*.

30 Insulting each other's mothers is a common trope amongst young lads. It reminds me of Richard Dreyfuss talking about it in his voiceover in the beautiful and mint film *Stand By Me*. Remember that bit? If you've not seen it, it's great. A lovely colleague, Brenda Wragg, and I used to use it as a media text at GCSE. That and *The Matrix*. Kids were chuffin' buzzin', weren't they?

(1994). The language from the film had been their inappropriate takeaway. Unfortunately for me.

I did not know what to do. So I did the only thing I could do: look at my curriculum as an English teacher, through the eyes of a bothered grown-up who wanted these children to just think differently about the world. I found myself knocking on the door of the English stock cupboard.[31] When I realised the coast was clear, I nipped in. It was more than a cupboard. It was like one of those small offices where kids do one-to-one catch up. I was like Indiana Jones going into the darkest recesses of the room. In the darkest, dullest corner of that space, I found the salvation I needed and what I wanted my class to be exposed to.

And it was a book on my syllabus. A book about:

- Childhood
- Hope
- Prejudice
- Community
- Hate
- Parenthood
- Loss
- Grown-ups
- Darkness and light
- Love
- Botheredness

It's a great story. It has people, in a place, with lots of problems:[32]

- **People:** A widower and his children.
- **Place:** Maycomb, Alabama, at the time of the Great Depression.
- **Problem:** There's going to be a miscarriage of justice.

Yes.

---

31 Had to knock in case the PE teacher and the English teacher were in there. #WorkAffair.
32 This is an example of taking an existing story and applying the story wheel from Chapter 4.

To Kill a Mockingbird by Harper Lee.[33]

Now, this book is hard for these kids. That is not supposed to be a patronising comment, it's just that I know I'll need to protect them into the text, rather than just throw it at them and expect them to 'get it'. *To Kill a Mockingbird* is a challenging study as it's distant. Distant in terms of time – the Great Depression of the 1930s – and it's distant in terms of simple geography – we're thrown into an old America. It's also distant in terms of themes: segregation, hate, race and so on. If our class were a football team, this was suddenly like playing away and all the supporters' coaches had broken down at Sandbach. It's a hard text to these kids in the way that *A Kestrel for a Knave* is accessible. I had to teach it differently, and I was pedagogically freestyling.

Now, do you remember the story *To Kill a Mockingbird*? The thing is (and I'm not wanting to upset anyone here) that the first chapter is a real slog. It's hard work. I'm there, reading it aloud to Troy, Robert and the rest of this merry band. I'm doing my best and skipping through the text absolutely knowing the potential love for this book is being obliterated every second I read. I can feel the atmosphere in the room cool, and that irritated shuffling begins as I try to make my voice dance a tune as if to provoke some eyeball interest. Nothing.

And then there's the knocking.

I'm trying to ignore it but struggling.

---

33 The strange thing with this story is that my dad, a great teacher, instilled in my brother and I a love for both *A Kestrel for a Knave* and *To Kill a Mockingbird* when we were kids. It's more evidence that stories are indeed 'psychologically privileged' and emotional. I remember Sunday afternoons watching *To Kill a Mockingbird*.

Eventually I relent and look up from my text. It's Troy. He's banging his head on his desk as if he's laying down some deep bass track. Oh man, I don't need this pressure.

'Troy?'

His head-knocking stops, and he lifts himself to look at me. He has the gait of someone waiting to be hanged. He then throws his whole body back in his chair,[34] and proclaims,

'Sir! God![35] This is SO BORING!!!!'

And I get it. I really do. I probably even said as such to him.

I really get it. Genuinely. It's just that back then, my toolkit was limited. Time froze and I looked back at my text as if Troy hadn't spoken for everyone in the room. Including me!

Just as I was about to launch back into the turgid prose,[36] however, Troy spoke again:

'Do an accent.'

'What?'

'Do an accent, Sir.'

'An accent?'

'Yeah. It's American.'

And he folded his arms expectantly. Young, massive Troy.

You know that rush of possibilities you get when a child suggests something? I've got that right now, in this moment. I know the lads are looking at me, waiting for me to make my move.

So I make it.

America it is. Not any America, oh no. The America of the Great Depression. The Southern imaginary seat of Maycomb County, Alabama. Sure, I can do that.

No chuffing problemo, my friend.

---

34 Four legs not two, young man!
35 Appealing to a higher body of support here.
36 Don't forget, I chuffin' love this book. That first chapter is rock though.

Why is it no problemo? Simple. This is my world. This is the world of my childhood. This is wasted youth coming to the rescue of a desperate (but serious) educator. This is me at 12 on my Grifter meeting my pals at Chaddy Fields and all speaking with the voices we've heard from the TV. American voices. Imported TV shows were the absolute fodder for us kids in the early 1980s.[37] And at last, I realise that the so-called wasted youth wasn't wasted at all. It's led me to this point. To save me from the wrath of Troy.

And so, I kick in with the greatest Southern-states accent these kids have ever heard. I suddenly find something new for my toolkit. An accent. Not great for every reader of this book, but enough for some. I'm blessed with a particular skill, and it has now, in this moment, become a motivator and a new behaviour management tool for my toolkit.[38] As I read, I look around the room and I see something that mentally throws me, although I keep reading.

The boys are listening.

What's interesting is that they've put their own texts aside on their desks and are now focused on me. They're children in a story. They're *investing* because of the accent. And I just crack on. I love this. I'm finding it hard to articulate the feeling now, but do you know when you're absolutely nailing it as a teacher and feel fabulous? It is that. That's how I am in this moment.

And so, we plough through the most brilliant of novels that is *To Kill a Mockingbird*. And the lads are *in*.

---

37 I'm talking about *CHiPS*, *The A-Team*, *The Fall Guy*, *The Six Million Dollar Man*, *The Dukes of Hazzard*, *Knight Rider* and *Tales of the Golden Monkey* – the latter being a completely mint *Indiana Jones* rip-off. Like *Bring 'em Back Alive*. Some of you youngsters will have to google some of this great shit. I feel sorry for you because you missed all this. This, and having a Grifter.

38 Not featured in any books about behaviour management, that I know of. I've only read behaviour management books by folks who know what they're on about, mind you. I recommend Dave Whitaker's (2021) *The Kindness Principle*, Mark Finnis' (2021) *Restorative Practice*, Sue Cowley's *The Calm Classroom: 50 Techniques for Better Behaviour* and anything by Paul Dix. Bill Rogers is also top notch.

Spoiler alert[39]

Our adult hero in the novel, Atticus Finch,[40] loses the case where he's been defending an innocent man. Tom Robinson,[41] a Black man, has been accused of raping a White woman. Atticus loses the case. And all my kids are gutted because they'd really got themselves immersed in the book. They loved Atticus. They sympathised with Tom. They knew that the latter was completely innocent.

There's a moment in the novel, after the verdict has been declared, where Atticus simply sits at the front of the courthouse as the jubilant White community leave, supported by the Ku Klux Klan and punching the air. 'What do you think about that?' I ask the class of gripped, bottom-set lads.

Troy, never letting me down, speaks for everyone when he says, 'They're all bastards, Sir.'[42] He's not wrong, but it does pass through my mind that I could do with him expanding on that point for a decent GCSE examination response. I get a small yellow sticky note off my desk and write on it quickly in black marker:

> Atticus Finch
> has lost the case.

----

39 Me walking into a showing of masterpiece *Schindler's List*, and one of my companions saying, 'Is this going to be depressing?'
40 Played beautifully by Gregory Peck in the 1962 movie adaptation.
41 Played with warmth and dignity by Brock Peters, who would later appear in a couple of *Star Trek* movies (*Voyage Home* and *Undiscovered Country*, if you're asking). He also voiced Darth Vader in the radio dramatisations of the *Star Wars* saga (*Star Wars*, *The Empire Strikes Back* and *Return of the Jedi*, if you're asking).
42 My Word edit tool has warned me that this word is offensive. I'm being managed by technology as I write. Apologies if it's offensive to you, but, frankly, this is a great example of Troy's communal knowledge. He was right good at swearing.

I take the sticky note and place it on the back of my blue classroom chair, facing the class.[43] I lift the chair and put its spindly legs on my desk. It's high up now and the lads are looking at it, a little confused as to what might be coming next.

I look at Robert and ask the whole class a question: 'If we could reassure Atticus at this very moment, what might we say to him?'

I really want Robert, the new kid, to step up, but his eyes fall, so I glance around. There are a lot of falling eyes. I think they think I'm trying something out from that course I went on the other week. I'm not. It's just something that's fallen into my head. Like a silent crash. I repeat the question again, motioning to the chair.

I'm about to remove the chair back to its normal spot when Troy suddenly gets up proclaiming, 'Oh, I'll do it!' as if he's taking one for the team and defusing a bomb. He comes to the front and at the same time, as if on the opposite end of a compass point, I drift to the back of the classroom, all eyes now on the big lad. He does some sort of theatrical pause and then gently lays a hand on the top of the chair. His voice, accented like comforting treacle, breaks the tension:

'Tha's done alreight.'

(Pause.)

'No one could ask for more.'

(Pause.)

'You're a good man.'

And I'm at the back of my class watching this boy. And in my mind, I'm carried through fields of gold to the soundtrack of Beethoven, just like Robin Williams in that film. *This is why I teach*, I think to myself, wondering if I'll remember this moment in the future when I'm old. There's so much to remember. Why would I remember this? In teaching, there can feel like there's no time for memories.

What this was about, amongst other things, was articulacy. It was all about the language of reassurance. These boys had to reassure someone, and they weren't used to doing that. They weren't required to do it in their day to day. They were used to just

---

43 Get yersen a decent chair if you've got your own classroom. Primary teachers practically create their own thrones consisting of cagouls, hoodies and winter coats.

insulting each other's mothers. So, this was a shift. An invitation to use language a little more gently, shall we say. Does that make sense? Troy was not an actor. We weren't putting on a play, we were just stepping into an imaginary space for a moment. And actually, it made teaching the novel a little easier, because these hard kids started asking me if we could perhaps meet some of the other characters from the book. Maybe Boo Radley.[44] Maybe Dill.[45] I mean, they all loved Dill.

And so, in this moment, this vignette, I understand what a helpful curriculum and syllabus look like. As the teacher, they are my servants. The communal knowledge, which is basically taboo language picked up from a lent-out copy of *Pulp Fiction*, can be challenged now. The children can be respected, but the community can be challenged. Harper Lee's *To Kill A Mockingbird* is my way of doing that. In that snapshot, the curriculum is my tool as I seek to lead the children through the complexity of literature. The curriculum helps.

As I've said elsewhere, we must work towards creating curriculum that offers rich experience and one that doesn't turn the tables on us, where we become cyphers for other people's visions and agendas. We must not allow our precious schools, and the teachers and children within them, to become servants of the curriculum. The curriculum should not be a black hole, sucking our souls away, demoralising our good nature and morphing us into content providers,[46] splashing around in a pool of poor pedagogy that stinks.[47] That place is where professional fear thrives, and we need to avoid it, at all costs.

Fear of coverage, fear of assessment, fear of children.

So, there's the story of my Year 10s; of Troy, of *A Kestrel for a Knave*, of quiet Robert and Harper Lee. I've laid it out for you in the hope you'll see where the botheredness rests.

---

44 Robert Duvall in the movie. I'll never forget Boo's first appearance in the film, hiding behind a door having saved the children from the villain. Duvall is a class actor. He's the guy advising Marlon Brando in *The Godfather*, advising Sean Penn in Dennis Hopper's *Colors* and advising his men on the beach in *Apocalypse Now*. See also *True Confessions*, *The Lightship*, *The Judge*, *The Road*, *MASH*, *The Godfather Part II*, *Falling Down* and *The Eagle has Landed*. He's a mint actor. Hard as nails.

45 John Megna in the movie. Died tragically young after making a shift from acting to teaching. The character of Dill Harris was apparently based on author Harper Lee's childhood friend, writer Truman Capote. I'm just throwing that out there.

46 We have the internet to help us with content.

47 Of shite.

And there's a coda, of sorts.

Fast forward to 2019. I'm in a decent juicer in Barnsley – the Jolly Tap on the Arcade.[48] I'm having a few beers with some pals when I get a tap on my shoulder. I turn, and there before me stands a very big fella. I look up so I can see his eyes and simultaneously I get a rush of recognition, like someone has thrown a bucket of warmth over me.

Although a giant, the gentleman's demeanor is humble and very polite. He extends a hand and I take it because I know him.

'It's Robert,' he says as a gentle direction.

'I know,' I respond. And the hairs on my arm go up.

He buys me a pint and reminds me of the story about Year 10; of Troy, *A Kestrel for a Knave*, Harper Lee, sticky notes, chairs on tables, and of him, sitting at the back, shy of his skin and being witness to a young teacher trying his best to corral racist language and attitude, batting it away with a bit of dramatic convention and control.

Robert has not forgotten. I have because there's always so much to remember.

'I was doing my best,' I proffer.

'I know you were. It was hard.'

48 A bar of distinction.

Robert doesn't know it, but he's lifting me right up and, again, I'm being carried through fields of gold. Teacher impact is an element of the job that is often used as a sales pitch for the profession and then, once you're in it, appears sidelined.[49] Indeed, when suggesting we take the word *botheredness* seriously, we run the risk of being seen as not operating in the real world or not understanding the real situations in real schools. And yet, it's key for the delivery of a curriculum that has been agreed by the institution. It's been published on the website and now needs to be brought to life. We don't just need folk to 'get into teaching' and stay a couple of years, we need heroes who will stay some distance.[50] And that is the big challenge.

Surviving, not thriving

Bonni Gourneau (2005) suggests five effective teacher attitudes. These include:

- **Genuine demonstration of care and kindness:** teachers should have sincere interest and concern about their pupil's well-being.

- **Willingness to share the responsibility involved in a classroom:** teachers can establish a shared environment by allowing students take responsibility and some form of freedom in the classroom. Like negotiating a dilemma. Like responding to the Ku Klux Klan.

- **Sensitively accepting diversity:** this has to do with empathy, sensitivity, encouragement and understanding the children in the room. It's also knowing where they've come from to be sitting at the desk in front of you.

- **Stimulating the pupil's creativity:** teachers should develop the attitude of stimulating creativity amongst pupils by listening to their suggestions, opinions and ideas for lesson activities. It's the establishing of a true learning culture in the classroom.

- **Fostering individualised instructions:** this attitude discusses the teacher's ability to provide learning opportunities for all pupils. Basically, planning for the children in the room.

---

49 'Everyone remembers a good teacher' rather than 'Everyone remembers that teacher who used to batter you'; 'Get into teaching' rather than 'Get out of teaching'.
50 Yes, I know. I clocked up 16 years. It's no lifetime, but it's a decent chunk. Back off, etc.

As I look through the list, I nod and am completely down with it. What I could perhaps add is the mindset of what Valerie Hill-Jackson et al. (2019, 4) call *organisational prowess*.[51] Nicely put, isn't it? Organisational prowess. I think of the astronauts in Ron Howard's *Apollo 13*, the true story of NASA devising a strategy to return the titular spacecraft to Earth safely after it undergoes massive internal damage, putting the lives of the three astronauts on board in jeopardy. They had to operate within the boundaries and bureaucracies of their own organisation. It's often left to ace character actor Ed Harris to work within these constraints.[52] Navigating an organisation and getting attuned to it isn't something that's shared widely on teacher training courses. Situational awareness is completely understanding the climate and culture of the place you find yourself in.

Just to be clear, when I talk about *climate*, I'm referring to how the school affects everyone. If it's normal for adults to shout at each other, that is the climate set by the organisation. It's the attitude and mood music of the day to day. If you think your school is a war zone and the children are the enemy, that is the climate that has been set. Your belief in it, your seeing of it as 'how it is', is the culture. School culture is the assumptions that are reinforced by the behaviours of those in the building. It can be the embracing of the rut and lead to a genuine lack of botheredness.[53]

If you aren't sure whether you're in a rut or not, this might help. It's taken from the work on school culture by David Hargreaves (1999) and works towards a professional understanding of either why you're buzzing with botheredness or bereft of it. Where are you?

---

51 This is a good piece, drawn from the research of Martin Haberman.

52 See also *The Truman Show*, *A History of Violence* and his turn as the I-have-my-demented-reasons-for-doing-what-I'm-doing character in Cage classic *The Rock*, where he essentially blows his top at the organisation he works within but can no longer understand. As a teacher, you don't need to blow shit up if you don't understand your school anymore. You just move on. Moving on is better than getting stuck in a rut.

53 A movie I loved as a young lad was the oft-repeated-on-TV classic *Logan's Run*, where inhabitants of a future world are executed on their 30th birthdays. Everyone accepted the executions as it's how the place worked. I'm talking about the future in the past tense, but you get my drift. I also loved the film because there was a bit where Jenny Agutter as runaway Jessica gets changed. It made me go all funny when I was about 11.

SOCIAL CONTROL

	HIGH	LOW
HIGH	HOTHOUSE	WELFARIST
SOCIAL COHESION		
LOW	FORMAL	SURVIVALIST

Hargreaves (1999)

Or as I like to put it …

SOCIAL CONTROL

	HIGH	LOW
HIGH	STRESSED OFF MI HEAD	BOTHERED
SOCIAL COHESION		
LOW	INTIMIDATED	BROKEN

adapted from Hargreaves (1999)

- **Stressed off mi head:** what happens when you're crying in the mirror just before work because you're worried that some kid might not have brought in their homework.

- **Intimidated:** when you feel really apprehensive about what is going to come out of the assistant head teacher's mouth when you rock up with baby food on your top because you've had a rushed morning with your own kids.

- **Broken:** when you get your head down, keep it down and don't want to cause any bother with or for anyone: 'There's nothing to see here. I'm just trying to get to half three. I'm a rut-embracer.'

- **Bothered:** when *you feel you can*. You're professionally resilient and possess a realistic, hopeful and healthy optimism.[54] You're also able to operate within a bureaucracy with organisational prowess. You are mint.

If I just throw you back to Robert and Troy's Year 10 class very quickly, I hope you can see the curriculum adventure we were on. And I hope you recognise two concepts:

1   I warmed up the curriculum, taking the potentially cold and distant text of *To Kill a Mockingbird* and serving it up to them using bespoke, inductive pedagogy.[55]

2   The curriculum was of service to me and my class. Not the other way round.

We also have that idea of the three aspects of knowledge (critical, classical and communal) wrapped around three elements of curriculum (*should, could* and *must*). When entering into conversations around curriculum, we should keep these ideas in mind. I also need to remind myself that 'good teachers are not good soldiers' (Dodge, 2014), but I'll crack on anyway.

---

54 Some good stuff here about resilience: https://www.apa.org/topics/resilience.

55 What I haven't done in this chapter is tell you how to teach the Harper Lee classic. That's okay, isn't it? It's not that I'm not bothered, it's just that the book is not the point of the chapter. The topic in the classroom could be anything. The fact that it's secondary doesn't matter either. This could all have been about rivers and mountains. ☺ The question is how we induct, say, city kids into learning about rivers and mountains. I'll stop there.

BRIDGE OF BOTHEREDNESS

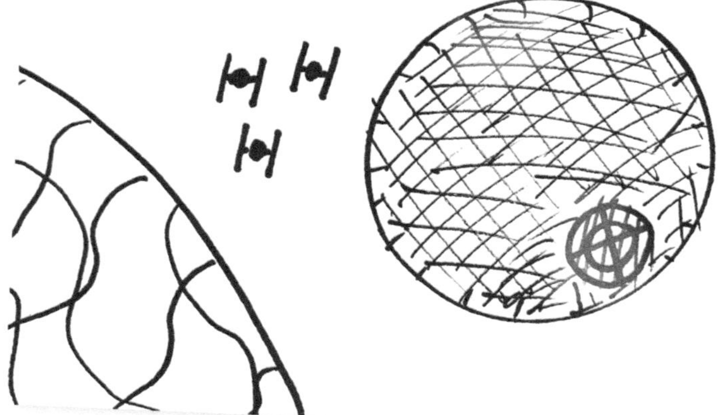

STAR WARS

Education isn't everything, for a start it isn't an elephant.

Spike Milligan (1974, 166)

My criterion for accepting a role isn't based on what I would like to do. I try to consider what the audience would like to see me do and I thought kids would adore *Star Wars*.

Peter Cushing (quoted in Miller, 2000, 155)[1]

And Peter Cushing was right. Kids loved *Star Wars* when it hit the screens in 1977 and love it today as the universe has continued to expand. Cushing's role as Darth Vader's boss, Grand Moff Tarkin, is a juicy essay in villainy and one that exposed him to millions of new fans across the world. Me included. I was 7 and obsessed. Not having a load of money in our house, I made do with the action figures I managed to pick up at jumble sales and was able to get new ones for birthdays.[2] For Christmas 1979 my dad got me the Imperial Troop Transporter, which never actually appeared in the original Star Wars film but enjoyed more screen time in the *Mandalorian* TV show. It was my favourite toy ever. Still is. I have it boxed these days, sitting on a nice shelf in the room where I'm writing this paragraph. You see? Obsessed.[3] I know it might be incredibly

---

1 Peter Cushing is probably one of my favourite actors. He also played an excellent Sherlock Holmes. I remember sitting with my mum watching Cushing and his regular co-star Christopher Lee battle an ancient alien entity on a train in the delightful *Horror Express*, a Spanish/English co-production that also featured Telly Savalas as a lollipop-sucking Cossack.

2 See https://www.action-figure-resource.com/star-wars-ships-vehicles.html: a useful resource for the edu-nerds out there who still have their Star Wars toys in the attic. For the younger readers, you'll see the how deep the rabbit hole goes with this stuff. Beware, it may cost you money. ☺

3 If it wasn't already obvious, I'm also obsessed with movies. And music. See the back of this book for my favourites. Music and movies are like tangible bookmarks of my life. What are yours?

nerdy to keep the box that my toy came in for over four decades, but that is the thing about botheredness – it's not just an education thing; it's a thing that makes us human.

But we're here for the education stuff, so what about this: pause for a moment and have a think about everything you know about

KENYA

(I'm pausing, letting you think. I'll also refer you to footnote 29 on page 49. Go on. Take a look back.)

I know some of you might not know anything about Kenya and, you know what, that is completely *OKAY!* I'm going to stop you there, though, because I know some of you are shrugging off this activity and simply thinking it begins with the letter K. And you're right.

Now, the story behind this is that I did a day at a school in Bristol. It was a day of me talking about curriculum possibilities, motivational approaches and the like. A few weeks later I got invited back to the school to demonstrate what I'd talked about with the grown-ups in the real classrooms with real kids, which is what I do.[4] It's like teaching but on steroids.

On this particular day, the teachers I was going to work with were in primary Year 3, Year 5 and Year 1. The Year 3 teacher had been in touch, and I completely knew what I was doing in their classroom. Year 5 teacher – same. However, I'd heard nothing from the Year 1 teacher, Miriam.

Not a sausage.

Now, I can be a worrier. Picture the scene: I've got to my Holiday Inn in Bristol, just at the end of the railway station. It's like I'm putting the steps in, pacing my small room. It's like waiting to be hanged. My mind is spinning with the question, *What the heck is happening with Year 1 at 9 a.m. tomorrow morning?* At best, I might get a brief conversation with Miriam as the day starts, but I know what it can be like in a Year 1 classroom early doors. This is serious stuff, and I'm feeling tetchy. Simply put, I'm

---

4 So back off with your consultant-shaming, consultant shamers!

getting a bit panicky. I don't want to look a turd in front of the observing teachers tomorrow.

At about 10.30 p.m. I resign myself to the fact that I'll have to wing it the next morning. And winging it, as the wise know, is a total nightmare.

At about 10.31 p.m. an email drops in. It reads:

> Dear Hywel
>
> We are doing Kenya.
>
> See you tomorrow.
>
> Miriam

And that is it. Nothing more. Nothing less.

Great, I think. A sleepless night ahead. I'm about to break out my online-teacher-resource-site-of-choice logins, when I stop myself.

I google Kenya. And I get results. Not the English curriculum's view of Kenya, but the real country. I realise why we don't teach 'Real Kenya'; because it's a bit too distressing. And so, I'm standing in my pyjamas in the Holiday Inn wondering: *What is going to happen in Year 1 Kenya?*

I flick my search across to Kenya images and I find a photograph of two majestic lions sitting in the savannah. When I find that picture, my professional imagination kicks in and a sharp-elbowed question muscles its way to the front of my mind: *How do we know if the lions are happy?*

Then I go to bed and sleep soundly.

Fast forward to the next morning – 9 a.m. – and Year 1 are all on the carpet, staring at the visitor.[5]

The classroom is great. I'd describe it as totally 'Kenya'd up'. Miriam is definitely bothered about what her room looks like. It really is mint. I can see a couple of giraffes, a sunset and a shield.[6]

Now I talk to the class whilst admiring the space. What comes out of my mouth is as deliberate as it is inductive:

> You know a lot about Kenya, don't you? You know a lot, you lot.

They mirror my deliberate nodding, murmur smiling agreement and hands go in the air.[7] They have the critical knowledge at their fingertips and want to share it with me. And that is great. It's a positive footing from which we can begin. They're contributing some genuine Kenya facts and, as a result, Miriam and her teaching assistant are high fiving each other at the back of the classroom, much to the amusement of the other observing teachers.[8]

I ask the children

> Shall we do a story?

And their minds are blown. Not only do we get to regurgitate facts with this dude, but we also get to do a story! Are you kidding me?

---

5 Even though I've been doing it for years now, it's always funny talking to children as they look up to you from the carpet. If you do this every day, please never take it for granted. I'm still getting used to it. If I turn away from them to grab a whiteboard pen or something, they all shuffle a bit closer, then freeze when I turn back around. Like that children's game from long ago.

6 I know. Another one.

7 When you nod at kids, they nod back. This might *not* work with teenagers.

8 They're also buzzing because they're essentially free of pedagogical responsibility for 90 minutes. A bit like when you watch a film.

Let's say …

Let's say there are two lions in a zoo, in Kenya.

'Nairobi', a child offers without invitation. They love their facts these kids.

'Don't shout out,' I remind. 'Yes, a zoo in Nairobi. There are two lions in a zoo, in Nairobi.'

'Now, can you help me with this?' I ask. 'How do we know if the lions are happy?'

The children talk with their carpet partners.[9] 'How do we know the lions are happy?' I repeat, whilst leaning in from my chair to listen to snippets of their conversations.

---

9 I've just made 'carpet partners' up. I might write a pamphlet about it.

To my right, a girl throws her hand in the air. Then another girl to my left copies her. And then more hands, all holding responses to this abstract and peculiar question.

I go to the girl on my right and repeat the question for the six millionth time.

'Go on then. How do we know if the lions are happy?'

She looks at me and answers confidently,

'They purr.'

And that throws me around like a sock in a washer.

I'm no lion expert and, it turns out, neither are any of the adults currently standing with me in the classroom.[10] I'm looking for help, but everyone over the age of 6 has their heads down, looking at the mauve carpet tiles. I look back to the girl and I respond with my kind relentless challenge which, frankly, is all I've got:

'Do they?'

There's a short pause as the young lady considers my response. She then nods her head to herself, having found some sort of mental confirmation and proclaims a determined and certain,

'Yes. They do.'

'You know a lot about lions, don't you?' I venture and she replies that she does. She's up on her knees now. This kid is buzzing. She's a lion expert. The man in the suit said. For those of you with a cynical edge who might be finding this too syrupy, this is simply protecting the children into the context as discussed elsewhere, so hang onto your sling-shots. It's building enthusiasm and motivation for the complexity that will come later.

A boy at the back of the class is waving his arm at me like it's on fire. He tells me that when happy, lions wag their tails. This seems plausible until I think of my cat, Basil, whose tail-wagging is a signal of imminent scratching.

'Lions are different,' the boy clarifies.

To sum up, the two lions are happy because:

▧ They purr.

10 According to science writer Helen Pilcher (2020), lions don't purr. I'm gutted. ☹

They wag their tails.

And then there's the little *'I forgot'* girl to my left, still with her hand in the air. Miriam says, 'Ooh, I think Ashley's got an idea.'

The whole class look at little Ashley who has form in the hand-up-then-forgetting-when-asked stakes. I go for it anyway. 'Go on Ashley,' I encourage. She goes all wide-eyed and the class appears to have some strange communal intake of breath. The tension is destroying me.

'They smile,' she whispers.

Everyone melts. Everyone is buzzing.

'Let's say there are two happy lions in this zoo in Nairobi. They purr, they wag their tails and, crucially, they smile.

'They need names,' I venture. 'What shall we call them? Lions need names! We've all got names. What names should the lions have?'

I put a line in the sand: we're not having any lion called Simba.[11]

The children are carpet whispering,[12] and now Simba has been rejected, possibilities are endless. I'm offering a subliminal narrative underneath their chatter: 'We've got two lions, two lions, happy lions in the zoo, in Nairobi. They're happy, they're purring, smiling and wagging their tails … but what are the lions called?'

(Louder) 'What are the lions called?'

A lad who hasn't grown into his glasses yet throws his hand up and offers this gem:

'THUNDER.'

We all agree that Thunder is a great name for a lion.

'This is great. A great name for a mighty lion. Thunder!'

The boy grows into his glasses.

---

11 Simba was the name of every Alsatian on our street when I was a kid. There were four of them.

12 I've just made this up as well! I'll need a sequel to my Carpet Partners pamphlet – this is it! It's Carpet Talk, but quieter. ☺

Now, these are Year 1 kids. So I remind them that there are two lions, not one. Two of them. In a zoo. In Nairobi. Happy lions. 'One of them is Thunder. The other? What could his name be, I wonder?' (It's like I'm absolutely kicking a dead horse, and the kids are letting me.) 'Thunder and …'

Miriam, thinking she's helping, suddenly pipes up in a sing-song voice, 'Come on now, think of the weather!'

It doesn't help. The class just look confused, like the teachers are on crack.

'Thunder and … Thunder and … Thunder and …'

What feels like 300 years later, the tension is broken like a breached dam. A little lad proclaims the best name for a happy lion that Bristol can muster: Colin.

Chuffing Colin.

'Thunder and Colin, the happiest lions in Kenya. Living it up in a zoo! Two happy lions, wagging their tales, purring and smiling. Thunder and Colin.'

The exuberance drops a little and I move things on. It's now time to really hook the children in. They'll meet one of the lions.

'Would you like to hear Thunder speak?'

The children may be unsure about this but they don't show it; rather, they nod their heads and there's that shuffling as they ready themselves to listen. Some of them may even believe that I've brought a talking lion to the school with me.

Now, a younger, more creative, exciting teacher may at this point say, 'Okay kids, I'll become Thunder. In a moment.' And I'd walk into an adjacent stock cupboard and sprinkle myself in magic dust that _turns me into someone else_. Or I might bung on a full cowardly lion outfit borrowed off my pal Am-Dram Paul. Am-Dram Paul is into amateur dramatics and has a wealth of costumes at his disposal. The children would be amazed as I emerge from the cupboard, all snarling and purring.[13]

Suffice it to say, and as discussed elsewhere in this book, I do neither. I wait for quiet. For genuine settlement. I throw in a quiet 'Look at me', which always works wonders, and begin:

....

13 To be fair, the kids would love it. It'd be fun and a bit silly. And there's the problem: it needs to be more than that.

We hate it here in the zoo. The people are kind. They look after us. We get clean water. Fresh straw. And the meat is okay but it's never the same, is it? I look out of the bars and people walk past. Every day they walk. Sometimes they turn their backs. Take their pictures. And they point. They talk. And they move on. My friend just stares at the wall. Once, on that wall, there used to be a painting of the mountains. And the savannah. It's washed away, over time. All gone. But he still stares at the wall, remembering. We both remember a different time. A time when we'd run and when we'd hunt. And when we had our pride.

You could hear a pin drop. There has been a genuine shift in the learning atmosphere of the room. It's dramatic and has been achieved through the use of teacher-in-role. The voice of the lion (*people*) in the zoo (*place*) has revealed the *problem*. And the kids *get it*. I catch my breath to continue for a moment longer when I'm suddenly interrupted by a little boy who says,

'We're going to help you.'

I give him a detention for interrupting.

Except, of course I do not. I'm buzzing. This is where I want the class to be. It's where I want all classes to be when doing such work. The little boy has articulated his botheredness. It's why he interrupts. He has no choice. He's been stirred into action. He's heard the lion speak and wants to do something about it. He wants to help. He wants to contribute.

'How on earth can we help the lions?' I ask.

Now the children chatter away. The little boy who interrupted me has launched us all in the direction I'd wanted to go in anyway. He's feeling empathy; he genuinely cares about the fictional lions in our fictional zoo. Empathy is a great virtue and something we want our children to have – indeed, we may have it as one of our key values – but I think that it's trumped by compassion. We want children to feel empathy, but we want them to *do* compassion. *Doing* compassion lies at the very heart of what the world of botheredness is about. We don't want children to believe they're entering a world where there are no happy endings. We need to keep a check on our curriculum so that it isn't doing that. Projects can easily slide into what Dr Debra Kidd calls 'the curriculum of trauma',[14] where forests cannot be saved, plastic use cannot be reduced and the polar bears will starve.

In the story of our two lions, the children are being asked to react to a problem, a dilemma, that is presented to them – how can we make these lions happier? Now, that isn't going to cut it with older pupils, but you know what? It cuts it with Year 1. The kids are being asked to take all that knowledge that they've acquired around Kenya and do something with it. This is not just knowledge-rich work but botheredness-rich work. It takes a story, a context, a narrative to build a platform on which to give the knowledge of Kenya meaning to these small children. They've been well taught by Miriam; they have the knowledge, and now need to do something with it. Other than in a test or an exam. We need tests and exams, but knowledge can be in the moment – it can be tested in imaginative and creative conditions.

With botheredness built, this is where we went with the class in the time I was at the school. We looked at two big words. We looked at:

Captivity[15]

That is a big word. It's a reaching-up word, that. It's an aspirational word to bung in the young vocabulary. We also looked at:

Sanctuary[16]

The children wanted to move the lions from captivity to sanctuary. According to the simple mapwork we did, we could get the lions shifted to a large area outside the city where, let's say, a large animal sanctuary is being built.

'If we are going to move lions, what do we need to think about? What jobs need to be done in making sure the lions are safe when being moved? What does an animal sanctuary need to be able to offer the lions? How can we make sure these things happen?'

14 Personal correspondence.
15 That's a big word in Year 1.
16 Another big word for the Year 1 massive.

The key question for me, Miriam and you is, probably, where is the curriculum in all of this? Well, the topic written in the plans is *'Kenya'*, and I think it's fair to say that we are doing 'Kenya'. We are doing more though, are we not? So much more. How this stuff can be mapped out and structured will be explored later but let me just return to that little human who had the courage to blurt out an interruption to my monologue. He could not keep it in, bless him. He'd been moved from empathy to compassion, and in that moving he'd upgraded his levels of engagement with me, the classroom, the story, to one of being bothered – one of being invested.

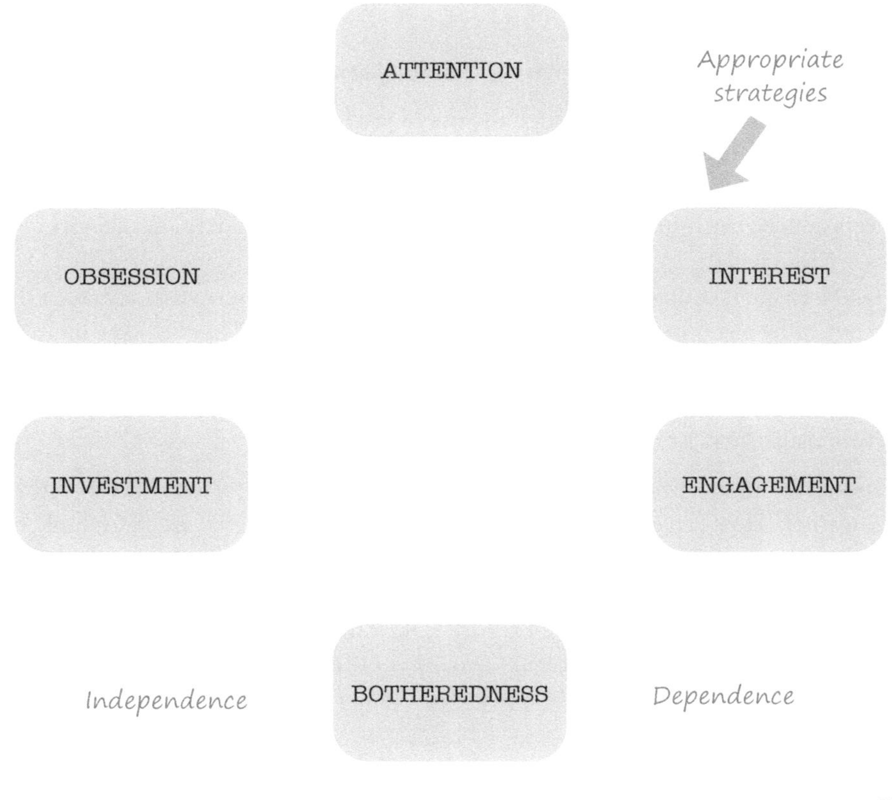

(adapted from Heathcote, 2011[17])

17 Dorothy Heathcote went through this 'circle of engagement' with me in person when I was a young teacher. Instead of *botheredness*, she used the word *concern*. As she spoke, I wrote it down. I later added the idea of dependence and independence when reflecting on how children react to the contextual learning work.

Dorothy Heathcote taught me that there's a whole world available to us that lies beyond the concept of engagement. As I've said elsewhere, I think engagement is simply the meeting of expectations around manners and compliance. When we get children bothered, better things can happen – it's the bridge to true investment in learning. It's cultivated engagement.

Going back to Kenya, this is how Heathcote's model plays out:

- **Attention:** achieved through routines and consistent high expectations.

- **Interest:** achieved through the use of an image alongside a powerful, inductive question.

- **Engagement:** achieved through the 'painting' of a scene based on the image.

- **Botheredness**: achieved through the use of teacher-in-role, in the moment and seemingly spontaneous. It isn't, of course. The monologue has greater effect because of its real-time unfolding of information. I could have easily just reproduced the monologue on a slide and read it to the children, but that would have lessened its impact. The act of listening is more demanding here. The children are learning to infer. They're being invited to immerse themselves in the context by an adult who is taking all of this very seriously. They're being invited to care for Thunder and Colin. Their sympathy is awakened, and their empathy mobilised. This careful 'sherparing' takes the class over the bridge of concern from engagement to investment.

- **Investment:** the teacher's stance is one of joint productive activity. We're in this together. 'How can we help the lions?' – the children are being asked to think for themselves. And it isn't straightforward. It isn't black and white. For example, what if the zoo needs the lions to attract custom? What if the zoo closes because the lions have gone? What will happen to the other animals?[18] The children will need to know and understand the small picture of the lions in the zoo but also the big picture of Kenya as a country. They'll need to know it and, crucially, will want to know it.

---

18 Thinking back to the story wheels, what you have in the story of Year 1 is this:
  - **People**: People responsible for the care of lions.
  - **Place**: A zoo in Kenya.
  - **Problem**: The lions are not happy.

■ **Obsession:** this is essentially 'Investment Plus'. It's when the kids are buzzing inside the context (the story-world zoo) but can see the world beyond it (Year 1's Kenya). This is when the bell goes, and a child looks at you and begs to stay to continue with the unfolding story. It's like the cliffhanger ending of a series and you stay up late for the next episode. Yes, curriculum delivery can be like that. It's simply an alchemy of story, stance and pedagogy.

CAPTION:

INTERMISSION #3

Tales of a Travelling Teacher

A reverie of professional learning misadventures

Dave Magoo

The fog clears and here we are.[19]

Year 1 are feeling funky and are dead excited that they have a visitor. Me.

I have learned much about Year 1 since flying the security of my secondary school nest. Year 1 mean business. When you ask them something, they react as excitable humans rather than the likeable lethargic teenagers I'm used to. Year 1, if you don't know, are around 5 and 6 years old. They take no prisoners, say what they think when they want and, to be fair, they will give you a few minutes grace to win them over.

And they sit on the carpet, shuffling and poking, picking and wiping. They are great because there is no guard to have up. The guard is down and the stream-of-consciousness replies to any enquiry can be joyful, confusing and, occasionally, bizarre. And sometimes, you know, they've just got to let it out.

....

19 This section was first published in Roberts (2019b). You'll notice a deafening echo back to the Year 1 Kenya narrative from Chapter 6 in this story. I wasn't going to include it but then thought it might offer a useful illustration as to how flexible these approaches can be.

And this class is no different.

In a Key Stage 1 classroom, I often feel like the lost Yank, Mac, in that brilliant film *Local Hero*, bewildered by locals. Or the tragic titular Withnail from *Withnail and I* who has gone on holiday by mistake. I sometimes feel like I'm in Year 1 by mistake.

We are doing 'Animals' as a topic and it's all very open. The lovely class teacher, Bianca, has assured me that the class will be enthusiastic and fun. She is not wrong.

I draw a giraffe on the flip chart and ask the children to talk about what it is.

'Is it a horse?' asks a jocular young fellow. Everyone laughs and I double-check my drawing. To be fair, you do have to be careful when drawing things for kids. Who can forget my attempt at drawing a lighthouse and adjacent abodes? I can't, that's for sure.

After a bit of cajoling, we all agree it's a giraffe. Behind bars. That's right! In a zoo! I eyeball the class and ask them how we might know that the giraffe is happy. They ponder and I ask them to share their ideas. The giraffe is happy because:

- He eats leaves.
- He likes getting his tail brushed (with a 'giromb' – a specialist giraffe comb).
- He drinks water.
- He smiles.

We start to think about the sign that is in front of the giraffe's enclosure. Should we give the giraffe a name? A girl, Lucy, shouts out 'DAVE!' I love this. A giraffe called Dave. What more could you want? The younger teacher in me winces, but I've learned to ignore him. On the front row sits Harry, with his horn-rimmed Krays-style specs. He has his hand up.

'Go on, what do you want to say?' I cajole once more.

'Dave Magoo!' he cries out, beaming.

'Dave *Magoo*?' I echo, my mind filling with cartoons from my own childhood.

All the kids find this hilarious. Bianca is shaking her head, smiling.

'Dave Magoo!' Harry repeats, sending the class into more fits. I'm finding it funny as well. Everyone is. I'm not sure why.

Then Lucy nails it. She declares: 'Dave Magoo! The happiest animal in the zoo!'

This is delightful and will definitely be what goes up on the sign in front of Dave's cage. We are all, to use a non-educational term, buzzing. But what do the other animals in the zoo say about Dave? The children are up and find their partners. After a few moments, the children are ready to speak as the other animals using the sentence starter 'We think Dave the giraffe is special because …'.

I use a metaphorical spotlight around the room, and we hear all the great things about Dave Magoo, the happiest animal in the zoo. The zoo's other occupants give him great reviews. (I need to move things on; to amp up a little healthy tension on these lovely kids.)

It's an old trick for me but it's one I use a lot. I'm going to do some expectation-shifting. I tell the class that I am going to talk as Dave Magoo, and this is what I say:

(*No funny voices. No acting. Just delivery of information*) 'I am so unhappy here in the zoo. The people are kind, but I haven't any space. There is no room for me to roam. To pace. I feel trapped. I am so unhappy.'

The children look on at me. I wait for a response.

Eventually, a serious young cove, Ned, whispers, 'We need to move you, Dave Magoo.'

I'll just leave that there, dear reader. And the fog descends.

You can't plan magic. You just need to believe in it.

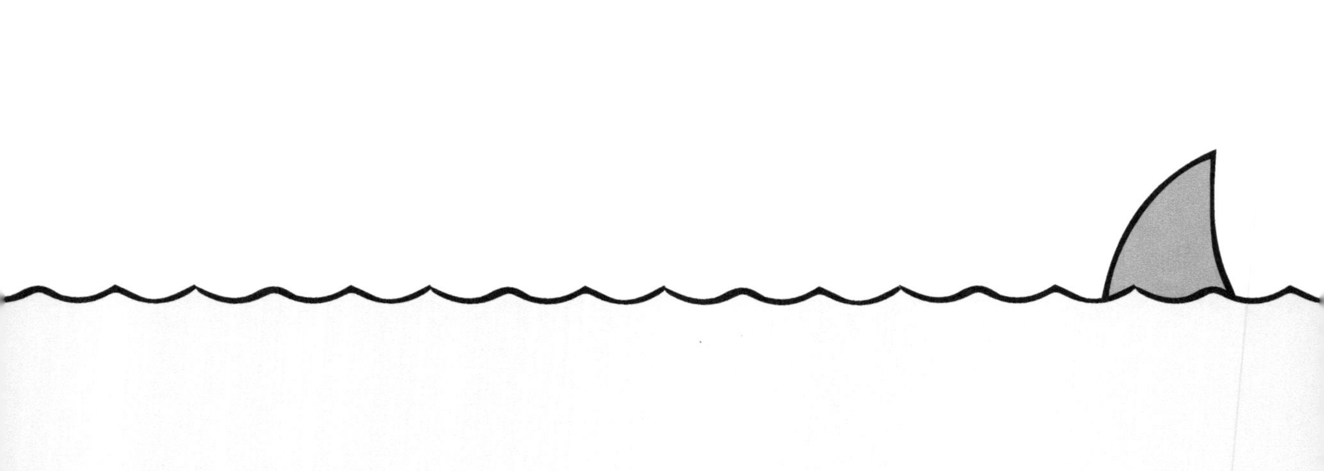

CHAPTER 7

FINDING HUMANITY

I went to the woods because I wanted to live deliberately. I wanted to
live deep and suck out all the marrow of life. To put to rout all that was
not life; and not, when I had come to die, discover that I had not lived.

Neil Perry[1]

The House by the Sea: Jimmy's Hill

- **People:** An old man.

- **Place:** In a house by the sea.

- **Problem:** He's being made to leave his lifelong home.

I really love telling this story. It's not just my story, it's Dr Debra Kidd's as well. Let's start at the beginning.

One day, the good Dr Kidd and I were leading a workshop at a teacher training thing. A roomful of pedagogically hungry trainee teachers, wide-eyed and coated in newness. The session went well with the mix of primary and secondary trainees. There was some laughing, some thinking and some old-fashioned telling.

At the end of the morning, one of the trainees – an earnest young fella – came up to us whilst we were packing up the tech and damned us with faint praise: 'That was all really nice. But. You can't do any of that for …' and he named a curriculum area that is renowned for being, well, quite a slog. I'm not going to tell you what it is just yet. He

1 *Dead Poets Society* dir. Peter Weir [film] (Touchstone Pictures, 1989). Words written by screenwriter Tom Schulman, who won an Oscar.

named a curriculum area and I didn't really know how to answer him straightaway. You know that moment someone is challenging you and you're desperately searching for something witty to come back with? I couldn't think of anything so just scrunched my forehead with concern and empathy. Dr Kidd asked me to quickly google an image. A house by the sea.

'I've got an observation on it next week,' he said, unable to make the connection between the curriculum and the image he'd been shown.

'Okay,' I reply. 'Give me a moment and we'll help you.' I turned to just zip up my laptop bag and then looked up. There he was, walking off down the corridor.

Should we call him back? Perhaps I should have done, but I didn't. Off he went into the sunset of anxiety and fingers-crossed planning. Typically, on the journey home, Dr Kidd and I thought of about _a million_ things the young teacher could have explored. Like when you've had a row and think of a brilliant last word long after the event.

Fast forward a few weeks later and we're in deepest Norfolk in a school on a Friday afternoon. It was a beautiful warm day and everyone was shattered. I had to model a story-led session based on the geography of coasts. Dr Kidd stepped in and said, 'Why don't you do that one about the house on the cliff?'

Of course!

I walked in and the teacher had a copy of the movie _School of Rock_ in her hand, and she was like, 'Oh, is it today?'

I felt sorry for her. I was like, 'I can go home, if you like. I'll go now 'cause it's 7 hours' drive.'

She said, 'Oh no, stay. We'll all be really quiet.' It was top primary and they'd just finished their national tests. Enough said?

The kids were ace. All the wall displays were covered but as I was doing the work, the teaching assistant was uncovering them, revealing the term's work. The teacher told me the curriculum area that the class had been studying prior to the tests. And it was the same curriculum area that the young, pressured teacher had mentioned to me. I suddenly had a million ideas to choose from.[2]

---

2   This is an exaggeration.

I invited the children to the front part of the class where I'd seated myself next to an empty chair. Some of the children sat on the carpet reminiscing about their early primary years whilst others pushed the envelope and lolled on tables. All were focused on me. I eyeballed them all and nodded at them close-mouthed. This is a way of focusing the attention of the room. I then started brushing the seat of the empty chair next to me with my open hand.

The children were quizzical but said nothing. They were waiting.

Let's say ...

Let's say there's an old man sitting in a house, in a room, by the sea. He's an old man. He sits on a threadbare sofa.

'What does *threadbare* mean? If it's threadbare, what is it?'

Responses:

- Old
- It's been well sat in
- There's stuffing coming out of it[3]
- It's seen some action[4]

The old man sits on a threadbare sofa. He brushes the empty seat next to him and mutters.

'Oh, Year 6, how old is *old* do you think?'

Responses:

- 31
- 53
- 80

---

3 This contributor pointed to what, in her head, was the side of the sofa. She's already invested in the narrative.

4 I know. The deputy spat her brew.

We settled on 80. An 80-year-old man sitting on a threadbare sofa, brushing it with his hand.

'If he's 80, when was he born? What year is 80 years ago?'

The children work it out and we create a timeline of events – this year at one end, his birth year at the other. We think of the events he's lived through.[5]

Responses:

- The moon landings
- The Second World War
- A pandemic
- The coronation
- The Olympics
- Live Aid[6]

'Oh, and he needs a name. What's a good name for an old man?'[7]

Responses:

- Albert
- Cyril
- Horace
- Barnaby

But the one we settle on is 'Jimmy, James on a Sunday'.[8]

I love that.

---

5   Timelining is a vital concept in the development of children's understanding of history. Using the story and a character can really help illustrate this concept. When teaching her version of this narrative, Dr Kidd uses timelining to great effect, emphasising two histories – the lived history of the character and the history of the world at large. Dr Kidd also manages to exploit maths skills in this activity. Can you see the possibilities?

6   Yes. A kid said Live Aid. Go figure! His dad had the DVDs apparently. ☺

7   Never accept names of pop stars/film stars/fictional characters. A name. A normal name. A name that fits the person described. Simple as that.

8   I imagine that the child who offered this beautiful name is thinking of their grandad.

So, Jimmy, James on a Sunday is 80, and he sits on a threadbare sofa in his house by the sea. And he mutters to nobody in particular.

'I'll speak as Jimmy,' I say to the class.

Dog hair. Dog hair and sand. Dog hair and sand.

Straightaway, a girl interrupts: 'Is the dog alright?' she asks.[9]

And I say,

Bessie's fine. She's a little dog. She lets herself out the back, runs down the steps, onto the beach, does her business and then comes back up and settles here next to me.[10] But she leaves it looking a mess. She's my best friend these days, so I'll let her off.

I love this time of day. At this time of day, the sun pours through the window – look. It turns everything to orange, and it reflects off the sea and this room becomes bathed in that warm glow. And it illuminates a table over there – look[11] – it was a wedding present. A table in the corner. And on that table sits a toy that my father made for me when I was a little boy.

I pause the monologue/teacher-in-role/information sharing and set a quick talk task: 'What could that toy be? What might his father have made him when he was a little boy?'

The kids are all chatting, theorising what a man might make for his little boy. Maybe something from a piece of wood? They naturally begin to contribute ideas.

9 This girl is already invested.
10 The business always raises a giggle.
11 I'll never tire of pointing at things that are not there.

I must tell you about a boy in the class at this point. Aaron is the kind of boy who is distracted by air, and yet his hand is straight up.

'Go on, then,' I say, gently.

'A PS4.'

And my heart breaks but I don't need to do anything because the rest of the class turn on Aaron. Poor Aaron. He faces a tirade of people saying his name. And he's very defensive. He's like, 'Shut up! Shut it!'

A girl takes control as I sit on my sofa and watch, like I'm an old man watching TV. 'Listen will you, Aaron? You're ruining it.'

I raise my hand and offer a calming 'shhhh'. I sit up and continue my speaking as Jimmy, James on a Sunday.

There is a PS4 in an Argos carrier bag ...

(pointing)

... under the table. That's what you've seen. My daughter, Jenny, arranged for that to be delivered here. Ready for when she brings my grandson, her son, Jake, here, to visit me. I've never met him. They live so far away. But it's just to make sure that I've got something to give him. When he sees it, I'll probably win Grandad of the Year! So, you're right, there is a PS4. I've no idea what it is or what it does. It's just sitting under there, collecting dust.[12]

(pause)

....

12 That kid, Aaron, bless him. His contribution is innocently made. It's well meant. He isn't trying to undermine anything – he just isn't great at listening. He's a lad. I could get unprofessionally sulky with him and tell him to listen more or to 'stop ruining it'. But in his idea of the PS4, he helps me introduce an extra layer to this old man; some more detail for the children and more reasons for them to invest and care about him. There's also the touch of the 'behaviour managements' here by bringing Aaron the Outlier back into the classroom. There's some emotional tension underneath what I'm doing, and I want him to feel it: they want to know – why hasn't his daughter been to visit? How old's the kid if he's got a PS4? You know, he's not a baby. Where does his daughter live? His idea is then championed rather than ignored. This stuff takes practice. The novice teacher in me would have probably just been pissed off with him.

'So, what other toys might there be? That his father made for him?'

Responses:

- Slingshot
- Boat
- Ship
- A nutcracker[13]

- Wooden train
- Wooden car
- Wooden motorbike

A wooden boat. Let's say it's a carved wooden boat. My father gave that to me before he went back out on the boats himself. He'd been away for such a long time, and when he returned home, he said nothing. Just stared at the fireplace. I was so thrilled with this small wooden boat. It meant that my father was truly home. I ran down the steps to the beach and let it set sail. I launched it with huge fanfare, not realising the tide was going out.

And I just sat there, my hands clawing the sand, watching it bob away. I was heartbroken.

(beat)

The next morning, my father brought it again to me. It was absolutely soddened with water. And he spoke to me gently. He said, 'Always be careful what you place on the outgoing tide.' And I didn't know what he meant by those words until today. Until today. And I look around this room and simply see memories of my life. Memories of a life well lived. I was born in this house. Got married and brought family up in this house.

(pointing around the classroom)

I can see a pile of letters over there.

Down here, the seashells we used to collect. All in a jar.

---

13 A nutcracker! They mean one of those ornamental soldiers. A toy soldier would be appropriate.

And back there I can see the wallpaper that just didn't match. Her eyes were going in the end. But who was I to stop her? She wanted to hang the wallpaper! None of the flowers match up!

(Jimmy chuckles)

'What else could be in this room that reminds this man, Jimmy, James on a Sunday, of a life well lived?'

This is another inclusive talk task, and a way of ensuring the class are keeping up with the unfolding narrative. The children talk to each other again and come up with ideas. We get some sticky notes, and each child writes an idea on one. We then stick them around the room – Jimmy's room … our classroom. This is scene painting.

Responses:

- Pictures
- A cabinet
- A chair
- An old fishing rod
- Unfinished knitting
- Lines on the door frame
- A grandfather clock
- An air freshener
- Vinyl records
- A TV
- A laptop

To share these sticky-note responses, I, Mr Roberts the visiting teacher, go and have a look around and read some of them out, asking for more details. Just like Aaron's PS4, this is so that the world of Jimmy, James on a Sunday, can be expanded. This is, essentially, a gallery.

Let's look at the class's ideas a little more closely:

Pictures

Paintings and photographs. 'Paintings and photographs of what?'

I then invite children to stand up and get into good working groups to create the images.[14] This is still image, freeze frame or tableau (see Afterword). As discussed elsewhere, they don't get a lot of time from me to do this task.

The class create photos of:

- The honeymoon when Jimmy and his new bride were in Paris.
- Wedding portraits.
- The newspaper photo celebrating the time Jimmy got a medal for rescuing someone from a sinking boat in the bay.

What does creating the images do? Is it just fluffy fun? I don't think so. It deepens the story of course, but it also continues to grow our absolute connection with the old man.

We could even grab a camera and take pictures of the class's 'photos'. Put them in a book! Create Jimmy, James on a Sunday's photo history! There are many possibilities for written work here – the labelling of the photographs, a 'what happened next' story, a diary entry. Just a thought.

Vinyl records

Vinyl! Vinyl! A load of vinyl!

Some classics.

Some good old classic vinyl. The soundtrack to *The Sound of Music* with Julie Andrews and Christopher Plummer on the front.

And maybe some ABBA.

And there's a record player. It's built into a furniture unit. You lift a lid and there it is. There's a record still there. The wood is scratched on top and has pale rings on it from forgotten cups of tea.

---

14 By good, I mean that they'll work well together.

Lines on the door frame

Scratches. Perhaps made by a kitchen knife. Above each line is a date a year apart.

A child's idea, maybe echoing something from their own home. It's a beautiful detail that needs that smoothing out; that detailing.

I offer the idea that there's a letter 'J' above the highest date: 'J' for Jenny, Jimmy's daughter, the idea for whom came from Aaron, the boy distracted by air. There's a delight in such synchronicity, isn't there?

Grandfather clock

What time does it say on it? Is it still going? There's a ship above the Roman numeral XII on the clockface. It rocks from side to side when the clock ticks. It'd be a ship in this room, wouldn't it? A ship on the sea?

A display cabinet

This is pretty much how this went:

GIRL: There's a display cabinet.

ME: Oh, yes? What is displayed in it?

GIRL: I don't know.

ME: Go and look.

(Laughing, she runs off to her friend who stands waiting at a computer table in the far corner of the classroom. They have an exchange, and she then runs back to me)

GIRL: It's got trophies in it.

ME: Who are the trophies for?

(Smiling, she rolls her eyes and returns to her friend, then comes back to me, exaggerating her breathlessness)

GIRL: They're running trophies that Jenny won at school. She practised on the beach and Jimmy and his wife would have tea watching her run. They'd have a picnic.

We both laugh. She's made a lovely image. A beautiful memory of a time long gone.

We have also pulled together some golden threads of that tapestry of impossible-to-articulate momentary understanding. We're on a wavelength. And my stance is enabling it.

Unfinished knitting

Unfinished knitting. A child in the class had suggested unfinished knitting. There's some genuine emotional prowess going on here. It isn't rushed. We're taking our time. When seeking definitions of what a joint productive activity might be, this is a good example of it; the teacher physically weaving amongst the children whilst helping them grow and develop their ideas.

I then sit back on my sofa at the front of the classroom and give them my final sharing of information, my last monologue, my ultimate teacher-in-role. And like the other inputs 'in role' as Jimmy, James on a Sunday, this is essentially me setting a task, giving them an instruction:

> I sit here and the orange of the sunset begins to turn to darkness. Still, I'm reassured by this room and all its memories. I see everything that is evidence of my life, a life well lived.
>
> *(Leaning forward and pointing at the children)*
>
> So, they can come knocking on my door as often as they want. They can tap on my windows. They can send me letters I'll never open. I won't let them in again, those liars. I'm not leaving here. I was born here, and I'll finish my time here. And nothing they can say will ever change my mind.

I allow a pause as the children start whispering to each other. Not all of them, of course, just a few. And the silent, attentive ones, glance at their peers.

'If you could ask Jimmy a question, what would you like to ask him?'

This is an invitation to a hot-seating exercise, which you may well recognise. Just to be clear, none of the children are in a state of confusion here. None of them are wondering which version of me is talking to them. They understand the process even though they're experiencing it for the first time in this sort of incarnation. Sure, they may well have done versions of drama activities before, but they haven't, according to their fab teacher, done it like this.

Hands begin to go up and I state clearly to them that they can only have one question and they should check with someone around them as to whether their question is any good or not. This lets us get rid of the poorer, shallower questions.

Or so I think. (Remember, the children have just found out that Jimmy is getting harassed by people turning up at his house.) The first question, from a delightfully smiley girl:

'Jimmy, please can you tell us again about your wedding?'

My heart sinks a little, but I'm still meaning business, so my face doesn't give it away. I tell her.

It was the best day of my life. Absolutely loved it.

And another child: 'Please can you tell us again about how you met your wife?'

We met at the fish market because I was delivering the fish, the catch that day. And I met her then. She was working on the market stall.

Aaron speaks. He asks this: 'Is it Death at the door?'

It's just liars and scammers.

'Who's knocking at the door, Jimmy?'

Who's knocking at my door? Nosy parkers and bureaucrats. The two worst combinations of people you can ever have the misfortune to meet on this planet. I'm not interested in their names. They need to just leave me alone.

'Where's Jenny?'

I don't want to bother her with it, do I? She'll only fret. They're so far away. No jobs here, you see? It's not easy. Australia is miles, miles, miles away.

There's a silent *boom* when children realise Jenny might as well be living on Mars. The whole idea of Jenny stemmed from Aaron's PS4 contribution, and it's now paying dividends. As the pennies drop, the children feel the weight of this emotionally pressured situation.

And who is knocking on his door? Banging on his window? Writing the letters he doesn't read?

I stand, smile and address the class, clearly as Mr Roberts.

'If you could help Jimmy, James on a Sunday, would you?'

They all want to help, of course.

Now all of this has unfolded – timelines, teacher-in-role, freeze frames, object descriptions, everything – in around an hour and a quarter. Just before playtime, I ask this question:

'Would you like to see where Jimmy lives?'

Apart from the sticky notes, here comes my other resource for this session – a projected image:

This is the turning point. This is what Dorothy Heathcote called a 'crux moment'.[15] We could call it an *Eastenders* moment, when the drums come in signalling a 'wow' event. The house teeters on the edge of a cliff. The children see it as Jimmy's house, and they want to do their best to help him. As they drink in the image, they articulate possibilities. They proclaim solutions (for example, 'we could move the house further back', 'we could build support struts') and have felt the real sense of a shifted perspective. The story has enabled that, as well as my stance. We have only heard one side of (not) the full story. And collectively, we realise that.

Pause. Just for a minute.

Have a think about what you've read so far in this chapter. I hope it's clear that this is not a lesson plan; rather, it's an account of a session where I was working with children whilst being observed by staff. It's an account of how to build botheredness. I regularly play this account back during staff development sessions, the invitation being to look 'underneath' what is being said. A professional comprehension if you like.

---

15 Personal correspondence.

When doing the staff sessions, I often ask what the worksheet would look like that would be an alternative to the lesson I've narrated.[16]

I think it could look like this:[17]

Coastal Erosion

Imagine there is a man called Jimmy who lives in house with a view of the sea. Trouble is, his house is falling into the sea! Oh no! Poor Jimmy! What can he do?

TASKS

1. Draw a picture in the box below of what Jimmy's house might look like.

2. Pretend you are Jimmy's friend. What could you say to him to warn him of the dangers of coastal erosion?

3. Role play a conversation between Jimmy and his friend.

4. Pretend you are someone who is encouraging Jimmy to move out of his house. How can you explain coastal erosion to him? Remember to use our keywords

5. Write a letter from Jimmy to his friend telling them what might happen next.

KEYWORDS:

Crack Cliff Cave Arch Stack Erosion

Your Coastal Erosion Drawing:

:-)

16 In England these sessions are still referred to as in-service training (INSET) days.
17 I created this worksheet to demonstrate how to drain learning of any emotion, but a friend of mine told me it's quite good. So, I've failed. ☺

Back with the class in Norfolk – where, at the time of writing, buildings *are* falling into the sea – and they're realising that they need to get Jimmy out of his house. When they hot seated Jimmy with their eventually well-thought-out questions, they found an old man who was cantankerous and difficult. A man who would not easily reveal his own fears and apprehensions. The class found his obtuseness challenging and, I think, it smacked them with its sharpness and realism. They did not know how to handle him. Because in the real world, people are difficult, aren't they? And classroom drama can be a rehearsal for this real life – the imaginative world overlapping the real.

The class write down what they've learned about the old man. I give them the time and opportunity to ask him more questions about his life as they write, and I answer the questions as I move amongst them.

And we have big fish to fry. How can we encourage Jimmy, James on a Sunday to leave his doomed house? What words are we going to use? It's desirably difficult, all of this, and the children are invested in it because they're bothered about Jimmy. They know they need to get him to leave the house and are mindful that whatever they do should be kind and thoughtful. This is curriculum warmed up, isn't it? Look at the children's hands in this photograph below from the session – they're genuinely grappling with this issue. This is difficult knowledge. How do you move someone who doesn't want to be moved? And for some people in the real world, this is their job. And difficult decisions, moral dilemmas and tensions in relationships are all part of life. With the story of Jimmy, we're practising this stuff, whilst doing some geography.

I ask a boy called Alan what we might do to resolve the situation. He shakes his head and proposes that we just need to jump in through the windows at night, put a bag on Jimmy's head and pull him out. At night. Like some SAS team on a midnight mission.

'Is that a kind thing to do, Alan?' I'm asking in the picture below.

'He's leaving us no alternative. It's all I've got,' replies Alan.

And that is fine. I asked him, and that is what he said. You cannot plan for organic conversations, so we have to respond in the moment. We can still do it thoughtfully, because, hopefully, that is how we live our lives anyway.

I quieten the class, knowing my time is nearly done. The narrative has shifted. Our story of Jimmy, James on a Sunday has stopped being about an old man's isolation and is now one of how a community can deal with coastal erosion. More on that in a moment. First, our final task:

We need to nail down the words we can say to Jimmy that will encourage him to leave his beloved home.[18] We know he's ignored our letters, our approaches and our appeals. He's a difficult man, but we need to operate with integrity and compassion. So, what can we say to him? What words will help him understand the gravity of the situation?

And once again, the class talk, unpick and grapple.

There's a sudden rush of voices as some girls approach me: 'Mr Roberts? Joshua has it. He has it!'

'Joshua has it?'

'Yes. Tell him, Josh. Tell him!'

I look at Joshua. A smiling shy lad. I nod at him and address the class:

'Josh has an idea.'

'Mr Roberts,' a girl interjects. 'Could we contact Jenny?'

I nod. It's a good idea, but I'm pressed for time in this session.

'What have you got Josh?' I ask, and the class are falling silent, watching.

Interestingly, Josh asks me to sit back down on my threadbare sofa. I do.

'Shall I be Jimmy?' I ask him as the class look on. 'I haven't let you in my house so how are you talking to me? On the phone?'

Josh looks heavenward, thinking.

'Or through the letterbox?'

---

18 In those words 'we need to', we find the essence of inductive practice.

He breaks a grin and nods. I tell him to stoop and make a letterbox shape with his hands. He does. As I glance across the class, I see they're watching Josh closely. He speaks the four words he's chosen. He speaks clearly, enunciating like an orator.

'Jimmy? Memories are portable.'

There's a gentle gasp, and I'm once again carried on the shoulders of children.

'The door is open,' Jimmy replies, and quiet, lovely Joshua of Norfolk steps towards me and begins explaining the impact of coastal erosion on my lovely old house. He uses his hand to emphasise the gravity of the situation. And all I do is listen.

Here he is, beautifully captured by the teaching assistant, explaining to me why memories are portable and that your home is in your head and heart. I couldn't shut him up. I didn't want to. I said, 'Shall I be Mr Roberts now?' because we were going to have to wrap things up.

Josh replied, mid-breath, 'No, no. Be James. Be Jimmy. Because I need to tell you about the garden in your photograph and how it isn't there anymore.' And he's proper banging on. One day, he'll be brilliant at negotiations as well as putting people at their ease.

This is another example of what can be referred to as *affectus* where we feel a sense of passion, of warmth, a sentiment, a mood, feeling or emotion.[19] This communal sense of being 'moved' is what it is to be human. It's where the critical knowledge is made flesh and transcends the cold, dead document that constitutes a published curriculum. There's no warmth in a cold curriculum we discovered earlier with the Vikings, but there is when we encounter the caged lions. Being affected affords children creative agency – a safe space where, as Boris and Peterson (2017) remind us, risk-free experimentation along with purposeful exchanges of ideas and knowledge can thrive. There's no final play, no parent-attended performance, just a joint productive activity in a classroom where we're in negotiation with the world.[20]

By operating in this way, by adopting this warm, inductive pedagogy, I feel I'm being my best teacher self, not what Giroux (2003) called a 'deskilled corporate drone', but a Sherpa of experience and knowledge. Not the cold, abstract, subject-specific critical knowledge of the *should* curriculum, but the human, humane, committed, responsive and compassionate knowledge that will support children and young people in navigating their lives. I am bothered. They are bothered. We are riding the waves of botheredness.

And coastal erosion.

Sympathy, empathy and compassion

Show children a photograph of a sea turtle with plastic impeding her ability to swim properly and they'll usually respond with articulations of sadness and proclamations of sympathy for the poor creature. And to make sure we've got the music curriculum covered, we'll do a soundscape of the sea. And then move on. This is not the curriculum of trauma mentioned earlier, but a good example of the pedagogy of poverty; the content is affective but in this teacher's hands, sterile. We move on from it without action or genuine thought. We understand the sea turtles are suffering and accept it.

---

19 Some Latin there for you. You can find some background to the ideas around affect theory (be careful though, it's a rabbit hole) in Shepard (2006).
20 There is an interesting piece about how process drama is used with trainee lawyers at New York University in Cooper Davis and Webb (2012). That inductive drama pedagogy gets everywhere doesn't it?

Brené Brown gives us an excellent description of *sympathy* when she describes it as to observe someone in a deep hole, whilst remaining on higher ground and talking to them from above. Someone who is sympathetic may also try to simply put what Brown calls a 'silver lining' on the other person's situation instead of acknowledging that person's feelings by saying, 'Well it's bad but at least …'. In other words, get a stiff upper lip and crack on.[21]

According to renowned psychologist Paul Ekman (Goleman, 2008), there are three elements to empathy – cognitive, emotional and compassionate. As I describe them here, you should be able to recognise the elements in the narratives I've offered so far. You'll also see that they're central to the whole idea of botheredness; they're the very bones of story, stance and pedagogy.

Cognitive empathy

This is sometimes called perspective-taking and is a key element of enabling children to understand issues that lie beyond the cold curriculum. Returning to my favourite movie for a minute, it's when we understand the mayor's reluctance in closing the beaches on the Fourth of July in *Jaws* (1975). We might not like it, but we understand it. Cognitive empathy helps children see things from another person's point of view. When we think of the story of Jimmy, we understand, following the reveal of his house, that the people trying to get him out are not *bad people*. We suddenly understand them because we recognise their perspective. Similarly, cognitive empathy occurs when we hear someone else's point of view, which may well differ from our own but we've developed the intellectual prowess to accept and understand it. Underneath this, I think, lies the skill of negotiation.

Emotional empathy

This is probably the aspect we all recognise. It's when we sit with another person's feelings; where, as Goleman (2008) writes, their 'feelings are contagious'. It's that moment we well up at our friend's tears. Or during an emotional scene in a movie we're experiencing. This echoes back to *affectus* – we're affected in our reaction. This

----

21 A really good animation from the RSA of Brené Brown's ideas around empathy can he found at RSA (2013).

actually can be quite tiring! Do you know when we say we might be 'emotionally drained'? That is the negative aspect of emotional empathy. I feel like that when I watch a particularly harrowing movie, like *Schindler's List* (1993) or *The Road* (2009). I'm moved by those films but am fatigued also. A bit like when I feel the need to make a cup of tea during the Children in Need television fundraiser. It's not that I'm not bothered, it's just that I cannot take any more sadness. After the children see a few plastic-ridden turtles, those turtles all start to merge into one.

Compassionate empathy

This is emotional empathy ramped up to something active. It's feeling becoming action. It's finding the middle ground I mentioned earlier. According to Goleman (2008), compassionate empathy is being 'spontaneously moved to help'. It's the state of feeling the emotional empathy but then engineering up to an action. In the narrative of Jimmy, this is when the children are considering the words we might use to encourage Jimmy to leave his house. In our botheredness work, compassionate empathy can manifest itself inside the safe space of the imagined story world, or it can begin there and ultimately bleed out into the real world and experience of the children. It's where the children in the class fundraise for an oceanic charity because they've looked at the plight of coral reefs or sea turtles thousands of miles away. It's where, following our encounter with Jimmy, we arrange a visit to the local care home across the road from school.

Back to Jimmy's hill ...

Well, we've finished. Joshua pretty much concluded the session.

Here are some of the things that we touched on in the session – the *should* curriculum, if you like:

- Understanding a history that has been lived

- Key moments in living history

- Coastal erosion

- How places change

- Descriptive, persuasive and formal writing

- Measuring and distance

As you reflect on what you've read, in terms of curriculum possibility, what else did the story of Jimmy reach out to?

The use of the narrative nods to my idea of the *could* curriculum, of course, but there's also the *must* curriculum to consider – the 'hidden', if you prefer. In Jimmy's story, the *must* curriculum is addressed by the deeper questions around old age, loneliness, isolation and family. As teachers, we should always examine the possibilities around widening children's experiences of the world. Knowledge is key to this. When we present children with the people, the place and the problem, we understand that it's the acquisition of knowledge that will help them in resolving the difficulties the story throws in their way. The children who worked with Jimmy had been studying coastal erosion as part of the school's geography curriculum. Now, this dry[22] area of the curriculum has been contextualised and the physical aspects of geography have melded into the human. We need to know about coastal erosion in order to help Jimmy.

'That was all really nice, but you can't do any of that for coastal erosion,' the young trainee teacher had said after my and Dr Kidd's session in Doncaster. And when I arrived in the classroom in Norfolk a few weeks after, the teacher had said, 'Oh god, we were doing coastal erosion and the rock cycle. You don't want to do that, do you?'

And I was buzzing. After the session, so was the teacher. She was buzzing and tired. It's quite a normal professional state that, isn't it? Buzzing and tired. If it isn't normal, you might need to use fewer worksheets. The actively compassionate outcomes were clear for all observing colleagues. In a short meeting, a debrief following the in-class session, we talked about the potential for written outcomes, or as we call it in the English education system, 'evidence in books'. I'm pretty sure this evidence is there so that people can point at it and say, 'Look! There it is! We're doing our job properly! It's there! Look! Look! So back off!', rather than as a celebration of learning and understanding. It's not our fault; it's just where we seem to be at this current time. Having said all this, the writing in books generated from the story in class will be powerful because the children have lived it. They've had an opportunity to cultivate their compassion and have practised their responses to a fictional scenario. From height notches

22 Sorry.

on the door frame to trophies won by a girl who has never lived, the children have participated in a world born from a collected imagination. I suggest to the teacher that one piece of writing the class might do is a social worker's report about Jimmy and his situation. Another could be Jimmy's letter to Jenny.[23] And maybe the surveyor's report outlining the impact of coastal erosion on Jimmy's cliff. We also talk about the need for knowledge and that the children must be taught about coastal erosion to navigate the narrative. I emphasise that the stories are not there to replace the formal teaching of a subject but, rather, be offered as a context to explore the topic or theme. This is where teachers are being invited to participate in a true creative act: the connecting of the seemingly unconnected – old people and coastal erosion; the history of a place with the geography of a place. We also talk about the fact that much of the session in class appeared to be a sort of 'living comprehension' where children were invited to infer, to reach up high to complex vocabulary that I modelled when I was using teacher-in-role as Jimmy – words like 'bathed' and 'illuminated'. The observing teachers also recognised the spaces where the children were given time to respond, reflect and ponder. This enabled them to empathise cognitively with what the story was offering them whilst also letting them find their own resonance within the narrative – they talked of their own grandparents, for example; their world and Jimmy's world overlapping and making sense.

We can't use stories for coastal erosion?

Turns out we can.

Activated compassion, the negotiation of dilemmas and young Joshua telling Jimmy that it'll all be okay are firmly rooted in one idea – connectedness. And to be connected is to be bothered.

It is rehearsal of life.

---

23 Thanks again, Aaron.

CHAPTER 8

TRANSCENDING THE ORDINARY: WHY HAS THIS BEEN ALLOWED TO HAPPEN?

The ever lasting
gob stope/s tastes
Like dust.

chloe

Curiosity is the engine of achievement.

Sir Ken Robinson[1]

As the story grew, it put down roots into the past and threw out unexpected branches.

J. R. R. Tolkien (1954, 13)

There's a school on one of Sheffield's hills. It overlooks the city and is flanked on all sides by a sprawling housing estate. The school, like many others, is an oasis of safety and optimism for the children who attend it. Everyone is working hard. Everyone.

I've been invited in to work with Year 3 following an INSET day I'd done at the start of the year. Now, I know you may be reading this thinking that I'm about to serve you up yet another primary-focused anecdote and you're a teacher in higher education or are focused on upper high school. I get that. I really do. I can honestly say this story is for you. It's a simple account of botheredness being established step by step. It's a lived example of how 'imagineering acetate' (more on this later) can become a humanly driven experience.

And it all starts with a book.

A famous book.

The Year 3 class have read it with their teacher, and they've absolutely loved it. In fact, the teacher, in her email prior to my visit, wrote, 'They have all fallen in love with a book', which I think is a beautiful thing for her to notice.

Cutting to the chase, the children sit before me on the carpet. I have my whiteboard pen at the ready and have brought with me two tasks:

1   We are going to make a map using the template of a mini roundabout.

2   We are going to create a pitch by finishing this sentence: 'The city we are planning is amazing because …'.

Yes! We are going to be:

CITY DESIGNERS

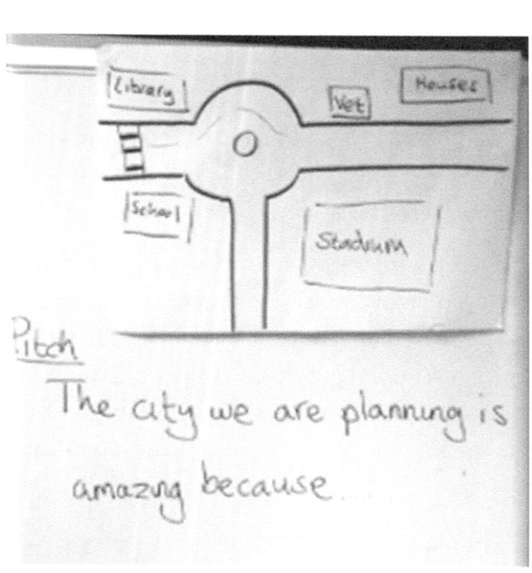

(No expense spared as you can see)

Let's say we're people who are in charge of making cities really exciting and interesting places to live.

We make fantastic cities. And Sheffield is a fantastic city already, but we've been asked to make it even more wonderful! I think this is something we can do.

So, if we're going to have a fantastic city, if we're going to rebuild Sheffield, what sort of places might we've? And we can have anything because we're in charge.

What shall we have?

Straightaway, a child responds with 'A BP garage!'[2]

I do a gentle double take and urge the class to throw out more ideas as I capture them on the whiteboard.

'A Subway!' proclaims a child, and they're not talking about a concrete underpass. It's a sandwich shop _inside_ the BP garage.[3]

Okay, we have a Subway and a BP garage so far. We can have anything we want. What shall we have in our fantastic new city?

A girl raises her hand and I nod her way.

'Streakers!' she says, pleased as punch.

It was an odd response, and I was almost lost for words, when the class teacher filled me in: 'It's a hairdresser.'

I learn later that what the children have offered me is _their world_. They've told me the places they know. You see, when they come out of their massive estate, they turn right. And there, on the busy road, is the BP garage with the Subway franchise built in. It's

2 Other fuel companies are available. It's just the one that he said.
3 Other sandwich shops are available. It's just the one that she said.

where they sometimes get their tea. And then past a few houses, there's Streakers Hair Design where Nana gets her roots done. And then they turn immediately right, and they're at school.

And that makes me feel melancholic.

I'm asking children for a view of the world and they're giving it to me.

Okay. We have a BP garage, a Subway, and Streakers Hair Design. You can have anything else you like. Really! What other amazing places could we have in our fantastic new city?

A child raises her hand and whispers, 'We don't have a zoo. Please can we have a zoo?'

'YES! WE CAN HAVE A ZOO!'

And then the floodgates of ideas, hopes and dreams are opened, and our city begins to find its feet. We even have a castle because we learned about them in Year 2, and they're ace. Our list of places in the fantastic new version of Sheffield is really taking shape!

The children then move to their tables and add details, words and sketches to their own mini roundabout template. The list we've created on the whiteboard protects some of the children into doing this as those ideas help them get going.

Just before morning play, we shift tasks to our 'pitches' that we write on our mini whiteboards – 'The city we are planning is amazing because …'.

CHILD: The city we are planning is amazing because we're going to have hot tubs.

ME: Where?

CHILD: Everywhere.

Fair play!

They went to playtime all knowing that collectively we'd done a great job of pitching our fantastic new city. When they returned, I'd joined all the mini roundabouts up on the floor, creating a visual of the proposed city of fantastic-ness.[4] This is an approach that is as old as the hills but is one of those simple ideas that has fallen out of favour. It isn't neat, it isn't ever finished, but it could go up on a wall or be kept in a draw and pulled out and remade when needed. It's also *our* map, not a downloaded colouring-in exercise. The template aspect of the road enables us to create an imaginative world. A place. A setting.[5]

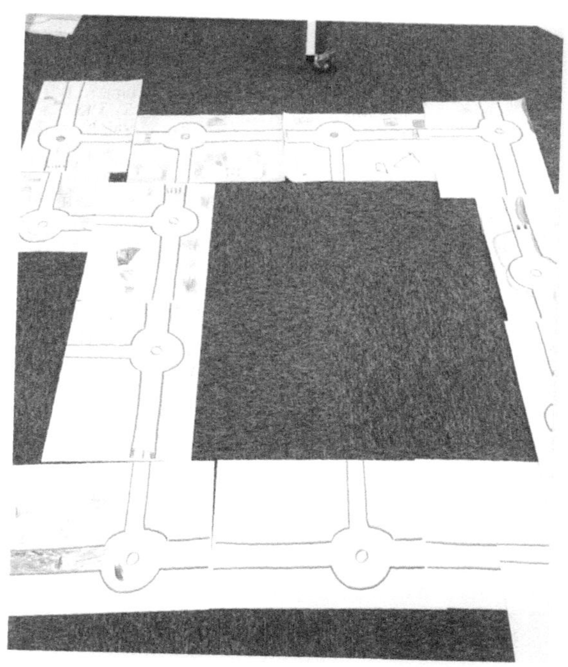

4   I know it looks like Milton Keynes but bung a volcano into the big gap and we could all agree it is Pompeii. Or stick a castle in that gap and we have a curriculum focus. What if the council were turning the castle into a supermarket? Are we all okay with that? We're not? The other thing with this mapping approach is that it's so simple. It's another way of getting children hooked into an idea and it's key that they create it together.

5   In my book *Oops! Helping Children Learn Accidentally* (Roberts, 2012), I share ideas around mapping that incorporate coastlines, islands and mountain ranges.

The children love seeing this, absent-mindedly hanging their coats on the hooks on the wall. A boy called James walks *through* the map, treading on some of the sheets with his damp shoes.[6] I tolerate it because he's completely aghast, like he can't believe what he's seeing. He's heading, as the crow flies, to the A4 sheet in the top left of the picture. This is his sheet. He calls to me.

'Mr Roberts, where does that go? Where does that road go?' He motions to the road going nowhere.

Perfect, I think.

The children settle because they're hooked in. They want to know what the visiting teacher is going to ask them to do next. I did tell them before playtime that there was an important job we needed to do.

'Mr Roberts?' James pipes up again, thinking I must be ignoring him. I'm not. I'm gathering my thoughts. And then we're *in*.

'That's interesting you ask that, James. That goes to a part of the city we don't talk about. Until now.'

Some of the children get excited and some are just eyeballing me, willing me on.

'James? Look at the palm of your hand. I'm going to FaceTime you.'

And he turns to the class teacher and says, 'I haven't got my phone.'

'That's why I said look at the palm of your hand, James. No worries. Let's say I'm FaceTiming you.'

He nods and looks at his palm. Other children join in. I can't lie: it's a nice moment. The teacher captured it here:

---

6   He has nothing to do with Jimmy, James on a Sunday.

Let's say …

James, you need to get your team together. At the end of that road is an old, abandoned factory. It's long been forgotten. People don't even remember what it made.

It's a place of forgotten memories and forgotten people. It's an ugly place. No one has set foot inside for many, many years. Until now.

James – let's say you're going to take a team inside the old place to see if there's anything of value inside.

The place is due to be knocked down next week. Before you get in the building you'll need to get through the nettles and weeds that have grown in front of the old iron gates.

And you need to know that we cannot trust the stairs and there's no electricity.

Is this something we can do?[7]

As James nods at the palm of his hand, some children have cast their eyes to the corner of the classroom. On the wall is a big sheet of paper – I mean a massive sheet – on which I've written the words

NETTLES AND WEEDS

The children clock it now, but it's been up there all morning.

---

7   This is a great question, especially if it's asked by an adult nodding their head.

We do some other list-making tasks including a response to the question: 'If we are going to go inside the old, abandoned factory, what do we need to take with us?'[8]

Responses:

- Rope

- Telescopic ladders

- Snacks[9]

- Ikea bags

- Wheelbarrow

- GPS

- Mobile phone (camera, torch)

- First aid kit

- Good shoes

- Tools

- Ball of string[10]

- Camera

… amongst other ideas. I sometimes use this session I did as a workshop with adult educators, and they pretty much come up with the same list!

8 This is another great question that invites everyone to that middle ground discussed elsewhere. When I did something very similar to the story I'm telling here in a school in Edinburgh, the first thing a child said he'd take into an abandoned building was an Uzi – a submachine gun. He then rat-a-tat-tatted the whole class with imaginary sprayed bullets. I told him that we never have guns in our stories. He stopped shooting, wiped a hand across his brow, and said, 'Oh. A hard hat?' I nodded. The younger teacher in me might have balked at 'Uzi' and I could see myself abandoning the task before it had even taken root. Sometimes we need to give classroom approaches just that – the chance to take root.
9 Food-related contributions can be a pain. I've learned to ride with them now, but they used to really get on my nerves. In Edinburgh a child offered 'sandwiches' and I asked her what she'd have on her sandwich. 'Sliced Peperami', she said.
10 In Edinburgh, a child said 'A loaf of bread' so that we could drop a trail of breadcrumbs as we go deeper into the factory like a Celtic *Hansel and Gretel*.

The session in Sheffield is moving at a pace and we're now all staring at the large sheet of paper stuck up on the wall.

Pull it down.

The children look at me, mouths opening.

Rip it down. I'll recycle it. Just tear down the nettles and weeds.

The kids cannot believe it. They launch into their task with gusto. Not all of them, of course, but the job gets done. In fact, it halts because the paper-rippers discover something: underneath the first sheet is a second, smaller piece of paper. On that is a drawing of the old factory gates.[11]

And on the old factory gates are two letters.

The initials of the once-famous factory owner:

Hear that?

It's the sounds of pennies dropping.

Realisation catches fire through the children and some scatter. Others sit excitedly on the floor. Some just stare at the letters. All quickly understand.

There's an overflowing of exuberance, and the teacher takes my elbow and asks me if I'd like her to step in to calm them down.

'Are they being naughty?' I ask, genuinely.

'I don't know!' she replies, breaking into an uncertain grin.

James is on his back chanting 'I'm Charlie Bucket!' over and over. Some kids are just dancing. I need to get a grip! I grab an imaginary torch and begin describing, using teacher-in-role, what I can see through the front door of the factory. The children sit, participate and some, as you can see in the image, are still jubilant that the book they've loved so much is alive and kicking *right now* in their classroom. Some kids have night-vision goggles, and some are just desperate to get inside the factory. This is investment. This is joyful. This is meaningful. The BP garage is a million miles away. All that matters is getting inside the factory. So that is what we do.

Other stuff happens. When I say that, I mean, we do some other tasks. For example, the children write down describing words for how they feel when they step into the cold, old building. The two sticky notes I remember are:

Fearful

Scarred

Now, we all can see that 'scarred' is written in error. The writer meant 'scared'. They're in the heat of it, so it's an understandable mistake. It's a mistake any teacher worth their salt can pick up and highlight to the child at the appropriate time. That time is _not_ now. We have a job to do. If I weighed the merit of these contributions, they'd both weigh the same, and now, that is more than good enough. The children are at peak botheredness, and yet it gets better.

A few freeze frames (see Afterword) later and we find ourselves in a great hall.[12] This is where we're going to find things. And it's where we're going to have to decide what we might take away and save before the place is demolished. As I say this to the children, I notice some of them furrowing their foreheads, glancing at their friends and shaking their little heads.

Perfect.

I tell them what I've found:

There is a painting on the wall. It is the portrait of a boy. Sadly, the frame is warped and broken. Rainwater has seeped behind the glass and the image is damaged. If you look closely, you can see the outline of a smiling boy being carried on the shoulders of a grown up.[13]

12 Still images/tableau – the children created the living statues of something happening in the darkness of the factory; for example, a group were sat eating their sarnies, another group rescued someone falling down a hole whilst another group were swatting away bats.
13 I'm actually describing the cover of the VHS release of *Willy Wonka and the Chocolate Factory*. This one: https://warner-home-video-uk.fandom.com/wiki/Willy_Wonka_and_the_Chocolate_Factory?file=51APZHBSDML._AC_SY445_.jpg.

I hear James whisper the name Charlie Bucket to nobody in particular.

Shall we take it? Is it worth saving?

'It's knackered,' says a child. A Year 3 child. I don't know what to say to that, so I ask them to write their objects down on the sticky notes, giving them some more examples as I go: a pencil on the end of a string, a fine desk with a leather top.[14] I soon realise that they don't need too much from me. They get it. They understand. Look at what Chloe has written on her sticky note:

'The everlasting gobstoppers tasted like dust.'
Chloe

---

14 This note creating develops real investment in the narrative situation. I outlined it early in the coastal erosion story. Like mapping, it's an easy win.

And what Summer wrote on hers:

'The chocolate river has dried up. Why has this been allowed to happen?'
Summer

There's a lot to love in these two examples. I'm always grateful when a colleague captures what is happening during one of my sessions. I think this photograph above is a favourite of mine. Here are two children reading Summer's sticky note. They're taking it in. And beyond the imaginative world of a small orange square, an abandoned chocolate factory and the team with a job to do, we have the real world. The real world of the children, their teachers, their families, me and our ordinary lives. For now, though, all that is forgotten. It's left behind. We are above it, held high by a curriculum and pedagogy of botheredness. Just like Troy reassuring Atticus Finch in an earlier chapter. We are motivated. We are invested. We might even be obsessed. 'Why has this been allowed to happen?' We settle at our desks and consider Summer's question. I then propose another.

Are we happy that the chocolate factory is being knocked down?

Unsurprisingly perhaps, we are not! And then I point. The children move from their tables to the front of the class. I know we're hitting lunchtime, so I want to tie some things up whilst opening some doors. Well, one door. One door in particular.

There is a light coming from under the door of a room at the top of the rickety staircase. Is there someone there? Who might it be?

Hands are up.

I can hear the familiar sounds signalling a primary school lunchtime. Shouts of children and the scraping of chairs in other rooms.

> We push the door to find a man sitting in the dull yellow of the room. We don't see his face. A top hat rests on his lap. We hear him sniff. And then he looks at us.
>
> 'Can you help me?' he asks.[15]

The session finishes.

'I'm Charlie Bucket,' says James as he leaves, coat on. Back to reality.

15 The teacher had to intervene at this point which is totally fair! 'Two lines! Sandwiches and hot dinners!'

CAPTION:

INTERMISSION #4

Tales of a Travelling Teacher

A reverie of professional learning misadventures

Rhythm and poetry

The fog clears and here we are.[16]

It's the closing days of the century and we are experiencing a professional development day. We are having a practical day on 'Creativity' via an external provider with a jazzy name. Training days are strange events as you get to see people in their normal non-school clothes. You'd never pictured them in dungarees and a checked shirt, but here they are, looking like an extra from *Deliverance*, talking about the millennium bug and its potential impact on the school servers. It was overhearing that conversation that led me to backing everything up on floppy disc. They weren't going to catch me out. Another teacher, Molly, always wore wedding outfits. I have no explanation for that. And then there was Rod, an aging woodwork impresario with a natty line in potentially offensive t-shirts with slogans like:

- I like school. When it's shut!!!

- There is only one 'F' in Ofsted.

- I shout because you are STUPID!

- I put the 'stud' into study.

- My pen is huge.[17]

There was another teacher, Mike, who for no reason anyone could fathom, always dressed as an American footballer, complete with shoulder pads, when the kids

---

16 This section was first published in Roberts (2017b).
17 I mean, for fuck's sake.

weren't there. He was a complete professional in every other way, but looked slightly out of place, especially when he put his helmet on. Like I say, it's an INSET day. Anything goes.

I was looking forward to this day as I felt it would be right up my street. Sadly, by the end of the event, as the visiting providers packed their first generation Berlingo van, I felt slightly bemused as to how the day had played out. This hadn't been my sort of creativity – it had been some wacky version of creativity designed to keep children amused and busy rather than thinking, understanding, asking questions and imagin-ing. Having said that, a few clearly enjoyed it a lot. There was a lot of laughing and it's always good to lean back and let someone else get on with it, isn't it? I went home and, like many an INSET gone before, forgot about it and self-medicated on Asda Shiraz, contemplating the beauty of a now four-day week.

By Wednesday, the dreams and reveries of the Monday INSET had been forgotten, by me anyway. As every day, in walk 11R – my form. And a right group of individuals they are too. Buzzing because they had Monday off, less buzzing because it's now Wednesday and the week is dragging. Jade is wanting me to check through her essay on *Of Mice and Men* whilst Terrie (named after her dad) is complaining about last night's episode of *Buffy*. In walks Paul Whitefield. He's often straggling in a few min-utes after he's supposed to, but I know where he's been.

'Been thinking, Paul?'

I await his usual response confirming the fact that he's been wandering around school 'thinking' but I don't receive it. I look up from Jade's essay.

'You okay, Paul?' I ask.

He nods and approaches my desk. I give him my full attention as something is clearly up.

'Sir. What happened on Monday?' he whispers.

Conspiratorially, I lean to him and reply, 'We had an INSET …'.

Paul raises his hand and nods his head. 'I know, Sir. But what *happened*?' His eyes now burrow into my own and I feel rather on the spot!

'Well,' I attempt, 'we did some work around creative strategies to …'

'Sir,' he interrupts, 'whatever happened needs to stop. And stop *now*.'

My eyebrows rise, and so do his.

'It's only Wednesday and I've already done four raps. Two of them have been in science. Frankly Mr Roberts, these are things I cannot un-see. Can you let someone know?'

I nod.

He nods and takes his place between Brett and Warren, who both greet him with hip-hop hand gestures and 'Whassups'.

And I smile whilst the fog descends.

CHAPTER 9

PAY NO ATTENTION TO THAT MAN BEHIND THE CURTAIN

A hunch is creativity trying to tell you something

Often attributed to Frank Capra

Creativity should never be allowed to become a byword for shallow pedagogy or knowledge-less learning experiences. I'm all for 'fun' but I also want impact. A lot of what I've shared in this book could easily slip into the realm of novelty and unlearning. It could, in less thoughtful hands, be distilled into 'make up a story'. It could be construed as 'keeping children busy' or 'make them laugh until lunchtime'. I hope I've successfully communicated to you that it's none of these.

If I showed you a pencil and an audio cassette, a creative act is one where you connect these seemingly disparate objects together. One finds a solution to the other's issue. In this case, trying to find 'Whole of the Moon' by the Waterboys. This paragraph may make little sense if you're under 40, but I've noticed the resurgence in sales of audio cassettes with major labels making new releases available on this ancient format. Anyway, I digress. My point is that creativity is something that we all tap into. It doesn't belong to one philosophy of teaching or how children learn. Being creative is what we're doing when we build a decent relationship with a class or when we consider how we're going to de-nettle an instance of curriculum complexity, or how we react professionally when the tech fails; and it *is* drama, music, dance and art, but it's also knowing what to say when a child is finding it all a bit too hard. It's uncovering accessibility, keeping challenge high with threat at bay. It's being genuinely inclusive and doing all you can to help children keep up. Remember the transformative teacher from an earlier chapter? We should all want to aspire to be that, but it's a creative act in itself to come to achieve that label and come to that conclusion about yourself. And how do _we_ make sure we can do all this _and_ sleep well at night?

A creative act is to simplify the complex

There's a useful lens to help us – the Standards of Effective Pedagogy and Learning from the Center for Research on Education, Diversity, and Excellence (CREDE) in the United States.[1] Before I share the standards, the Center's philosophy is this:

- All children can learn.

- Children learn best when challenged by high standards.

- English proficiency is an attainable goal for all students.

- Bilingual proficiency is desirable for all students.

- Language and cultural diversity can be assets for teaching and learning.

- Teaching and learning must accommodate individuals.

- Schools can mitigate risk factors by teaching social and learning skills.

- Solutions to risk factors must be grounded in a valid general theory of developmental, teaching and schooling processes.[2]

I don't think there's much to argue with here. It's about social, academic and human approaches to practice. There's help here for us to label the stuff that we do, and can do, in class.

Here are the standards. If you search the internet for them, most of what you'll find refers to _five_ standards. The creator of the standards, Professor Roland Tharp of the universities of Hawaii and California, added two further standards as a result of research. I find them to be a useful reflective tool and offer them here as such, and also perhaps as a lens to observe practice and plan learning.

---

1   Loads more information here: https://manoa.hawaii.edu/coe/crede/.
2   See https://manoa.hawaii.edu/coe/credenational/.

The CREDE standards are as follows:

1 **Joint productive activity:** the teacher and children collaborating on a joint product. A product can be tangible or intangible; it can be the imagined object found in the abandoned factory, or the employment of process drama to understand a different perspective, like the dragon in the cave.[3]

2 **Language and literacy development:** developing competence in a full range of communication types across school. Understanding that there's one way to address a visiting king, and another to address your friend.

3 **Contextualisation:** connecting new knowledge and experiences to prior knowledge and experiences from home, school and community settings. This is that keen act of creativity we hope to imbue in our students – the connecting together of the seemingly unconnected; the things we're learning in science suddenly becoming relevant in PE; the stuff we're learning in history suddenly needing that learning we've done in maths. It's the dissolving of silos.

4 **Complex thinking:** challenging children towards deeper cognitive models of information processing. This is everything I've shared with you in this book. It's the protection of learning, the holding back of nettles and offering children the stepping stones across the rough river of complexity.

5 **Instructional conversation:** teaching through collaborative dialogue and questioning; aka talking to children about what they're doing, employing kind relentless challenge and working with them in the middle ground.

6 **Associative modelling:** encouraging children to make connections between behaviours, ideas, concepts or procedures as part of more complex systems. This is the essence of employing stories, narratives, case studies and design briefs to our hooks, our planning and our pedagogy.

7 **Child-directed activity:** encouraging independent decision-making and self-regulated learning. This is the children deciding to go and see the dragon in the cave; it's the realisation that the old building needs to be saved; it's finding the right words when realising one has to negotiate. (Char, 2017)

What I really like about these standards is that they do offer us those labels for practice that we can often seek. At the beginning of the book, I talked about *phronesis* – that

---

3   Process drama is the opposite of theatre performance.

development of practical wisdom we have as teachers. I think these standards articulate elements of how *phronesis* might reveal itself in the classroom context alongside our ability to recognise them. Later I'll talk about 'imagineering acetate', where we can imagine placing transparent acetate over our formal planning so that we can sketch out possibilities in bringing that planning to life in the classroom. Here, I think these standards are like an acetate we can put over our lived classroom practice; the ups, downs, challenges, successes and so on. When I read through the list and reflect on my own classroom-based session, I find them a useful lens: I can see that my stance is one that supports joint productive activity, my pedagogy supports complex thinking and my use of a story supports contextualisation. And I think this is a creative act. It's a line in the sand. I want it to be part of my teacher self.

Our use of People + Place + Problem is a versatile story-making device. Again, it sits well with Tharp's standards and creatively arouses the professional imagination. Here's an example:

We're in an early years classroom. I've learned to love early years and recognise the skill and dedication of the teachers that work there. I'm no expert in the setting but I find myself there in order to understand if these approaches I share around building botheredness work with our youngest school-age kids.

Does it work?

And, of course, the answer to that query is a resounding *yes*.

I've been told by Lauren, the lead teacher, that the children have visited one of those city farms that very morning.[4] I ask Lauren what else the children have been learning about and she tells me that they've been talking a lot about the senses. Things are coming together in my head. I should say that this was all last minute and I hadn't expected to be working with the class when I arrived that day. Early years teachers are adamant though – they don't want to miss out. They're like the sirens from some ancient Greek story and I'm an enthusiastic sailor. I have little experience, just enthusiasm. And I'm confident in the People + Place + Problem approach, so feel I could do something with 'Senses'.[5] 'How hard can it be?' a stupid voice asks in my head.

....

4   You know the sort: a depressed alpaca and his mate, a pygmy goat.
5   As I said earlier, we should never wing it. That is the path of the mad. I feel this is different as I'm falling back on a repertoire of professional imagination. I'm definitely going to do something about the farmer on the farm they've visited. I'm going to fictionalise their lived experience.

So I stand there, in a primary school in Leeds city centre, wearing a Matalan suit and a fixed grin. All of the urchins ignore me. I mean, there's shiny stuff to look at, sand to sift and helicopters to fly. I'm just some bloke. Just one child eyeballs me. He *really* eyeballs me. I eyeball him back, grin still fixed. I feel like I'm standing on very thin ice.

'Who are you?' asks the shaven-headed little boy.

'Mr Roberts,' I reply. 'And who are you?'

'Billy Corker.'

'Have you been to a farm today?'

Billy Corker nods.

'What did you *see* on the farm?' I ask whilst pointing at my eyeball.

Other kids are gathering now that Matalan Man has starting speaking. They drift over like extras from *The Walking Dead* and ask me to repeat the question.[6]

'What did you see on the farm?'

Billy Corker, spokesperson for the hoard, answers with a strange Northern gravitas: 'It was a right mess.'[7]

This catches me by surprise as I expected him to say, you know, a cow or something. As I catch myself, Billy Corker continues:

'The gate didn't shut properly. The road was bumpy.'

Other kids now join in. It's funny.

'There was a crack in the window.'

'The Fruit Shoots were warm.'[8]

Basically, these early years children offer me a snagging list for the farmer.

6   I like *The Walking Dead* but haven't made it to the end yet. Still. I liked the bit in Season 1 where Andrew Lincoln as Rick Grimes rides into a city on a horse. Like he's a cowboy. Oh, and the bit where he's trapped in a tank. I also really like the actor Jeffrey Dean Morgan who plays the villain, Negan. He was in a cool sleeper of a movie you may have missed called *Texas Killing Fields*. It's mint. Oh, and whilst we're on it, Blighty's own David Morrissey excels in *The Walking Dead* as the treacherous governor.

7   Just prior to this response, little Billy Corker sucked in air between his teeth like a mechanic looking at mi dad's Allegro.

8   Apparently, the refrigerator was faulty. ☺

'Okay,' I say to the class who, by now, have meandered over and are giving me some attention, for which I'm very grateful. 'What did you hear on the farm?' I ask, cupping my ear.

Billy Corker's eyes dart around. He's my lynchpin. I know he'll respond with something. Bizarrely, he begins to hum. Well, I say hum, it's a kind of buzz. The other kids follow suit. I feel like I'm an innocent in one of those horror films where folk like me get lured into some awful trap. I see Nicholas Cage in that *Wicker Man* remake and think of the bees. THE BEES![9] The children are now staring at me, humming and buzzing. In my head, at lightening speed, I'm trying to figure out what it means.

'Did the farmer keep bees?' I ask.

The noise subsides immediately, and Billy Corker shakes his head. 'No,' he says. 'It's the motorway.'

I feel the ice cracking again under my feet. I try my level best to keep cool and throw out another senses-related question: 'What did you smell on the farm?'

I must have forgotten where I was, but in that instant I saw an observing teacher's eyes widen. She knew what was coming.

And it rhymes with 'kite'.[10]

As I pull my eyebrows from the ceiling, I decide to move full throttle into the filling of my lesson sandwich. These urchins have put me through enough. I ask them a simple question: 'Can we help the farmer with his farm?'

And, as expected, the children respond with one of those elongated *YEEEEEEEEEE EEEEEEEEEEEEEEEEEEEEEEEEEEEEEEEEEEEEEEEEEEEEEEEEEEEEEEEEEEE EEEEEEEEEEEEEEEEEEEEEEEEEEEEEEEEEEEEEEEEEEEEEEEEEEEEEEEEES SSSSSSSSSSSSSSSSSSSSSSSSSSSSSSSSSSSSSS*es that such classes and children do. Now I sit and I tell them that I'll speak as the farmer.

---

9   See page 45.
10 Shite.

Can you help me?[11]

The farm is not how I would like it to be. The road is bumpy, the gate is broken and there is a crack in the window.

We've all agreed to help the farmer. We're invested in him and his farm. The farm of the children's real-world experience has now morphed into this imagined place which we're going to map out using symbols, pictures and words, on sticky notes. We also compile some questions:

- What jobs need to be done?

- What things do we need to help us get the jobs done?

- Who else might be able to help us?

- Who else might we need to talk to?

- How will we know we've done a great job?

I use a sticky note to draw a scarecrow. I show it to Lauren, the teacher.

11 And a few children answer 'yes' straightaway. ☺

She tells me it's terrifying and that I should probably try again. I do a double take at my sticky note and realise I've drawn someone with a hat on getting crucified.[12] I follow her advice and create this masterpiece:

I'm not sure why he's wearing a hard hat, but there you go.

We look at all our drawings, symbols and words dotted on sticky notes around the classroom. When the children see my hard-hatted scarecrow, they become very excited. Billy Corker asks if we can speak to the scarecrow, and I answer yes.

This blows their minds. They cannot believe it. Billy Corker asks why the farm is such a mess and I, talking as the scarecrow, respond:

> People used to come here from all over the world. They don't now because the farm is messy, and things are broken. Can you help to make it great again?

***

12 *Children of the Corn*, anyone?

And the session goes on to its natural conclusion where we pose for a picture for the local newspaper in our heads. And then it's playtime and coats are retrieved and supervisors supervise the children outside. I feel like James Brown, the soul singer, at the end of a gig, full of funk and needing to be escorted backstage.[13] We end up in the staffroom where I slump into a chair whilst attempting to hold together some professional dignity. That was a hard session. Lauren leans in, full of the joys, and in her best teacher voice proclaims:

'You've done REALLY WELL!'

To be fair, it's what I need to hear. Now, we debrief my session, which everyone is complimentary about. I talk through the concept of:

- **People:** The farmer.
- **Place:** The farm.
- **Problem:** It's a mess.

We consider the approach in terms of investment and motivation; of botheredness. Conversation then drifts, as it inevitably always does, to the little characters in the class.

'What about Billy Corker?' I ask, smiling. 'What a brilliant little human. If it wasn't for him, we'd have never got going.' I venture to the listening teachers that Billy Corker properly saved my skin.

'It's really unlike him,' says Lauren, to my surprise. 'We thought we might have to intervene straightaway. Billy doesn't kick off, he just displays anxiety. He might get under a table or get behind a curtain when something different or unplanned is happening. He doesn't like strangers. Particularly men.'

I'm aghast. Billy Corker? Are we talking about the same kid?

So, what happened to Billy Corker? Why did he not get under a table, hide behind a curtain or require some adult intervention? Well, the simple answer is I don't know. In fact, none of us could say. We just pondered and created theories and speculations. Nothing solid because that is what happens in real-life classroom situations: the unpredictable. Billy Corker was somehow not just held but lifted by a creative

---

13 James Brown nailing a performance: https://www.youtube.com/watch?v=vruy2GRUsV8.

curriculum that resonated with him, meant something to him and helped him be bothered.

My teacher decisions – building on the children's experience on the farm, using teacher-in-role, sticky notes, joint productive activities – were the small creative acts we can all do in our classrooms, drawing on varied and pedagogically sound toolkits and approaches.

I was just trying to teach, but Billy Corker – well, he was living it, safe inside the protective shell of a story.

What a legend.

CHAPTER 10

ACETATE IMAGINEERING: BOTHEREDNESS PLANNING

This has been a book about stories, stance and pedagogy, all wrapped up in the word *botheredness* – and it isn't over yet. A bit like the multiple endings of Peter Jackson's *Lord of the Rings*,[2] this is going to go on a bit – with useful stuff, I hope. Stuff that will help you put what I've offered so far into action. You'll have noticed, I'm sure, that there's an undercurrent of earned teacher instinct in what I've shared so far. Anecdotes unfurl like a pack of magician's playing cards. Theory and research are dashed out like the writer actually knows what they're on about. Buzzwords and the writer's 'truth' are laid bare, and it's the way it should be – always has been, always will be.[3] This is an educational book after all.

If you've got this far, much of it'll have landed well with you, I hope, but I know what you're waiting for. I know what you need. You want the chuffin' planning. You want to see what I've written, written up.

So, at heart, I'm a secondary teacher. That is where my professional learning journey began. The thing is this: my secondary practice, my secondary *phronesis*, has blended into my practice in special and primary settings as my career has progressed. This is the true definition of *phronesis*, of botheredness. A learning constant. If you're a

---

1   *Raiders of the Lost Ark*, dir. Steven Spielberg [film] (Paramount Pictures, 1981).
2   Which I love, by the way.
3   For 'truth' read 'opinion'.

secondary teacher – particularly one working with our 11–14-year-olds – take a look at what follows and ask yourself this:

How might I engineer and imagineer this stuff up?[4]

It's just that pesky professional imagination that needs to kick in, is it not? Even though I've likened 'curriculum written down' to Jack Nicholson at the end of *The Shining*, you want to see what I'm banging on about written down. Like crack addicts, teachers need the planning hit. We can get the theory and the research, can't we? We can understand and appreciate fresh approaches? We can even appreciate someone else doing it,[5] whilst being filmed by a documentary crew![6] Can't we?

But what does the planning look like? Well, the short answer is that up until recently I simply was not sure. We have the story wheels outlined in Chapter 4, but they act more like professional provocations that get the elements of a story together in the teacher's mind rather than the whole plan of intended teaching and learning.[7] They shake the professional imagination a little.

What follows are some examples of planning that are intended to inspire and provoke rather than to be simply copied.[8] These plans were commissioned by a large trust of schools during the first COVID-19 lockdown of 2020. Wellspring Academy Trust asked me to support them in writing creative plans that would inspire the staff as well

---

4   We might not need to teach 'Victorians' in Key Stage 3, but we might want to create a scheme of work around 'Childhood'. Engineered and imagineered up, the plan here will help. ☺
5   You can see me talking about building botheredness in a classroom – also featuring a debrief with professional colleagues – at Roberts (2021). This video was produced by Lucy Thwaite.
6   My education hero is the Real David Cameron (@Realdcameron on Twatter). He invited me up to Aberdeen and we did some work with teachers around using story as a way of hooking children into their learning. The film about the work can be found at Roberts (2020). It's mint and was made by the ace and skilled Rachel Thibbotumunuwe, learning manager, Aberdeen City Council.
7   This design brief, or context, if you're struggling with the very word *story*.
8   You don't want to be the teacher equivalent of Gus Van Sant when he made that shot-for-shot remake of *Psycho* in 1998. Chuffin' dreadful and devoid of imagination unless you want to see the likeable Vince Vaughn pulling his pudding, as my mate Dave of Doncaster would say.

as the children.[9] It was in the writing of these plans that I articulated the concept of the _should_, _could_ and _must_ curriculum outlined in Chapter 5. These narrative plans sit solidly in the _could_ curriculum with knowledge organisers existing alongside. So, as you read through these, bear in mind that they're not the whole teaching and learning story – rather, they're botheredness-builders and should be seen as such. Each plan is set out within a template that includes:

- A narrative hook
- A 'Let's say'
- Stages
- Narrative
- Purpose

A narrative hook

This is the application of the _People_ + _Place_ + _Problem_ story wheel.[10] It's the genesis of the narrative.

A 'Let's say'

This is the kick-off of the narrative with the class, as outlined in Chapter 4.[11] It's the magic bit; the bit that gets the kids interested, engaged and, hopefully, invested.

---

9   This would be the education heroes Katie Pierce, Katherine Heaton, Kev 'Spreadsheet' Scott, Natalie Wathen and gaffer Sam Bailey. We Zoomed through the COVID-19 pandemic and worked towards creating a robust, experience-led, narrative-focused curriculum that would completely hcok the kids of West and South Yorkshire into their learning. The **should** curriculum was already sorted by the time I was invited on board, in the form of knowledge organisers. The _narrative_ curriculum (as we call it) offered the _could_ aspect, whilst outcomes from both helped tick the boxes of the **must**.

10 Three blokes on a boat hunting a killer shark: People + Place + Problem.

11 Let's say we're people living on a small island on the American coast. We're a town preparing for our Fourth July festivities. Unfortunately, the police chief wants to close the beaches at the height of our holiday season because of a shark attack. How can we get him to change his mind?

Stages

Rather than apportioning blocks of time to the unfolding story, the planning presents it in stages.[12] Think of them as chapters of a story. Some chapters are long. Some are short. Stage 1 is often a scene setter; for example, getting the class to think about life in Victorian Wales after being introduced to the broader aspects of Victorian Britain through the taught *should* curriculum. Stage 2 deepens the imaginative narrative.

Narrative

This is the story itself.[13] This is you as the teacher getting your children invested in a curriculum area by allowing the development of an imaginative context that can either be rooted in the fantastical realm (rescuing dragons, for example) or rooted in the real world (preserving beautiful places, for example). It can cross them all. The story – the narrative – sits in the centre of it all.[14] Narratives can exist in the worlds we believe will support us and the children achieving our learning goals. It's the narrative – the mobilising of People + Place + Problem – that gets children hooked in, that gets them bothered.[15]

---

12 There's a nice breakdown of *Jaws* at Miyamoto (2020). This breakdown relates to the stages of the classic *The Hero's Journey* by Joseph Campbell. My breakdown (as it were) can simply be thought of as chapters of a story.

13 The absolute articulation of teacher as storyteller. This is the key aspect of the approach: a story that unfolds, that engages and encourages investment from the pupils by offering them a context to buy into.

14 The idea of different worlds operating inside the classroom comes from the work of Dorothy Heathcote and Tim Taylor. Tim's book *A Beginner's Guide to Mantle of the Expert: A Transformative Approach to Education* (2016) is a masterwork.

15 An example of an online world-creation project can be found here: https://www.storymakersco.com/reimagining-home-project. Produced during the dark days of COVID-19, this resource supported families who suddenly found themselves home schooling. It was created by Dr Lisa Stephenson (@lisa_stephenso on the Twotters) and colleagues at Leeds Beckett University.

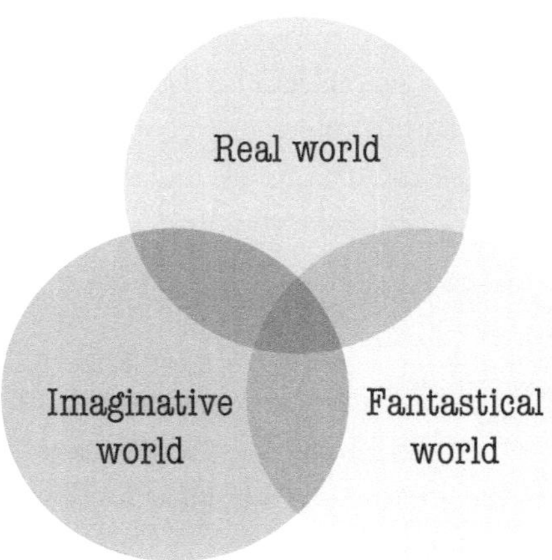

Three worlds

Purpose

And this might be the most important column. This is the one you throw at the colleague who is being a bit of a drain,[16] and saying things like, 'Why do we need to do this? What's the point? What's it achieving?'[17] This column in the planning nails down the reasons for doing what you're doing. It's flying the flag for the professional imagination, possibility and perspective, echoing the second story wheel from Chapter 4. When that looks-12-years-old-senior-leadership-team-clipboard-carrying observer asks you why you've spent 20 minutes talking about the dangers of coach travel in seventeenth-century England, you can explain to them that you're laying the foundations for a deeper understanding of the 'Crime and Punishment' historical study you're doing with the focus on highway robbery. This is instead of colouring in a template drawing of a highwayman.

---

16 The opposite of you, a radiator.

17 This seems to happen less now in my work, but I do remember being in a school where a bloke who wore a brown leather jacket like Dennis Waterman circa 1981 *every time* I saw him, and who had sat through a full INSET day *and* observed me working with his children *all fucking day*, said to me at the end of it all, 'Yeah, but why do this?' Well Dennis, *this* is the *why*. This is the *purpose*. You're etched on my memory. You, your leather jacket and your Twankle subscription.

These then are our planning elements, _but_ they're not a rule you have to follow. They're here to help, to inspire and to offer exemplars of what _could_ happen in your class. The sharp-eyed amongst you'll see that the following are rooted in primary humanities, but these examples can be easily engineered up for secondary, down and across. I want the following to inspire your thinking and shake your professional imagination.

For other examples of narrative planning, please check the _Uncharted Territories_ book (Roberts and Kidd, 2018) and also Debra Kidd's (2020) _A Curriculum of Hope_, the latter being chock-full of exemplars and in no small way the inspiration for the following plans.

I'll say it one more time: these are not a replacement for formal schemes of work or lesson planning.

Let's say you have the scheme of work printed out in front of you. You then get some transparent acetate and decent felt tips. As you look through to the scheme of work, you use the acetate to capture your ideas, over-writing and deepening the _should_ curriculum by imagineering your _could_ curriculum.

Topic: The Romans

Age group: Upper primary/special

The class are presented with the following:

Let's say we are soldiers in the Roman army. We are not citizens of Rome so we cannot be legionaries. We are paid much less than the Roman legionaries and are simply soldiers drawn from many other parts of the vast Roman Empire. We are part of the invasion force mounting an attack on a cold, unforgiving island near Gaul (France). They call it 'Britain'. They have an army waiting for us and the landing might be difficult. We are to establish a camp on a beach.

A narrative hook

- **People:** Roman soldiers newly arrived in Britain during their first invasion in 55 BC.

- **Place:** A beach in what we now call Kent.

- **Problem:** We might not be welcome here.

Stage	Narrative		Purpose
1 A Roman invasion	*We are the Roman soldiers arriving on a beach. The invasion of Britain has not been as easy as we thought it might be.*		Teacher-in-role. Reflecting upon and considering innovation. Children protected into the past.
	1	If we're lowly soldiers in the Roman army, where might we be from?	Timelines and research. Using images to see what a Roman soldier might carry in his kit.
	2	If we lived in 55 BC, what wouldn't we have that we take for granted today?	Children building on knowledge already established around the Roman Empire and Julius Caesar.
	3	How did we travel from mainland Europe to the south coast of Britain?	Scene painting the beach using teacher-in-role: the cliffs, the shelter and the potential for a safe camp.
	We hear the description of where we've landed on the beach (teacher-in-role).		Links to geography. 'Occupational mime' (see Afterword) demonstrating jobs that need doing.

Stage		Narrative	Purpose
	4	In groups we survey the scene described to us. We need to organise our camp. If we're going to arrange ourselves efficiently, what do we need to do first? What things might we have with us that will help us organise the camp?	List making. Organisation. Still images of the camp and 'thought tracking' (see Afterword). Descriptive writing around the life of a lowly Roman soldier.
	5	As soldiers, what are our responsibilities to each other? To our leaders?	
	6	What rules do we have in our camp?	
	7	We're going to be here a while. The Celts (Britons) have not noticed the arrival of our particular troop. What jobs do we need to do?	

Stage	Narrative		Purpose
2 A message and a woman	*On the third morning we awake to find a message written in the still-wet sand. It reads: 'Go home. You are not welcome.' There is just a single pair of footprints around the message.*		Healthy learning tension. Children in role discussing reactions to the message. Speaking, listening and articulacy.
	8	What is the meaning of the message?	Researching who lived in Britain in 55 BC. Thought tracking.
	9	Who might have left it for us?	Children making the character of the woman on the cliff. A female warrior. They can name her authentically. We know she has a spear. What else might a Celtic warrior have with them?
	10	Should we be worried?	
	11	What do we do now? And how do we stay safe?	
	12	Children comment on how they feel *internally* about the message.	
	High on a cliff, looking down on us, stands a woman. She's in silhouette. We can see she hold a spear. She says nothing.		'Role on the wall' opportunities (see Afterword). Children thinking about what they may say to the woman. They're imagining the situation and are in role as the Roman soldiers. Reflection.
	13	Who is she?	
	14	Did she leave the message?	
	15	How did she walk through our camp to the wet sand without us seeing her?	
	16	Should we speak to her?	Measured responses: some children may opt to attack the warrior. This needs to be discouraged in favour of diplomacy and negotiation.
	17	If we're going to speak with her, what should we say?	
	We invite her to speak with us. She nods and makes her way down the cliff towards us.		

Stage	Narrative		Purpose
3 The agreement	18	Recap on what we've done so far – the first Roman invasion of Britain, the beach camp, the Celtic warrior. Recall and summary.	Organisation of ideas. Hot seating with appropriate questions. Listening. Teacher-in-role. Decision-making and sitting with dilemma. Dealing with difficulty. Discussion.
	19	The Roman soldiers ask prepared questions of the Celtic warrior.	
		The warrior then asks us this question: *How long are you staying here? As you saw in my message in the sand, we are not keen for you to stay. You need to decide and decide carefully. My warriors are all around us. You are few. We will crush you if you do not leave. If you join us, we will make sure you are safe.*	

Stage	Narrative		Purpose
4 Deserters or freed slaves?	20	Recap on the offer made by the warrior – to join the Britons.	Recall. Researching origins of Roman conscripts – many will never have been to Italy and would be of different ethnicities. Subtle links to forced migration. Arguments. Conscience alley (see Afterword). Finding compromise. Right and wrong – grey areas – dealing with difficult decisions. Teacher-in-role. Whole class improvisation around formality of the surrender.
	21	Why might a group of Roman soldiers desert their emperor?	
	22	We are not citizens of Rome. How did we each end up in the Roman army?	
	23	What punishments might we face for desertion? What if some hope to desert and others do not?	
	24	How can we change each other's minds? (The teacher can take this in any direction. We'll assume here in the plan that the children decide to desert the camp after they see the Roman ships subjected to heavy attack further along the coast.)	
	25	How do we surrender to the warrior and her people?	

Stage	Narrative		Purpose
5 The Celtic tribe	*The Roman invasion is thwarted. The deserted soldiers are stranded, having surrendered to the Celtic warriors.*		Demonstrating interaction with sources. Consolidating learning through the writing of a journal. Writing in role. Links to literacy. Demonstrating abstract historical skill using evidence and imagination. Role play. Speaking and listening. Presenting.
	26	Research Celtic tribes during these times, focusing on *how* they lived.	
	27	Write a journal/diary entry for one of the Roman soldiers on his experiences in the camp. What do they see? How do they interact with the enemy? Perhaps they hop to escape!	
	28	The Roman soldiers, allowed to live freely amongst the Celts because of their surrender, plot to escape to a new life elsewhere. Why would they do this? Where might home be for them? What is *home*?	
	29	Children do a sequence of still images recounting their escape to real freedom. This could be represented as a comic book.	

Resources

BBC Bitesize – https://www.bbc.co.uk/bitesize/topics/zwmpfg8/articles/zqbnfg8.

Ancient Origins – https://www.ancient-origins.net/history-famous-people/eight-things-you-should-know-celts-0011579.

Romans in Britain – https://www.romanobritain.org/4-celt/clb_tribe_dumnonni.php.

Topic: The Vikings

Age group: Primary/special

The class are presented with the following:

Let's say we live in the time of the Vikings. We have travelled up-river to the shores of a distant and fertile land. We have decided to settle here in the shadow of some great mountains. From where we stand, the mountain resembles a dragon's claw. A cave, visible to the eye, we have named Dragon's Cave. Now we settle on these flatlands, we have to devote our time to what we do best: farming.

A narrative hook

- **People:** A Viking community.

- **Place:** A settlement by a river in the shadow of some mountains.

- **Problem:** Our water supplies have run dry.

Stage	Narrative		Purpose
1 The settlement	*Let's say we are Vikings.*		Timelines and research.
	1	If we live in the time of the Vikings, when are we?	Reflecting upon and considering innovation. Children are protected into the past.
	2	If we lived then, what wouldn't we have that we have today?	Scene painting the settlement using teacher-in-role: the mountains, rivers and trees.
	3	What technology can you imagine the Vikings would have?	Perhaps using mapping strategy (see Afterword). Links to geography.
	We hear the description of where we've landed in the shadow of some mountains (teacher-in-role).		Building on knowledge already established around Vikings and how they travelled.
	4	Where might we be? Where did the Vikings travel to?	Creating lists of responsibilities through research and discussion.
	5	When we decide to make this place our home and a place to farm, what factors do you think we might have considered?	Occupational mime demonstrating jobs that need doing. Organisation.
	6	When establishing a settlement, what do you think we need to do first?	Still image and thought tracking. Naming places using the models of Dragon Claw Mountain and Dragon's Cave. Teacher seeds in the idea of Viking sagas.
	7	If we're Vikings, what jobs do we need to do in order to establish our settlement?	
	8	What shall we call our new home?	

Stage	Narrative		Purpose
2 The Viking community	9	We are the Vikings. What have we named our settlement?	Teacher ensuring that when children name places there's a sense of authenticity about it. Opportunity to look at prior learning.
	10	What is the hierarchy of the village?	Roles and status in Viking society.
	11	What rules might we have in order to live well?	Class all in role.
	12	What do we farm?	Still image and thought tracking.
	13	Present to the rest of the class your own element of settlement life as if you're contributing to a documentary about Viking village life	Presenting ideas. Comparing sources. Teacher, in role as the chief, delivers the message.
	14	How does this view of Vikings as hard-working farmers compare with other depictions?	Children play back what they've heard and process it. Children speculating/ theorising about what has happened to the water.
	The chief calls a village meeting: *We have some worrying news. All the rivers and streams that provide for our village have run dry. The shields from our long ships have washed away and the vessels themselves lie forlorn on the dry riverbed. The only clue we have is the smoke that emerges from Dragon's Cave, two day's hike away. What should we do? What is going on?*		Why do we need the water?

Stage	Narrative		Purpose
3 The hike	*Let's say we need to hike into the mountains to investigate the smoke coming from the cave. Dragon's Cave.*		Organisation and responsibility. List making. Problem-solving. Resilience. Class in role. Thought tracking. Children writing accounts. Description, metaphor, simile. Healthy learning tension.
	15	If we're going to travel up to the cave, how long might it take to get there? If we have to stay outside overnight, what should we take with us? How do we ensure that we'll be safe?	
	16	We'll need shields and axes.	
	17	Who goes? Who stays behind?	
	18	What roles do we take when setting up a mountainside camp?	
	19	As we approach the cave, what are we thinking about? How do we approach the cave?	
	A deep rumbling sound comes from the cave. We react to it. The bravest of us approach the mouth of the smoke-filled cave. And there we spy warm red eyes watching us closely.		

Stage	Narrative		Purpose
4 Dragon protectors	We hear the dragon speak: *I thought you would come. Fear me not. I have enough to think about. Behind me are my children, thirty-three of them. Newborn dragons, with rumbling tummies and burning throats. The only way to soothe them is the cool water of this mountain. You may slay me, but help my children.*		Teacher-in-role. Children responding to what they hear. Discussion. Compassion. Processing new information. Compiling good questions to ask when hot seating the dragon, avoiding trivia. We could ask:
	20	How do we react to the dragon?	1 How can we help you?
	21	Compile questions to ask her/ hot seat.	2 We need the water as well. Can we compromise?
	22	The class discuss options – leave the dragon alone/ help her.	3 How old are you? Investigating and research mission statements.
	23	Teacher steers the class towards helping the dragon with the class becoming dragon protectors.	Designing a dragon protector's shield – links to art. Instructional writing.
	24	As dragon protectors, what is our mission statement?	
	25	If we're going to protect the dragons and restore our water sources, what jobs do we need to do?	
	26	How do you look after a baby dragon?	

Stage	Narrative		Purpose
5 A Viking saga	Write your own Viking saga that tells of the new settlement, the successful farming, the mystery of the lost water and the discovery of the dragons in the cave.		An opportunity to demonstrate genuine new learning. Writing in role. Links to literacy. Demonstrating interaction with sources.
	27	Demonstrate your Viking knowledge.	Demonstrating abstract historical skill using evidence and imagination. Presentation skills.
	28	Show off your writing skills – use vivid description where you can. Maybe tell the saga from the point of view of one of the Vikings.	
	29	Illustrate the story.	

Resources

Ranker – https://www.ranker.com/list/viking-history-facts/mike-rothschild.

BBC Teach – https://www.bbc.co.uk/teach/school-radio/english-ks1-english-viking-sagas/zkyqd6f.

VKNG – https://blog.vkngjewelry.com/en/fafnir/.

Topic: Hot and cold places

Age group: Primary/special

The class are presented with the following:

Let's say we are a company who advise people on what they should pack in their suitcases for their trips around the world. These days people want to travel all over the world – hot places, cold places, places that are dry as deserts or as wet as rainforests. They really will go anywhere! Our job is to help them when they are thinking about what they need to take when going away. We are a helpful team and we want people to help our planet whilst exploring it.

A narrative hook

- **People:** We help people pack the right things for their holidays.

- **Place:** The United Kingdom (where in summer we should pack for the autumn)

- **Problem:** We sometimes get mixed up ourselves!

Stage	Narrative		Purpose
1 The Hot Cold Wet Dry Travel Company	1	Our company is called the Hot Cold Wet Dry Travel Company. We help people with their holidays. How can we *look* helpful? How can we *sound* helpful? Do we have a motto/mission statement/logo?	Children investing in joint productive purpose. Social and emotional literacy. Creating a visual anchor for imaginative talk, research and study. Links to visual and written literacy. Gathering communal knowledge. Thinking about questions and information gathering – articulacy and oracy. Conversations around the comparisons between UK and other countries in the world. Introduction of keywords; for example, climate, weather, equator. Troubleshooting ideas and following instructions. Still images and thought tracking.
	2	If we're a company that helps people prepare for their holidays – particularly in terms of what to pack – what do we need to be good at? What do we need to know?	
	3	If we're to advise people on what to pack for their holidays, what information do we need from them?	
	4	What don't we need to pack if we're going to a hot place? What don't we need to pack if we're going to a cold place?	

Stage	Narrative		Purpose
2 The hot holiday	An email has arrived. It's from a group who wishes to travel the world. Can we help? The email is presented to the class: *'We are a group of six who would like to travel to four different places in the world. We are very interested in the weather and climate of different countries. We would like to go to a hot place, a cold place, a dry place and a wet place. Is this something you can help with? We need to know what to pack! Thank you so much.'*		Taking ownership of the context using drama role. Information presented to class via teacher-in-role or by a simple slide. Reactions to the email. Organising a response. Research skills – pupil autonomy. Opportunities for discussion – listening skills, oracy and articulacy. Responding in role – links to literacy and writing.
	5	Can we help? If we're going to help, what do we need to think about? What places spring to mind straightaway that we could recommend? What do we need to find out? Shall we reply to the email saying we can help?	Processing information and writing in role. Building geography skills; for example, map reading. Creating lists of hot countries. Making links and owning new knowledge.
	6	Where are the hot countries in the world? How are they linked to the Equator?	Links to computing skills; for example, a virtual suitcase for each destination in the narrative.
	7	Can hot countries also be wet (for example, the Amazon Rainforest)?	Desirable difficulty. Geography focus on different places.

8	If the six holidaymakers are going to a rainforest, what should we advise they take with them? Why?
9	Can somewhere be hot *and* cold (for example, New York)?

Stage	Narrative		Purpose
3 The cold holiday	*The trip to the rainforest has been organised. What place can we recommend as cold?*		Building on geography skills. Listening, oracy and articulation. Working effectively in a group and responding to a difficulty – there's an understanding about hot, fluctuating hot and cold, but now just *cold*. Research opportunities around Greenland. Links to computing skills; for example, a virtual suitcase for each destination in the narrative.
	10	Why are some places hot and some cold? What is it like where you are? Is it ever hot? Can it also be covered in snow? What weather can you remember where you live?	
	11	A really cold place is Greenland. Would this be a good destination for the holidaymakers? Is it 'green'? Where is it?	
	12	When going to Greenland, what should we recommend they take with them? What don't they need?	
	We have organised two destinations. Where else should we send the six holidaymakers?		

Stage	Narrative		Purpose
4 Postcards	*The trip to the Brazilian rainforest has been organised. The trip to Greenland has been sorted. What places can we recommend as hot and dry? Or cold and warm?*		Reflecting on work done. Using keywords. Researching answers to challenge. Group work skills.
	13	Where in the world is hot and dry? What place could the holidaymakers go to that has a desert but also tourist attractions? a Focus on Egypt, its climate and the fact that it lies in the Sahara Desert. b Focus on New York and how it can be very cold and very warm, depending on the season. Help advise the holidaymakers on what they should pack for their globetrotting trip! Share these ideas as an online presentation, creating a script of the information you want to get across to the holidaymakers first. Write postcards from the holidaymakers telling us about the weather and climate of the places they visit.	Processing information whilst responding to a task. Global learning. Reinforcement of understanding of climate and weather. Collating ideas and organising a presentation. Links to literacy, oracy and writing – formal and informal language. Understanding and development of knowledge around geography of the world and where the UK sits in relation to other countries.

Resources

BBC Teach – https://www.bbc.co.uk/teach/class-clips-video/geography-ks1--ks2-climate/zjdthbk.

Climates to Travel – https://www.climatestotravel.com/climate/england.

Weather Atlas – https://www.weather-atlas.com/en/united-kingdom-climate.

PBS – https://www.pbs.org/wnet/nature/blog/alps-facts/.

Britannica – https://www.britannica.com/place/Alps/Climate.

Oddizzi – https://www.oddizzi.com/teachers/explore-the-world/country-close-up/egypt/climate-3/.

Topic: The Plague

Age group: Primary/special/secondary

The class are presented with the following:

Let's say we are villagers in a place called Eyam. It's a small village in Derbyshire. The year is 1665 and all is not well in our country, England. The place has been ravaged by a deadly plague coming from the capital city, London. The Great Plague has taken many lives and appears incurable. There are many theories as to how it's spread. It seems very contagious. We must make sure that our small village is safe and remains plague-free. This is something that we can do. We can hopefully remain untouched by this cursed plague and carry on with our quiet lives.

A narrative hook

People: Villagers in the North of England in 1665.

Place: Eyam, Derbyshire.

Problem: The plague has arrived in our village.

Stage		Narrative	Purpose
1 The village of Eyam	1	If we live in 1665, what don't we have that we might take for granted today?	Opportunity to reflect back to the study of the Great Fire of London in Key Stage 1.
	2	What might life be like in a small village compared to a big city at this time?	Protection into considering the past. Application of knowledge and prior learning.
	3	If we're working in a small village, what jobs might we do (for example, farmer, baker, tanner, lead miner)?	Links to geography. Occupational mime. Imaginative application of historical knowledge.
	4	Who are the key figures in our village? (These are the named individuals in the story of Eyam; for example, Reverend William Mompesson, the Hancock Family, Marshall Howe – this resource is useful to teachers: https://www.historic-uk.com/HistoryUK/HistoryofEngland/Why-Is-Eyam-Significant/.	Research skills – Eyam and the plague. Using historical sources. Use of a prop – a bundle of damp cloth – to be passed around the class.
	5	A damp bundle of cloth is passed around the class. It's nondescript. How can we dry the bundle if it's 1665?	

Stage	Narrative		Purpose
2 A plague and a difficult decision	*Young George Viccars is the first victim of the plague, having placed the cloth bundle in front of a fire, awakening the plague-carrying mites dormant within. Over the course of winter 1665 and into the spring of 1666, the plague snipes away lives in the village, spreading from house to house.* The class are established as a village meeting in the church.		Children taking ownership of the context using various drama roles. Emphasising of historical context – rural 1665. Children in role as concerned citizens of Eyam. Understanding formal settings. Listening skills. Oracy and articulacy. Reflective thinking. Suspension of belief. Responding in role – links to literacy and writing. Teacher-in-role. Processing information.
	6	Why might the village be called to a meeting?	
	7	What things are we bothered about? What are our worries? What if we were impatient with the man calling the meeting, Reverend William Mompesson? How do we get a point across without being rude?	
	Teacher uses teacher-in-role to speak as Mompesson: *The plague has gripped our village. I know I am not a popular man and your trust in me is not complete. But I have called upon a man you do trust, your old rector, the Reverend Thomas Stanley. He and I agree that there is only one possible course of action to stop this terrible blight spreading across the North of England*		

Stage	Narrative		Purpose
	8	What plan have the Reverends Mompesson and Stanley decided upon?	
	9	How do we change people's minds? How do we see persuasive language being used in our own lives?	
	Reverend Mompesson speaks: *It is clear that the plague has found a home here. And yet Sheffield, Leeds and Manchester remain plague-free. It is us in this room who can stop the spread. Therefore, we propose a village-wide lockdown. No-one is to enter or leave the village after tomorrow. The decision is yours.*		

Stage	Narrative		Purpose
3 Reactions and decisions	10	If you're a family, should you stay or go?	Opportunities for role play, improvisation and conscience alley.
	11	How can you persuade someone to stay/go?	Oracy and articulation. Balancing an argument.
	12	If you go, what will you take? What will you leave behind?	Writing opportunities.

Stage	Narrative		Purpose
4 A cruel summer	*August 1666 sees the highest number of deaths in the village, all recorded in the Bills of Mortality – an account of who dies when. Although Mompesson is an unpopular man, the village gets behind his plan.*		Information could be shared with the children via teacher-in-role – like a 'this is where we are now' speech.
	13	What is life like for a village in lockdown?	Other information could be included: for example, Elizabeth Hancock burying her husband and six children in a field next to her house as the graveyard has been closed; or Marshall Howe taking the job of sexton, responsible for the burial of corpses.
	14	How do we sustain ourselves? Where might we get support for our families? Where would we get support today?	Parallels with the recent COVID-19 crisis. Opportunity to talk about the role of government and the NHS, the latter non-existent at this time.
	The Earl of Devonshire at Chatsworth, a few miles away, has arranged for delivery of food and drink to us in Eyam. There is also a well where passers-by can leave coins.		Researching treatments of the plague, such as having sores rubbed with vinegar and use of leeches. This could be presented as a note/PowerPoint/recording.
	15	How do we treat our sick in the village?	'Then and now' work using historical sources; for example, an image of the plague doctor compared with an image of a caring nurse.
	16	What is a plague doctor? What do they look like? How does their appearance make us feel? How do they look compared to healthcare professionals today?	Drawing out clear understandings of how the history of medicine is constantly progressing; for example, vaccines and their impact and history.

Stage	Narrative		Purpose
	17	How do people rally together in a time of crisis? When have you been faced with a difficult decision?	Visiting the Eyam Museum website. Writing opportunities around storytelling, empathy pieces; for example, diary entries, letters. Drama opportunities around scriptwriting, enactments, whole-class improvisation.
		The plague leaves Eyam in November 1666. Over 250 people have perished, but in the act of lockdown and self-isolation, a huge death toll in the North of England has been stopped.	
	18	How can we make sure that stories like this are preserved for the future? How do we remember the past? How do people ensure their place in history?	

Resources

BBC News – https://www.bbc.co.uk/news/uk-england-35064071.

Historic UK – https://www.historic-uk.com/HistoryUK/HistoryofEngland/Why-Is-Eyam-Significant/.

The Roses of Eyam (read by Robert Lindsay) – https://www.youtube.com/watch?v=lOym6OYsy5o.

A tour around Eyam plague village, Derbyshire – https://www.youtube.com/watch?v=ls3NF9ORQjM.

Topic: The Second World War

Age group: Primary/special/secondary

The class are presented with the following:

Let's say we live in a prosperous town in the North of England. The year is 1939. The trouble in Europe does not really affect our lives. We have the factory in the middle of town where most of the men work, and we have all the shops we need on our main street – the butcher, the grocer, the haberdashery, the bookshop and many more. This is a great place to live and work. The factory is the beating heart of the town and it's owned by a decent gentleman who looks after his workers.

A narrative hook

- **People:** The people of a prosperous town in the summer and autumn of 1939.
- **Place:** A prosperous Northern industrial town.
- **Problem:** War is coming.

Stage		Narrative	Purpose
1 The prosperous town	1	If we live in 1939, what don't we have?	Teacher-in-role. Timelines and research.
	2	Research life 'between the wars'. What was life like in 1939?	Reflecting upon and considering innovation. Children protected into the past.
	3	What was happening in Europe? What concern was it of ours?	Building on knowledge already established around the First World War. Mapping to build the 'place' of the prosperous town.

Stage	Narrative		Purpose
	4	Have towns changed much since 1939? What might we see then that we might not see now (for example, horse and cart as well as motor vehicles)?	Links to geography. Occupational mime demonstrating life in the town, the jobs that would be done and the role of the factory as the 'beating heart'.
	5	What would a high street look like? What shops might there be in 1939?	Opportunities for writing around a day in the life in the town, the shop, the factory. Using images as a way of looking into the past; for example, using an original photo of a busy pre-war street, the class can focus in on one person and think about what they'd like to know about them. They can create questions they'd like to ask the person, for example: Who are you? What are you doing in town? Have you a family? Where are you? What about the other people in the photograph? Opportunities for in-role writing.
	6	What would young people do at this time? What was school like? How old would you be when you started work?	
	7	Map out the town using the mapping.	

Stage	Narrative		Purpose
2 Rumours of war	*Life in the factory is challenging but the work is good and puts food on the table.*		Researching industry in 1939. What would make a 'prosperous' town.
	8	What might the factory produce?	Possible teacher-in-role: describing the factory and its importance to the life of the town.
	9	Why would it be men that were mainly employed in our factory?	How the factory supports other businesses in the town.
	10	What would the role of women be at this time?	The announcement of war in September 1939.
	War is announced on 1 September 1939.		Reacting to the announcement of war. Speaking, listening and articulacy.
	11	How might the workers in the factory talk about the start of the war? How would they know about the conflict (this is in the days before the internet and 24-hour news)?	Prepared improvisation of factory workers reacting to the news of war. How would we persuade our friends to join up with us? What choices would be available to young men at this time? The army? Navy? Air force?
	12	Who would do the fighting against the enemy? What were their qualifications and skills? Was anyone allowed to go and fight?	Thought tracking. Researching conscription and national registers. Conscience alley.
	13	What is *conscription*?	Opportunities for role on the wall.
	Men would talk to each other and encourage one another to sign up to go and fight.		Language of persuasion; for example, prepared improvisation between a mother and her son.

Stage	Narrative		Purpose
	14	Why would men want to go and fight? Who and what would persuade them to do so?	Analysing argument; for example, pros and cons of signing up to fight. Researching conscientious objection.
	15	Would the factory owner be encouraging his workers to go and fight? How would other people in the town react to all the men of fighting age leaving?	

Stage	Narrative		Purpose
3 The march	*Some shops close. The factory owner looks from his office window and sees his workers marching up the main street as the soldiers they now are.*		Recalling and summarising. Organisation of ideas. Hot seating with appropriate questions for the factory owner. Listening and discussing. Reviewing the map of the town to look at the impact of the war. Decision-making and sitting with dilemma. Dealing with difficulty. Researching how factories adapted to produce munitions for the war effort.
	16	What might the impact on our town be with so many of the working men leaving? What shops might close on our street map?	
	17	As we stand watching them march by, what might we be thinking?	
	18	What is bravery? Who are heroes?	
	19	What can the factory owner do to preserve his factory?	

Stage	Narrative		Purpose
4 A changing town	20	The factory owner needs our advice. What are we to recommend he do to keep the factory open during the war?	Children sharing their Stage 3 research around the changing purposes of factories.
	21	What does the British government need factories to do to support the war effort?	Prepared improvisation outlining to the factory owner the merits of a female workforce. Articulacy and oracy. Arguments.
	22	Who is left behind in our town?	Conscience alley. Finding compromise. Organising and presenting research.
	23	What jobs need to be done now that we're at war (for example, female wardens inspecting gas masks)? It would be good to perhaps have a slideshow of images showing women at work in the munitions factories of the towns and cities, and in the fields as part of the Women's Land Army.	
	24	Research the Women's Voluntary Service and the jobs they did to support the war effort. What other organisations were there for women to be part of (for example, the Auxiliary Territorial Service and the Women's Royal Naval Service)?	

Stage	Narrative		Purpose
5 Stories from home	25	Create a scrapbook of letters for the town's museum. The scrapbook will be made up of letters from the front line of battle and the front line of domestic support (the home front).	Consolidating learning through the writing of letters from soldiers in Europe and those left at home in the town. Writing in role. Links to literacy. Demonstrating interaction with sources; for example, recruitment and propaganda imagery. Demonstrating abstract historical skill using evidence and imagination. Role play. Speaking and listening. Organising and presenting ideas.
	26	What do we need to think about when producing our letters?	
	27	We are writing in role – who are we? What's our story?	
	28	What research do I need to do to make my letter an important historical document (for example, from what place am I writing? War-torn Europe or the factory canteen)?	
	29	To whom am I writing?	
	30	Children create their own authentic historical document that tells the story of the town, the people in it and the impact of the Second World War.	

Resources

My Learning – https://www.mylearning.org/stories/women-at-war-the-role-of-women-during-ww2/resources.

BBC Bitesize – https://www.bbc.co.uk/bitesize/guides/zqf4srd/revision/5.

Topic: Biomes and climates

Age group: Primary/special

The class are presented with a person sitting on a chair, holding a photograph album. They speak to the class:

Let's say I'm the owner of a garden centre that has fallen on hard times. No one visits anymore and I cannot look after the various greenhouses. The place is becoming overgrown, and I've noticed that the glass on a number of the greenhouses has been smashed. It hasn't always been like this. Once, people would flock from all over Yorkshire to get here. From Harrogate, Sheffield; all over. We even had the Queen visit one time. All the photographs are in here. Happy times. But times that are gone. I need help to make this garden centre great again. Is this something you can help with? The greenhouses need repairing. I thought we could turn this place into somewhere where children could visit and learn. How might that work? Can you help?

A narrative hook

- **People:** A team of climate and biome experts.

- **Place:** A garden centre.

- **Problem:** Visits to the garden centre have dropped and help is needed to revive its fortunes.

Stage	Narrative		Purpose
1 The forgotten garden centre	Words on the whiteboard as children enter room. Letters are missing: **G RDE CEN RE**		Teacher-in-role, setting the scene so children get an image of the old character sitting in a shed and bemoaning the state of the garden centre. Teacher-in-role emphasises that the concept of a cutting-edge garden centre with climate zones and biomes is the way forward, building on class knowledge, prior learning and expertise.
	1	Teacher describes an old person sitting on a chair in a run-down shed. This is the owner of the garden centre. They speak to the class and the thrust of the narrative is set.	
	2	The garden centre was once famous, attracting many visitors. Children recreate images of times gone by when the place was popular; for example, preparing for the Queen's visit, families busy admiring the gardens, workers tending to the gardens.	Still image and occupational mime; fostering imaginative application – layering knowledge creatively. Hot seating with *good* questions. Group discussions. Listening. Responding to 'let's say' question.
	3	Why might people have stopped visiting? What questions might we want to ask the owner? How do they see the place becoming great again?	
		Let's say the owner wants to bring the whole world into one place; all the different climates – how could this be done?	

Stage	Narrative		Purpose
2 Mapping innovation	*A brand-new garden centre is to be established that has the concepts of climate and biomes at its heart.*		Recap on previous session reiterating the idea that we're responsible for the planning of a new garden centre. Considering the branding of the new place. Links to literacy and design. Researching mission statements – what is the new venture hoping to achieve? Who is it for? Taking ownership of the context. Occupational mime – children in role. Children 'showing' the jobs that need doing. Troubleshooting ideas and drafting plans. Recycling and upcycling. Thinking beyond a remit – applying imagination. Group presentations.
	4	What should we call the new proposed garden centre?	
	5	What is our mission statement?	
	6	Could we make a marketing logo?	
	7	The new garden centre hopes to attract visitors to see its climate zones and biomes. Create a plan of the garden centre and consider how we can achieve this aim. What do we need to consider?	
	8	Could we use some of the old greenhouses in our new plan? How might we utilise existing pathways?	
	9	What else will attract visitors? Shops? Animals?	
	Plans are presented to the owner who gives feedback.		

Stage	Narrative		Purpose
3 The greenhouses	10	There are a number of greenhouses that will act as biomes. What different climates might we choose to represent within each greenhouse? We need the following: Arctic tundra Desert Deciduous forest Taiga Tropical rainforest Tropical savannah Mountainous	Researching. Responding to hook in groups. Sharing and curation of geographical knowledge within context. Working to timescales. Application of imagination. Using research tools and gathering real-world case studies. Working as a team. Linking to literacy, conservation, codes of conduct, rules. Opportunity to look at how real-world organisations manage visitors. Teacher troubleshooting children's responses – kind relentless challenge.
	11	If we're going to create a biome, what do we need to do first? What are our key considerations? How will our biome be managed and the life inside protected? How do we want visitors to behave in each biome? Is there a guidebook that is required?	
		Ideas for each biome are presented to the owner, who gives feedback.	

Stage	Narrative		Purpose
4 Making the garden centre great again	*When new attractions open, they are generally inundated with visitors, but this can often tail off. We don't want that to happen to our new garden centre.*		Teacher-in-role as a marketing manager addressing the team. Children reacting to what they've heard. Reviewing biome ideas and considering what they need to do in order to make the garden centre sustainable. Reflecting on geographical knowledge – human and physical. Taking responsibility. Empathy with challenge = active compassion. Discussion and consensus. Using real sources; for example, the Countryside Code (UK). Unpicking the term 'planet-friendly lifestyle'. Researching real-world examples of information sharing; for example, posters, banners, displays, social media and websites focusing on conservation, geography and scientific knowledge.
	12	What are the unique selling points of our new garden centre?	
	13	How can we make sure people are interested in what we do?	
	14	Each biome is an attraction to our visitors. What can we do to make a visit to, say, the desert biome interesting and exciting?	
	15	What could visitors perhaps purchase from each biome?	
	16	How can we ensure that a visit to our garden centre will be educational?	
	17	How can visitors be encouraged to live more planet-friendly lifestyles?	
	18	How can information be displayed to visitors?	
	19	Produce an information leaflet linked to your biome.	

Stage	Narrative		Purpose
	20	Create a script for a short advert selling the new garden centre and, in particular, its biomes.	
	21	Prepare a fact sheet that could be given to small children. Try and make it fun and interactive as well as informative.	
	22	Plan an official opening of the new garden centre!	

Resources

The Eden Project – www.edenproject.com.

Blue Planet Biomes – https://www.blueplanetbiomes.org/.

UC Museum of Paleontology

- The tundra – https://ucmp.berkeley.edu/exhibits/biomes/tundra.php.
- The grasslands – https://ucmp.berkeley.edu/exhibits/biomes/grasslands.php.

BioExpedition

- Biomes – https://www.bioexpedition.com/biomes/.
- The grasslands – https://www.bioexpedition.com/grassland-biome/.
- The savanna – https://www.bioexpedition.com/savanna-biome/.

Topic: Rivers and mountains

Age group: Primary/special

The class are presented with a tourist who has arrived in their precious mountain community:

Hello! I represent an organisation that is promoting the natural beauty of our planet. Every 11 December is International Mountain Day and we would like you to join in this year! It will guarantee you lots of tourists coming to the area to climb and it will be great for your local economy. You don't have to do anything except guarantee their safety and offer them a warm welcome! Let me leave you this leaflet.

A narrative hook

- **People:** A mountain community.

- **Place:** The foothills of a grand mountain.

- **Problem:** 11 December is International Mountain Day. How do we ensure that our mountain home is protected?

Stage	Narrative		Purpose
1 The place where we live	1	Map out a horizon of a mountain range. Foreground the image with rivers and trees.	Mapping. Application of knowledge and prior learning. Geographical skills.
	2	What geographical features could we imagine from our maps (for example, treelines, scree, snow caps, valleys, tarns, forests, erosion, glaciation)?	Imaginative application – layering knowledge creatively. Links to literacy. Building a context and taking responsibility.
		Let's say we are people who live very simple lives in the mountains far away.	
	3	What names would we give to the places on our maps? Choose good names that our ancestors might have called these places. What would the forests be called (for example, Dark Forest, Yeti Valley, the Forest of Silence, Dragon Mountain, Rolling Rocky River)?	

Stage	Narrative		Purpose
2 Who we are and how we live	*A simple life is one where we live off the land. We do not want for or have any technology.*		Myths and legends; how the landscape influences the stories we tell.
	4	Describe the simple life we live. Discuss how we might live.	Taking ownership of the context.
	5	Name our community. Make it appropriate. Perhaps link it to a story that we might tell the children of our village about the landscape and its history.	Occupational mime – children in role. Children 'showing' the jobs that need doing. Teacher emphasising the idea of zero technology and the need to live off the land.
	6	If we're the people of this community, what jobs need to be done in order to thrive?	How does the natural world affect our celebrations (for example, harvest)?
	7	What might the rules of our community be? What do we do with people who break them?	Teacher-in-role.
	8	What do we celebrate?	
	9	How did some of our special places get their names (reflecting back to Stage 1)?	
	10	A tourist arrives. They're very enthusiastic, but we're suspicious.	

Stage	Narrative		Purpose
3 International Mountain Day	11	We hear the tourist's invitation to participate in International Mountain Day in December. How do we react? Are we all happy with the thought of a load of climbers and sightseers coming to our community?	Responding to hook. Discussion – pros and cons of International Mountain Day. Researching. Teacher troubleshooting children's responses – kind relentless challenge. Links to literacy – presenting opinion and argument. Real-world research. Impact of humans on the natural landscape. Dealing with difficulty. Links to literacy, conservation.
	12	Community meeting – what do we decide? Class steered towards involvement whilst compiling a list of issues.	
	13	How have other mountain communities been impacted by tourism (for example, Everest)? How is negative impact tackled in these examples?	
	14	Community seek solutions to issues around overcrowding and waste.	
	15	Decision to go ahead.	
	16	Class create leaflet promoting International Mountain Day.	
	We have a problem.		

Resources

The Countryside Code – https://www.gov.uk/government/publications/the-countryside-code.

Visit Norway – https://www.visitnorway.com/plan-your-trip/safety-first/mountain-safety/the-mountain-code/.

NOW SHOWING

BERGMAN
BOGART
HENREID
THEY HAVE A DATE WITH FATE IN
Casablanca
Directed by
MICHAEL CURTIZ
"STOP HITTING
ME WITH THOSE
NEGATIVE WAVES,
MORIARTY!"
STAR WARS
©Hymelr
©hymelroberts
'kes'
Pu'
JAWS
THE 6 66 OMEN
Freddy
The
Elep
ELM ST.

Knowing is a process, not a product.

Jerome Bruner (1966, 72)

Movies make magic. They change things.

bell hooks (1996, 1)

I arrogantly recommend some films you really should watch

I love lists. Especially film lists.[1] I've decided to make 2009 the cut-off date for this list as that's the year I left full-time teaching.[2] That is the only logic at play here and it isn't that logical to be honest. It just seems like a good idea. A lot of the films on this list are from my childhood, teenage years, early adulthood and then my adventure as a grown-up. I find lists cathartic.[3] Why not make your own? It could be a list of movies. Or maybe a list of songs. Or international football teams. Or a list of favourite places you've visited. What list are you bothered about making, that maybe you could pass on to someone else? Remember making mix tapes when you were a kid? Analogue

----

1 I know this is an education book, but I hope you'll tolerate this. I'm really bothered about movies. I think my love of movie lists stems from when I was 12 and got a book token. I bought *The Hamlyn Book of Horror and S.F. Movie Lists* by Roy Pickard from the WHSmith in Middleton. We'd gone there to look at the new multistorey car park.

2 The 2009 cut-off means I can't have the delights of *The Secret Life of Walter Mitty*, *Three Billboards Outside Ebbing, Missouri*, *Skyfall*, *Interstellar* and *Midsommar*, amongst many others.

3 See Roberts (2012) for evidence of this.

playlists that reflect you and your world; that's all I'm about right here. I also find myself in the privileged position where I can do this (unless the editor kicks off).

My favourite movie of all time is Steven Spielberg's *Jaws* and you'll find it on the list. It isn't just because it's a great movie – it's the tapestry of emotion it weaves when I reflect on its impact on my own life. It has its place in my consciousness *and* uncon-sciousness. It's only a film, I know, don't worry. When I was just 5, my dad took my brother and I to the Mayfair cinema to see *Jaws*. It's spring, 1976. I remember him holding my hand during the scary bits and him spilling his Trophy bitter when Ben Gardner's head rolled out of the submerged boat. The Mayfair cinema had a bar which was quite forward thinking at the time. Oh, and you could smoke as well. Everyone cheered when Brody does the deed at the end (spoiler), blowing Bruce the shark to smithereens. We piled into the Vauxhall Viva and got home, going straight to bed whilst singing the iconic score. In the middle of the night, my brother Big Al sneaked into my bedroom and grabbed my legs, shouting, 'Shark! Shark!' It was traumatising. I slept again when I was 9.

We went to Presto supermarket the next day still talking about the movie.[4] On the shelf was the *Jaws* game where you had to retrieve objects from a plastic shark's mouth before it snapped shut. We begged my dad for it but it was too expensive.

My dad was a great man. He saved and presented us with the Game of Jaws at Christmas that year. We were elated. It was like a horror version of Buckaroo.

In 1985 I started learning the double bass. First tune? You know it!

When I think of the film *Jaws* today, I think of my dad. Him holding my hand. Loving the moment – his warmth and humour. When working with teachers, I sometimes show a clip of the movie – maybe the shark cruising below the *Orca*. I tell them the story of the cinema trip, the game, the Christmas. I remind them that to many chil-dren, they are the significant adults; the most important grown-ups the children know. Metaphorically, they hold children's hands in the way my dad held mine.

As a lad growing up, cinema became the route out of drudgery for me. I'd get lost in black-and-white Universal movies, Willis O'Brien's special effects in 1933's *King Kong*, Amicus and Hammer films, and the *Moviedrome* series on the BBC. Nerd-level

---

4 A long-disappeared supermarket chain that was taken over by Safeway, who then became Morrisons. You're welcome, supermarket fans!

knowledge of movies got me through my degree and my PGCE back in the day. It got me through my probation year. Cinema even helped me build rapport in class. It supported the development of my teacher persona. Of my stance. Other folk have sport, food, gardening and the like. I've got my movies. What have you got?

The other day, in the attic, I stumbled upon the Game of Jaws in all its plastic 1970s glory. It's nostalgia – kitsch, I know. But it's so much more. When I look at it, I feel my dad's hand touch mine.

Movies, like a lot of culture, are an attempt to reflect back to us our humanity and the various states of the world we occupy. Books, art, dance, theatre and music – they all do it. I think teaching and _how_ we teach does this job as well. As teachers, we're a reflection of the world we want our children to be in receipt of. And I want a world where people are bothered. So I throw these movies out and say to you – here is the world; the past, the present and the future. Other worlds, small worlds, big worlds, beautiful worlds, frightening worlds, all worlds, our world.

When writing, I'm constantly drawn to movies as the punctuation marks of my own life and experience. It's a collision of the personal and professional. And when I think of classes long gone, the children that occupied them – faces smiling or faces grim – play in my head as movies. They're my stars of old. Touchstones of a professional life lived and personal heart marked. Real people now walking in the world but who are forever young in my mind's eye, like fast-moving 35 mm film, laughing, blurring, looking serious, breathing, optimistic, thoughtful and ready. I hope they read this book. Like the movies I've listed here, they're an important part of my life and will be preserved forever.

The Kid (1921)

Charlie Chaplin could make me laugh and make me cry. And this is one of his best.

Bride of Frankenstein (1935)

This film is where you realise Karloff's monster is not the villain.

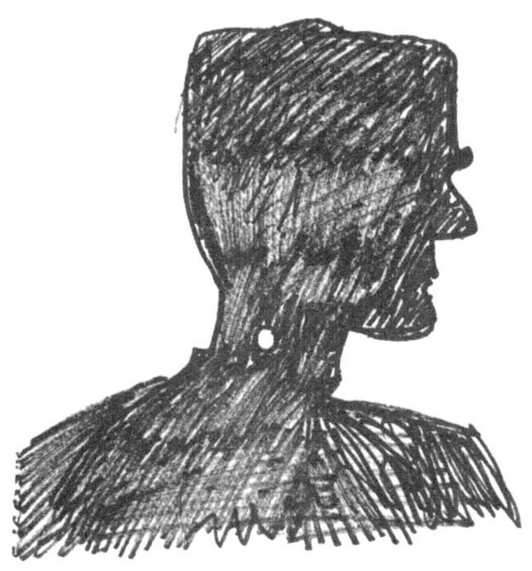

The Wizard of Oz (1939)

A montage of childhood Christmases, cake and pop. And my dad's pipe smoke. And the scarecrow is my inspiration.

Casablanca (1942)

Bogart. So cool. But it's Claude Rains who ticks the boxes. What a dude.

To Kill a Mockingbird (1962)

A sublime adaptation of Harper Lee's classic. Another stalwart in our house. 'Hey Boo!'[5]

Kes (1969)

BBC2 broadcast this at 6 p.m. one midweek night in the mid-1980s. My dad sat me down just before it started and said, 'You need to watch this.' He was right. Everyone needs to watch it. God bless Ken Loach, Lynne Perrine, Brian Glover, Colin Welland, Barry Hines, Tony Garnett, Freddie Fletcher, Dai Bradley, Chris Menges, John Cameron, Barnsley; the whole damn lot of them.

---

5   *To Kill a Mockingbird*, dir. Robert Mulligan [film] (Brentwood Productions, 1962).

Kelly's Heroes (1970)

The film that introduced me to Donald Sutherland. In this he plays an incongruous hippie called Oddball. In school the next day, we were all Oddball. 'Why don't you knock it off with them negative waves? Why don't you dig how beautiful it is out here? Why don't you say something righteous and hopeful for a change?'[6]

The Wicker Man (1973)

Edward Woodward's realisation that he's been set up. It's an unforgettable film with so many moments that shock, thrill and impress. The story behind the film is almost as great as the movie itself. And the music, oh the music. Summer is a-comin' in.

Don't Look Now (1973)

Donald Sutherland and Julie Christie with Nic Roeg's eye and Pino Donaggio's score. Sublime. I tried showing it to a few mates in the late 1980s but they couldn't concentrate because of Donald's haircut. Some people, eh?

---

6 *Kelly's Heroes*, dir. Brian G. Hutton [film] (Metro-Goldwyn-Mayer Studios Inc., 1970)

Young Frankenstein (1974)

I actually do need breathing equipment to help me with my breathing when I'm watching this classic. As a kid, I didn't want to be Han Solo, I wanted to be Gene Wilder.

The Godfather: Part II (1974)

De Niro and Pacino before they appeared in *Heat* (1995) and, er, *88 Minutes* (2007). It also features a brilliant turn from John Cazale.[7] This is one of those films they tell you to watch. Watch it.

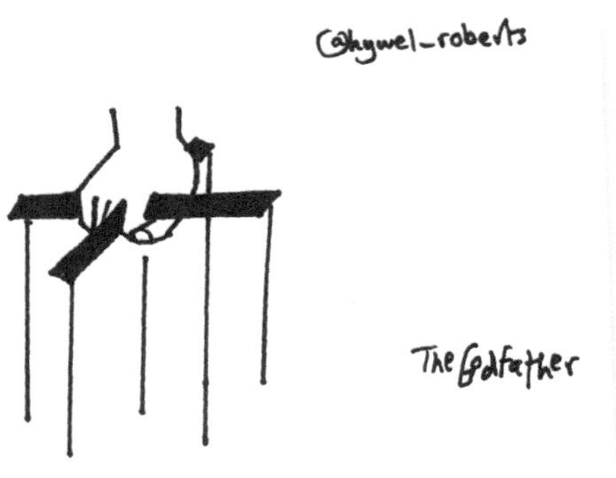

The Rocky Horror Picture Show (1975)

Tim Curry emerging from a lift with a cocky grin, surly welcome and an unforgettable tour de force that burns onto your retinas. The definition of showstopping. I met Tim Curry in 2021. I said to him, 'We're huge fans of yours in our house,' and he replied, 'I hope you've got a big house.'

---

7   John Cazale's last film was *The Deer Hunter* in 1978. He was ill on set, dying of cancer. The studio found out and wanted him kicked out. Michael Cimino, the director, and leading actor Meryl Streep threatened to quit. They filmed his scenes early. He died shortly after filming was completed. He was 42.

The French Connection II (1975)

The first one is outstanding. I could not believe the ending. No spoilers here, but this one picks up straightaway and features Gene Hackman going loco at the hands of a granny drug dealer. It's mint.

Jaws (1975)

Quint: 'Cage goes in the water, you go in the water. Shark's in the water. Our shark.'[8] Three men in a boat redefine the blockbuster.

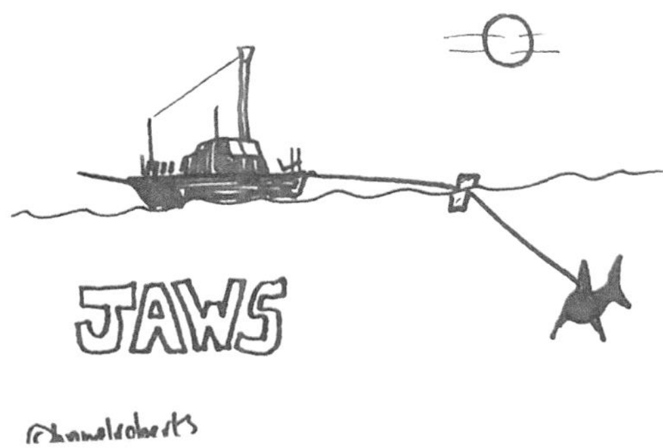

The Omen (1976)

David Warner is in this, and he's cool. Can film music be scary? Er, yes. Don't lose your head.

---

8   *Jaws*, dir. Steven Spielberg [film] (Zanuck/Brown Productions, 1975). I'm ready now to write my teacher book *JfL: Jaws for Learning*. I'm just waiting for that phone to ring.

Close Encounters of the Third Kind (1977)

I love Richard Dreyfuss in *Jaws*, and I _really_ love him in this. Spud mountain.

Star Wars (1977)

It's *Star Wars*, innit? Second-best *Star Wars* movie of the entire franchise.

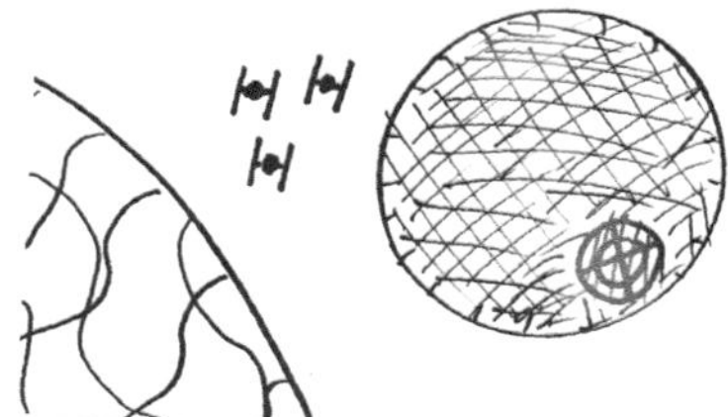

Alien (1979)

I watched this on repeat, alongside *Southern Comfort*, instead of revising for my O levels. It's a slow burn, and brilliant for it.

Monty Python's Life of Brian (1979)

Me, Big Al, Chris and Richard laughing our socks off listening to the vinyl version of this movie in Richard's bedroom circa 1981. I was one of those irritants who knew the dialogue off by heart. Performing 'Always Look on the Bright Side of Life' during assembly at my Church of England secondary school in 1987 is a great source of rebellious pride.

Murder by Decree (1979)

Look, I love Peter Cushing, Benedict Cumberbatch and Basil Rathbone as Sherlock Holmes as much as the next bothered movie nerd, but Christopher Plummer _nails_ it in this brilliant, understated mash-up of Conan Doyle and the Victorian 'Jack the Ripper' identity conspiracy.[9] It's also got Donald Sutherland in it.

....

9   John Neville and Peter Cook were also decent Sherlocks.

The Fog (1980)

Ghost ships, fog and a worm-riddled sea captain pushed me to the edge. Just great atmosphere and a cool spook story. 'That's Blake's gold.'[10]

Southern Comfort (1980)

There's trouble on the bayou as blank-shooting national guardsmen fall foul of local backwoods folk. Ry Cooder's nailing the soundtrack and I'm holding the grubby VHS box in my 15-year-old hands instead of revising for my O levels.

The Empire Strikes Back (1980)

Me in the back of the car having seen this on the big screen. It's November 1980. I'm crying because I'm desperate to watch it again, but we have to go home. The AT-ATs. Boba Fett. Han Solo's winter coat.

The Long Riders (1980)

Made at a time when the western genre was box office treacle, the cowboys in this all wear really cool coats. Me and my dad got a couple of similar ones and wore them to our local in the early 90s like a right couple of weirdos.

An American Werewolf in London (1981)

Rik Mayall, David Scholfield and Brian Glover are regulars in Lila Kaye's Yorkshire boozer, the Slaughtered Lamb. In walk two American backpackers. The rest is cinematic history.

---

10 *The Fog*, dir. John Carpenter [film] (Embassy Pictures, 1980).

The Elephant Man (1981)

Anthony Hopkins' tears as he sees the deformed John Merrick for the first time. David Lynch has a field day with post-*Eraserhead* visuals.

The Monster Club (1981)

This little-known anthology movie was outdated by the time it was released. It's really a nostalgia trip with the familiar faces of Vincent Price and John Carradine rocking up and dancing to some disco. There's also zombies, vampires and death by whistling. And if that doesn't pique your interest, I don't know what will. See also *The House of Long Shadows* (1983) where Price and Carradine are teamed with Peter Cushing and Christopher Lee.

Raiders of The Lost Ark (1981)

A rollicking pulp adventure with absolutely everything you could possibly want in a movie. If you don't like this film, you may well be dead.

Time Bandits (1981)

It's got David Warner in it (again), and he's well cool. And Sean Connery. And Shelley Duvall. And Michael Palin. And David Rappaport. It's a proper romp.

Eye of the Needle (1981)

Donald Sutherland as a murderous Nazi spy holding out on a remote Scottish island, getting his heart melted by Kate Nelligan. It's old fashioned and the cinematic equivalent of a cup of tea.

The Thing (1982)

Me and my brother, Big Al, round at Mark Appleton's house watching this on VHS. It's 1983. I love it. It's aliens and horror. I'm buzzing. We then watch the original *Friday the 13th* and I fail to sleep for the next week.

Blade Runner (1982)

Harrison Ford with a shaved head. Rutger Hauer as a renegade robot having an existential crisis. Vangelis nailing a dreamy 'futurescape' score. I had no idea what was going on until I read the Marvel comic book adaptation.

Local Hero (1983)

As mentioned in Intermission #3. This is a film of beauty and warmth. You can feel the sand between your toes. 'I'll make a good Gordon, Gordon.'[11] And Denis Lawson is mint.

Psycho II (1983)

Richard Franklin made this belated sequel to the Hitchcock classic on the back of his cult classic *Roadgames*, which starred a post-*Halloween* Jamie Lee Curtis, daughter of Janet Leigh – Norman Bates' shower-murder victim in that original frightmare. I loved watching this on repeat. It was another alternative to revising. I was more bothered about movies than learnin'.

---

11 *Local Hero*, dir. Bill Forsyth [film] (Goldcrest Films, 1983).

Trading Places (1983)

'Beef jerky time!'[12] Dan Ackroyd stealing a salmon whilst drunk, Jamie Lee Curtis chewing gum, Eddie Murphy blowing people's minds and Denholm Elliott, a classic British actor, clearly having a brilliant time.

A Nightmare on Elm Street (1984)

A genuine film of horror. Not yet a quip-spouting joker, Freddy Kreuger chills and terrorises with low-budget ease.

The Company of Wolves (1984)

David Warner is in this, and he's cool. There's also a brilliant werewolf transformation sequence. The Little Red Riding Hood tale zapped back to its grim roots via Neil Jordan and Angela Carter.

Splash (1984)

Big Al and I loved watching this on Sunday afternoons. We both loved Daryl Hannah, of course, but also adored John Candy and that young buck, Tom Hanks. There's a scene where Hanks and Candy play squash. Candy has a velour tracksuit and carries a lager. Brilliant.

Paris, Texas (1984)

'I knew these people … these two people …' [13] Harry Dean Stanton doing a monologue in a movie where not a lot happens, but you're emotionally crushed by the end. Like a dishcloth through a mangler.

---

12 *Trading Places*, dir. John Landis [film] (Paramount Pictures, 1983).
13 *Paris, Texas*, dir. Wim Wenders [film] (Road Movies Filmproduktion, 1984).

Back to the Future (1985)

We all wanted to be Marty McFly, didn't we? Released in summer 1985, it didn't hit VHS (therefore, your house) until April 1986. Check that out!

Brazil (1985)

Ace actor Jonathan Pryce escapes his life somewhere in the twentieth century by day-dreaming himself a flying white knight in shining armour. It's bonkers and brilliant.

Pretty in Pink (1986)

'Blane? His name is Blane?'[14] Harry Dean Stanton effortlessly stealing the show.

Stand by Me (1986)

'Two for flinchin'!'[15] An elegy to loss of innocence and a farewell to childhood. I used it with my GCSE English classes a few times. There's a bit where *Jaws'* Richard Dreyfuss sits in his pick-up reminiscing that always manages to break my heart.

Blue Velvet (1986)

It was like being hit in the face with a saucepan watching this for the first time. It ignited my love for cult movies, fostered a respect for indie films and turned Dennis Hopper into my poster boy. The actor Dennis Hopper, not Frank Booth, the nutter he plays in this.

14 *Pretty in Pink*, dir. Howard Deutch [film] (Paramount Pictures, 1986).
15 *Stand By Me*, dir. Rob Reiner [film] (Columbia Pictures, 1986).

Aliens (1986)

The universe expands for the *Alien* follow-up, respecting the original and upping the ante with multiple monsters. 'Game over, man!'[16]

The Mission (1986)

Jeremy Irons can be ice cold but in this glorious film, he warms up, playing the conscience of De Niro's guilt-ridden slaver. And you'll all recognise Morricone's score from that wedding you went to.

Withnail and I (1987)

I met Richard E. Grant at a book signing in Leeds. He was lovely. It was 1997 and he couldn't believe that people were only just discovering this classic. 'I don't advise a haircut, man. All hairdressers are in the employment of the government. Hair are your aerials. They pick up signals from the cosmos and transmit them directly into the brain. This is the reason bald-headed men are uptight.'[17]

The Untouchables (1987)

Costner, Connery, Garcia and the little fella, Charles Martin Smith, get their picture taken looking all hard and then get taken down by De Niro's Al Capone. All to the classic soundtrack of later Morricone.

Angel Heart (1987)

I had a Harry Angel (Mickey Rourke) t-shirt that I wore to death at university. This is a great Alan Parker movie. And another scary score, this time from Trevor Jones – all voodoo drums and snapshot movie dialogue.

16 *Aliens*, dir. James Cameron [film] (20th Century Studios, 1986).
17 *Withnail and I*, dir. Bruce Robinson [film] (Cineplex Odeon Films, 1987).

The Princess Bride (1987)

'As you wish.'[18]

Midnight Run (1988)

Charles Grodin is great as the on-the-run accountant pursued by Robert De Niro's heart-to-be-melted bounty hunter. It's really sweary and better for it. And Joe Pantoliano (*The Matrix* and *The Sopranos*) nearly steals the show as Eddie, De Niro's boss. 'See you in the next life, Jack.'[19]

Die Hard (1988)

A Christmas movie with Alan Rickman. Bruce Willis' wife, played by Bonnie Bedelia, is named 'Holly' and folk still deny it's a Christmas film.

Dead Poets Society (1989)

See elsewhere in this book. Me and Craig at the Mayfair cinema, Whitefield, Manchester, 1989. I wanted to be carried on the shoulders of inspired young people.

Field of Dreams (1989)

Ray Liotta emerging from the corn. 'Is this Heaven?' … 'It's Iowa.'[20]

The Fisher King (1991)

Jeff Bridges' washed-up shock jock assuages guilt by helping crackers modern-day knight Robin Williams find the Holy Grail in New York City. Terry Gilliam nails it. Everyone nails it, including Mercedes Ruehl – a fantastic actor we don't see enough of.

---

18 *The Princess Bride*, dir. Rob Reiner [film] (20th Century Studios, 1987).
19 *Midnight Run*, dir. Martin Brest [film] (City Light Films, 1988).
20 *Field of Dreams*, dir. Phil Alden Robinson [film] (Universal Pictures, 1989).

The Silence of the Lambs (1991)

People were screaming in the cinema when I saw this. It was a game changer. Everyone said it was a psychological thriller. It's a horror movie, people!

JFK (1991)

Oliver Stone's epic with career-best Costner and a host of outstanding actors from the 1980s and early 1990s. And Donald Sutherland.

Reservoir Dogs (1992)

Tim Roth messing up the back of the car with his own blood. Stealers Wheel, Harvey Keitel getting a taco, a gunpoint standoff, Michael Madsen singing in your ear and Quentin Tarantino blowing the bloody doors off indie cinema.

Jurassic Park (1993)

The last film I took my mum and dad to see at the pictures.

Schindler's List (1993)

Because it's *Schindler's List*.[21]

The Shawshank Redemption (1994)

The Stephen King novella brought to spectacular life. Me and my mate went to the cinema and we were the only ones there.

THE SHAWSHANK
REDEMPTION

Fargo (1996)

The woodchipper. 'You're darn tootin'!'[22] I just love films set in the snow. This is a chuffin' Frances McDormand classic.

Brassed Off (1996)

The great Pete Postlethwaite shines in this wonderful tribute to the Yorkshire coal fields and the brass bands that populated them. I congratulated PP on his performance in this film when I met him at a urinal at an ice cream parlour in Cornwall. He was very gracious.

---

21 I studied Thomas Keneally's book *Schindler's Ark* at A level, buzzed because I'd already read his *The Chant of Jimmie Blacksmith*. It taught me a lot. I was 17.
22 *Fargo*, dir. Joel Coen and Ethan Coen [film] (PolyGram Filmed Entertainment, 1996).

Twin Town (1997)

From Lily Allen's uncle Kevin: Rhys Ifans and Llyr Ifans wreak havoc around Swansea in a brilliantly funny and tasteless critically disappointing movie that I love.

Con Air (1997)

Nic Cage with the *best* character name ever: Cameron Poe. Come on! Peak 1990s.

Saving Private Ryan (1998)

Hanks. The soldiers doing a sweepstake on what he does for a living. He's their boss. Eventually, he reveals his civvy-street trade to them. You know what it is, don't you?

Black Hawk Down (2001)

City warfare made real by Ridley Scott. A host of familiar faces adds to the wrought drama and realism. War today, as always, is hell.

The Lord of the Rings trilogy (2001–2003)

It's a Christmas stalwart franchise in our gaff. Peter Jackson epitomised botheredness in his masterful retelling of the Tolkien classics.

Dog Soldiers (2002)

Sean Pertwee always lifts the spirits when he turns up in a movie, and what a great shift he puts into this joyous werewolf rollercoaster. Great premise, crackling script and truly frightening monsters.

Dead Man's Shoes (2004)

The revenge movie reimagined in Derby with a Citroën Dolly. A masterclass performance from Paddy Considine as a steel-eyed soldier and lost soul.

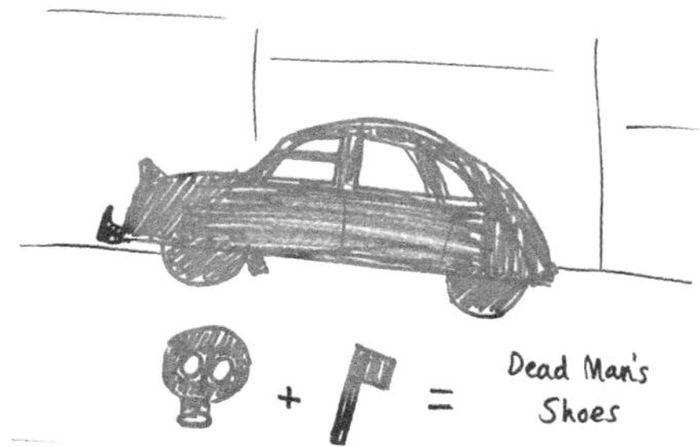

There's a list then. I might not have your favourites on here, so go and make your own list and share it back to me. The trailers for all these great movies can be found here: https://tinyurl.com/26yw4yyx.

I put a post out on that Twitter. It read:

I know movies aren't everything, but …

(Please complete the sentence for a thing I'm doing. Much appreciated!)[23]

23 Hywel Roberts (@HYWEL_ROBERTS), Twitter post (20 February 2022, 6.22 p.m.). Available at: https://twitter.com/HYWEL_ROBERTS/status/1495463951974506512.

Here are some of the responses:

I know movies aren't everything, but they can be. ♡ *#lovemovies*

They're as close to time travel as we can get … And as close to real travel as lots of people get. My friend's nan used to say she had travelled the world from her armchair …

I can't imagine life without them.

You'd have to imagine life without them

The best ones sure as hell remind you what it means to be human and that there is hope and wonder.

They are a good way to escape reality ☺

They unlock a door into a hidden world.

They can tell you a story in 2 hours that you will remember for the rest of your life.

Movies can be entertaining, educational, inspirational, make you think, make you laugh, make you cry, scare you and allow you to completely forget about your own life for 2 hours. A brilliant score/soundtrack for me is what makes a movie so much more than just a movie. #Jaws

They are definitely my favourite waste of time!

You had me at 'movies'.

They have the power to move us, and that's everything …

They're about everything.

I know films aren't everything, but they connect you to people and your past like nothing else. Memories of watching special films with my grandma for example.

I know movies aren't everything, but familiar ones can provide a huge source of comfort when you are struggling.

They have the ability to draw every conceivable emotion out of you in the space of a couple of hours – or send you to sleep!

They help us forget the bad and think of the good – especially when they are so bad they're good!

They help us not just see the world but feel the world.

All this energy and talk of movies and their importance. This has basically been a chapter about *passion*. And this is why, I hope, teachers will never be replaced by robots.

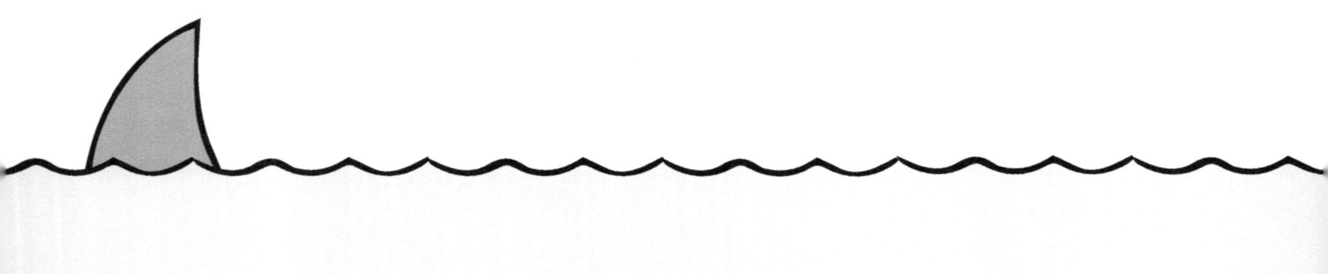

CHAPTER 12

OVER THE RAINBOW

I shall take the heart ... for brains do not make one happy, and happiness is the best thing in the world.

The Tin Man, *The Wonderful Wizard of Oz* (Baum, 1958, 31)

In 1998, for the *Wizard of Oz* listing on the TV network Turner Classic Movies, listings writer Rick Polito wrote: 'Transported to a surreal landscape, a young girl kills the first person she meets and then teams up with three strangers to kill again.' Polito's listing quickly became the most celebrated and amusing summary of a movie and spawned hundreds of copycat rebrands of well-loved movies.[1] I used to use the listing as part of my whole-school training events as a way of introducing the idea of perspective and how we could both be looking at the same thing but be seeing something totally different. Teaching, as discussed elsewhere in this book, is complex and incredibly subjective. In Chapter 3, I cited Ian Menter's paradigms of teaching, with the transformative teacher being the gold standard. I should, at this point, quote that great orator Billy Bragg: 'The temptation / To take the precious things we have apart / To see how they work / Must be resisted for they never fit together again'.[2] This is a decent warning to anyone who thinks that teaching as an endeavour can be broken down into bullet points on an A4 sheet of paper; when we get to a point where we're gaslit into believing that children will thrive in environments of posture-led learning,[3] and told (in England, at any rate) that there are only a small number of approved classroom approaches; where novice teachers are manhandled into believing that 'delivering' packages of knowledge is the same as teaching, and where government-approved

1   See https://ew.com/article/2012/10/26/wizard-of-oz-movie-description/: 'Talking lion befriends a warthog and avenges father's death' (*The Lion King*), 'Boy left to fend off robbers after parents abandon him' (*Home Alone*) and many more! It's a game you can play with yer mates!
2   Billy Bragg, 'Must I Paint You a Picture?' *Workers Playtime* [song] (Go! Discs, 1988).
3   For more on the debate around posture-led learning, see Morgan (2020).

education remora fish[4] shill the pedagogy of poverty for the price of a premium INSET day; where the professional imagination, the gathering of *phronesis*, the pursuit of professional impact and, of course, botheredness are dismissed as somehow trivial. And yet these latter ideas of imagination, wisdom, impact, stories, stance and pedagogy are probably some of the reasons we became teachers in the first place.

> But, for goodness' sake, don't look at these crazy hippy concepts, look over here instead! Look! Don't think! Here, drink this shiny research we've found for you. Here, feast on these stats we have about reading. Look! Listen! Don't speak! Don't think! Don't imagine! We'll do that for you! We'll look after you. Come and deliver.

We are more than this, are we not?

Just as a reminder for you, should you need it, here are four key elements to living a happy, fulfilled teaching life, unobscured by the nonsense distractions of external entities:[5]

1. Intellectual prowess

Knowing our stuff. Placing the acquisition of knowledge at the centre of what we do whilst ensuring we do not get seduced by terms such as 'knowledge rich'.[6] We're all passionate about our subjects. We want to know more about them. We want to find out things we can pass on. This subject knowledge – this critical knowledge – gives us, and the children we work with, momentum to move forward. To keep moving forward. To be architects of pasts, presents and futures. To be road builders towards the horizon. If we're science teachers, let's aspire to create scientists. If we're history teachers, let's create historians. If we teach physical education, let's help create healthy

---

4 'The shark and remora relationship benefits both species. Remoras eat scraps of prey dropped by the shark' (North Shore Shark Adventures, 2019).

5 By 'nonsense distractions' I mean the kind of stuff that can get teachers' knickers in a twist on social media, usually kicked off by someone who can't actually hold down a teaching job writing a dog-whistle post to wind everyone up.

6 How long have you taught? You've been interested in knowledge-rich teaching for that long. Add a bit more on, if you like.

and happy people, including those with a lifelong interest in participation. If we teach … you get the drift. Intellectual prowess is about a hunger for knowing more about your subject, your children, your setting, your job, your self. It's nurturing your botheredness.

2. Relational warmth

Knowing the middle ground. Being the radiator, not the drain. Understanding and recognising difference. Showing optimism and the ability to offer solutions. For humans, some days are easier than others. Botheredness thrives in a world where people are open to change and are seeking unity and fairness. Relational warmth is about being a trusted adult. It's about being a teacher.

3. Professional courage

This book is nearly done, and you can be on your way. As a result of reading it, what will you do next? What will you think next? A good model for reflecting at this point is this:

- What do I already do?

- What has resonated?

- What could I do next?

- What do I need to let go of?

Acting on what I've shared with you might well be an act of professional courage. Frankly, finding the time to read an education book is brave when you have a million and one other things demanding your attention. But to *act* on something you have read, written by someone you may have never met, that is a Herculean effort. Like intellectual prowess and relational warmth, it's something that can be continually developed and modelled to students. It's botheredness in action. It's no accident that in his piece 'The importance of academic courage', Ron Berger (2017) talks about maths teachers modelling courage to their students by sharing their own mathematics stories – how as students themselves, they navigated mistakes, misconceptions and confusions, and used courage to overcome so-called 'maths scars'. 'It's hard to overestimate the value of courage,' writes Berger, ' – this broader vision of courage – in education.' Try things out. When they do not work or go wrong, reflect. Try not to blame the method or the class, or yourself. Just consider what needs tweaking. That is an act of professional courage.

4. Self-care

Go home on time. You're no good to anyone if you're quite simply surviving. That survival mode we can find ourselves stuck in – a rut of treacle – can erode our botheredness and pour bile on teaching, our setting, our colleagues, our children and young people, and the love we felt for the job when we started. Seek a healthy tribe, ideally in real life, but there are great groups of people you can connect with on social media, of course. For my own self-care, I really try to curate my 'friends' and 'followers' carefully. It's because I'm brittle. Someone really took umbrage with an ill-written response from me on Twitter recently. I tried to explain myself, but they were having none of it. I had a sleepless night. I'm not kidding. That's how thin-skinned I am. We are all different, so that's a good enough reason to look after yourself and seek help if you're struggling.[7] We can also help our colleagues. As school leaders, we need to find our healthy tribes as well. We're all in it together, aren't we?

A way of remembering these four lenses that support the whole principle of botheredness is thinking about the key players in *The Wizard of Oz*.[8]

Intellectual prowess

The Scarecrow: The desire to know more, to think, to learn, to lead – and to do so with sensitivity and compassion.

Relational warmth

The Tin Man: The oil in the machine; the heart and soul of the space they occupy, touching the hearts and minds of others as they go.

7   See https://www.educationsupport.org.uk/get-help/help-for-you/helpline/.
8   See https://oz.fandom.com/wiki/Category:Oz_Book_Characters.

Professional courage

The Lion: A 'yes' person rather than a 'no' person. Someone who trusts their instincts, listens to their hunches and is willing to give it a go.

Self-care

Dorothy: Absolutely rooted in the real world. And sometimes just wants to go home. Nice line in shoes.

Print off the picture. Stick it on your desk. Remind yourself of who you are.

Someone who is bothered.

A CONCLUSION OF SORTS

CAPTION:

INTERMISSION #5

Tales of a Travelling Teacher

A reverie of professional learning misadventures

Becky, two seasons and the wardrobe

The fog clears and here we are.[1]

The autumn

It's primary team planning time at the SEMH school and pupil referral unit in Barnsley. We've successfully implemented our new vision for a curriculum over the last two terms and since September, things have been going well. We're now thinking about the run up to Christmas with our Key Stage 1 cohort. We want a book – that's easy and lots to choose from – and we'd like to focus on the change of seasons with the associated science work. As we sit chewing our Sharpies, staring at our brainstorm/thought-shower/ideas-vomit sheet, Christmas seems so far away.

The pace of the day-to-day in this setting is full-time full throttle. As a mainstream secondary teacher, I hadn't really thought about these 'special' settings much at all, but once I find myself in one on a regular basis, I'm genuinely awestruck at the resilience and professionalism of these adults, not to mention the mettle of the children in their

---

1 This section was first published in Roberts (2018).

care. In the classrooms I see relationships being honed and managed, as well as a curriculum being personalised and delivered for the kids in the room. I also witness good humour and warmth: the classrooms are oases for a lot of these children, the work is rich and, from my own humble point of view, I feel I'm really contributing.

We stare at the blank sheet as the October rain hits the windows with a depressing thunderous monotony. Then Dan, a gent who has given his life to the place, and has the wrinkles to prove it, says one word:

Narnia

… and we are off!

The room fills with the strangely attractive scent of Sharpie pens as we scribble down possibilities and I find myself coming into my own. What areas of the curriculum does *The Lion, The Witch and The Wardrobe* reach out and touch? This is one of my standard planning questions when dealing with a hook or a stimulus. The answer to the question is: *a lot*. And we scribble, laugh, reflect and then scribble again. The plan is forming. Winter is coming, and it'll be alright.

Sophie, a brilliant recently qualified Key Stage 1 teacher, starts talking about immersive environments and Dan's head theatrically hits the desk in a kind of I-Can't-Take-It-Anymore declaration.

'No,' he moans, 'please, no!'

'YES!' Sophie and I respond, in unison.

'We need a wardrobe,' I suggest.

'A what?' Dan asks, one of his craggy cheeks still glued to the desk.

'British Heart Foundation furniture shop at Town End roundabout. They'll have one,' offers Sophie.

'We'll need an old 'un,' replies Seth, a very agreeable support teacher, as he retrieves one of the school's minibus keys from his pocket.

'Yeah,' I concur, 'one that's haunted, forgotten and non-Ikea.'

Ninety minutes later, we are all back in the planning room, our presence dwarfed by a massive old wardrobe. To be fair, it's ghastly.

'Have we checked inside for skeletons?' I ask.

'Chuff me,' mutters Dan.

'Don't worry, Dan,' says Sophie, cheerfully, 'it'll soon be Christmas.'

The winter

Simply put, the wardrobe becomes more than just a wardrobe. And the classroom becomes more than a classroom. In their study of 'Ice Worlds', Sophie, Dan and the children gradually transform the classroom into a frosty kingdom of fake snow drifts, polar bears and penguins. The role play area has swamped the classroom and the vibe is great.

So, what about the wardrobe? Well, despite Dan's subtle mock-exasperation at my suggestions, they follow them to the letter:

- The doors of the wardrobe are removed and 'made magical' by the children who etch their names into them under the guidance of Alex, the Key Stage 4 design and technology whizz. They also create the image of a castle on one of the doors. When the doors are refitted, the wardrobe front looks like something from, well, a magical story.

- Unbeknownst to the children, the back panel of the wardrobe is removed and the structure made safe.

- Old coats, donated by staff, are hung on the rail inside the wardrobe.

- The wardrobe is placed in front of the classroom door – the entrance to the Ice World.

So, to enter the classroom, these sometimes angry, often vulnerable and seeking-to-be-understood little people have to open the doors and walk *through* the wardrobe. I'm there, in class, watching the children come through the hanging coats, wide-eyed and excited. It's magical and I'm finding the whole experience strangely moving as the children ask if they can go out and come in again!

And then little Becky Potter emerges, coats swinging on their hangers in her wake.

Becky Potter, a powder keg of emotion and wit, all 7 years of her.

'How long's that chuffin' staying there?' she asks, in her colourful South Yorkshire twang, shaking her head.

Dan, Sophie and I crack up.

'That's just what the caretaker said to me this morning,' whispers Sophie in my ear.

Becky Potter takes her seat and proclaims, 'Is it Christmas yet?'

'Soon,' Dan replies, smiling, and repeating, 'soon, Becky'.

And the fog descends.

Becky Potter will be about 17 years old today. And even though she might not remember me, I'm thinking of her. I hope she's okay. I hope it's working out for her and the world isn't as cold as it sometimes can be.

I hope she has a very merry Christmas. She's my very own ghost of Christmas past.

AFTERWORD

Some helpful terms

I'm not trying to turn everyone into teachers of drama but if you've got this far, you'll have seen that story, stance and pedagogy – the ingredients that make up *Botheredness* – are rooted in the 'getting up and thoughtfully doing' aspects of the classroom.[1] This is not a definitive list of drama conventions but a good place to begin.

Authentic fake

Creating a prop that looks the business. For example, the letter from the king that has been tea-bagged. If you know what I mean.

Conscience alley

The children form an archway by creating two lines and joining their hands. A character from the story they're exploring who is perhaps having to make a difficult decision, walks through the archway. The children offer advice and points of view to the character.

Flashback

Something that we've encountered in the narrative we're exploring is retold; an event from the past is replayed.

Freeze frame

See 'Still image'.

1　Check out John Somers' 2015 'Making the case for drama' presentation online at: https://slideplayer.com/slide/12845215/.

Hot seating

The interviewing of a person from inside the story that is being explored.

'Let's say'

Setting a scene by suggesting a time, a place and who we might be. A way of protecting children into thinking about knowledge contextually.

Role on the wall

There are variations of this, but here's what I do: draw the outline of a gingerbread man on a sheet. This represents the person we're thinking about. Fill the inside of the outline with what we already know and then write questions we have for the person on the outside of the outline. It's a good way of capturing a character – their motivations, emotions, hopes, worries and dreams.

Scene painting

Pointing to places in the classroom and suggesting images that support the establishing of a fictional and imaginary place.

Still image

Using their bodies, children create 'photographs' of a moment.

Tableau

See 'Still image'.

Teacher-in-role

The teacher gives information to the class whilst taking the stance of being inside the world of the 'Let's say'. Easily done with the words 'I'll speak as …'. No need for accents, exaggeration, pantomime, costume, Oscar performances or tomfoolery. It's the giving over of information and knowledge to the class and saves you spending your Sunday making a PowerPoint.

Thought tracking

A child, having been tapped on the shoulder, speaks their mind inside the context of the story.

Mapping

Using a template, children map out a place, which can then be joined to other templates to create a class map.

Occupational mime

Children mime a job or action that someone does to contribute to their community.

RECOMMENDED HUMANS

Here are some of my go-to edu-texts (they're all really good):

Cowley, S. (2017). *The Artful Educator*. Carmarthen: Crown House Publishing.

Dix, P. (2017). *When the Adults Change, Everything Changes*. Carmarthen: Independent Thinking Press.

Finnis, M. (2021). *Restorative Practice*. Carmarthen: Independent Thinking Press.

Gilbert, I. (2013). *Essential Motivation in the Classroom*. Abingdon: Routledge.

Kidd, D. (2019). *A Curriculum of Hope*. Carmarthen: Independent Thinking Press.

Taylor, T. (2016). *A Beginner's Guide to Mantle of the Expert: A Transformative Approach to Education*. Norwich: Singular Publishing.

Whitaker, D. (2021). *The Kindness Principle*. Carmarthen: Independent Thinking Press.

THE *BOTHEREDNESS* PLAYLISTS

The movie soundtrack – https://open.spotify.com/playlist/18VIJq5lSErl0ZkM9asbwJ?si=c6400e40b1054fa4.

The songs of the book – https://open.spotify.com/playlist/4a8wAIMZloGpPld6xOBDX3?si=6fd73a307d984c8f.

The movie trailer playlist – https://tinyurl.com/26yw4yyx.

BIBLIOGRAPHY

Babauta, L. (2013). Learn to respond, not react, *Zen Habits* [blog] (18 July). Available at: https://zenhabits.net/respond/.

Baum, F. (1958). *The Wonderful Wizard of Oz*. New York: Scholastic Book Services.

Benchley, P. (1974). *Jaws*. London: Book Club Associates.

Berger, R. (2017). The importance of academic courage, *Edutopia* (25 October). Available at: https://www.edutopia.org/article/importance-academic-courage.

Biesta, G. J. J. (2016). *The Beautiful Risk of Education*. Abingdon: Routledge.

Bolton, G. (1979). *Towards a Theory of Drama in Education*. Boston, MA: Longman.

Boris, V. and Peterson, L. (2017). What makes storytelling so effective for learning? *Leading the Way* [blog], Harvard Business Publishing. Available at: https://www.harvardbusiness.org/what-makes-storytelling-so-effective-for-learning/.

Bruner, J. S. (1966). *Toward a Theory of Instruction*. Cambridge, MA: Belkapp Press.

Bury, L. (2013). Noel Gallagher says reading fiction 'a waste of fucking time', *The Guardian* (18 October). Available at: https://www.theguardian.com/books/2013/oct/18/noel-gallagher-fiction-waste-time.

Campbell, J. (2008). *The Hero with a Thousand Faces* [audiobook], narrated by Arthur Morey, John Lee and Susan Denaker. Audible. Available at: https://www.audible.co.uk/pd/The-Hero-with-a-Thousand-Faces-Audiobook/B01BFBYWTM.

Char, S. (2017). How a preschool implements and sustains CREDE practices. M.Ed. thesis, University of Hawaii. Available at: https://ccre.ac.uk/download/pdf/211328831.pdf.

Clegg, A. (1972). Making the whole world wonder. Speech delivered at Bingley College of Education (3 August). Available at: http://www.educationengland.org.uk/documents/speeches/1972clegg.html.

Cooper Davis, P. and Webb, J. (2012). Learning from dramatized outcomes, *William Mitchell Law Review* 38(3): article 4. Available at: http://open.mitchellhamline.edu/wmlr/vol38/iss3/4.

Curran, A. (2008). *The Little Book of Big Stuff about the Brain*, ed. I. Gilbert. Carmarthen: Crown House Publishing.

Daskalovska, N., Gudeva, L. K. and Ivanovska, B. (2012). Learner motivation and interest, *Social and Behavioral Sciences* 46: 1187–1191. DOI:10.1016/j.sbspro.2012.05.272.

Dodge, A. (2014). Teaching as a subversive activity, *HuffPost* (27 August). Available at: https://www.huffpost.com/entry/teaching-as-a-subversive-_b_5724706.

Dweck, C. (2017). *Mindset: Changing the Way You Think to Fulfil Your Potential*. New York: Robinson.

Freire, P. (1995). Preface. In P. McLaren, *Critical Pedagogy and Predatory Culture*. London: Routledge, pp. ix–xi.

Gilbert, I. (2015). *There is Another Way*. Carmarthen: Independent Thinking Press.

Gilbert, I. (ed.) (2018). *The Working Class: Poverty, Education and Alternative Voices*. Carmarthen: Independent Thinking Press.

Giroux, H. (2003). Public pedagogy and the politics of resistance: notes on a critical theory of educational struggle, *Educational Philosophy and Theory* 35: 5–16.

Gobir, N. (2021). How unconditional positive regard can help students feel cared for, *KQED* (25 May). Available at: https://www.kqed.org/mindshift/57646/how-unconditional-positive-regard-can-help-students-feel-cared-for.

Goleman, D. (2008). Hot to help, *Greater Good Magazine* (1 March). Available at: https://greatergood.berkeley.edu/article/item/hot_to_help.

Gottschall, J. (2012). *The Storytelling Animal: How Stories Make Us Human*. Boston, MA: Mariner Books.

Gourneau, B. (2005). Five attitudes of effective teachers: implications for teacher training, *Essays in Education* 13: article 5. Available at: https://openriver.winona.edu/cgi/viewcontent.cgi?article=1085&context=eie.

Gutstein, E. (2012). Connecting community, critical, and classical knowledge in teaching mathematics for social justice. In S. Mukhopadhyay and W. M. Roth (eds), *New Directions in Mathematics and Science Education*, vol. 24. Rotterdam: Sense Publishers. DOI:10.1007/978-94-6091-921-3_15.

Haberman, M. (1991). The pedagogy of poverty versus good teaching, *Kappan* (1 December). Available at: https://kappanonline.org/the-pedagogy-of-poverty-versus-good-teaching/.

Haberman, M. (2004). Can star teachers create learning communities? *Educational Leadership* 61(8): 52–56.

Haberman, M. (2010). Eleven consequences of failing to address the 'pedagogy of poverty', *Kappan* (1 October). Available at: https://kappanonline.org/11-consequences-of-failing-to-address-the-pedagogy-of-poverty/.

Halliday, J. (2018). 'We batter them with kindness': schools that reject super-strict values, *The Guardian* (27 February). Available at: https://www.theguardian.com/education/2018/feb/27/schools-discipline-unconditional-positive-regard.

Harfield, T. (2014). Teaching the unteachable: on the compatibility of learning analytics and humane education, *LAK '14: Proceedings of the Fourth International Conference on Learning Analytics and Knowledge*: 241–245. DOI:10.1145/2567574.2567607.

Hargreaves, D. (1999). Helping practitioners explore their school's culture. In J. Prosser (ed.), *School Culture*. London: SAGE Publications, pp. 48–65. DOI:10.4135/9781446219362.n4.

Hartlep, N. and McCubbins, S. (n.d.). What makes a star teacher? Examining teacher dispositions, professionalization, and teacher effectiveness using the Haberman Star Teacher Pre-screener, Department of Educational Administration and Foundations report, Illinois State University. Available at: https://www.academia.edu/3481195/.What_Makes_a_Star_Teacher_Examining_Teacher_Dispositions_Professionalization_and_Teacher_Effectiveness_Using_the_Haberman_Star_Teacher_Pre_Screener?auto=download.

Hayes, D., Mills, M., Christie, P. and Lingard, R. (2006). *Teachers and Schooling: Making a Difference*. Sydney: Allen & Unwin.

Heathcote, D. (1978). *Collected Writings on Education and Drama*. Evanston, IL: Northwestern University Press.

Heathcote, D. and Bolton, G. (1995). *Drama for Learning*. London: Heinemann Drama.

Heyward, P. (2010). Emotional engagement through drama: strategies to assist learning through role-play, *International Journal of Teaching and Learning in Higher Education* 22(2): 197–203.

Hill-Jackson, V., Hartlep, N. and Stafford, D. (2019). *What Makes a Star Teacher: 7 Dispositions That Support Student Learning*. Alexandria, VA: ASCD.

hooks, b. (1996). *Reel to Real: Race, Sex, and Class at the Movies*. London: Routledge.

Hopkins, D. (2001). *School Improvement for Real*. London: Routledge.

Kidd, D. (2020). *A Curriculum of Hope*. Carmarthen: Independent Thinking Press.

Kleinfeld, J. (1975). Effective teachers of Eskimo and Indian students, *School Review* 83(2): 301–344.

Le Guin, U. K. (1996). 'The Creatures on my Mind'. In *Unlocking the Air and Other Stories*. New York: HarperCollins.

Leeds Beckett (2016). What is a teacher in the 21st century and what does a 21st-century teacher need to know? [video], YouTube (21 March). Available at: https://www.youtube. com/watch?v=SAr_g2dunfA.

Lightfoot, L. (2020). Outstanding primary schools fail Ofsted inspections under sudden rule switch, *The Guardian* (4 February). Available at: https://www.theguardian.com/ education/2020/feb/04/outstanding-primary-schools-fail-ofsted-inspections-under-sudden-rule-switch.

Marsh, L. (1970). *Alongside the Child in the Primary School*. Edinburgh: A & C Black Publishers.

Martello, J. (2001). Drama: ways into critical literacy in the early childhood years, *Australian Journal of Language and Literacy* 24(3): 195–207.

Mele, D. (2005). Ethical education in accounting: integrating rules, values and virtues, *Journal of Business Ethics* 57: 97–109.

Miller, D. (2000). *The Complete Peter Cushing*. London: Reynolds & Hearn.

Milligan, S. (1974). *'Rommel?' 'Gunner who?': A Confrontation in the Desert*. London: Book Club Associates.

Miyamoto, K. (2020). The hero's breakdown journey: Jaws, *The Script Lab* [blog] (24 January). Available at: https://thescriptlab.com/ features/screenwriting-101/12938-the-heros-journey-breakdown-jaws/.

Morgan, J. (2020). Behaviour management: the science behind Slant, *TES Magazine* (25 September). Available at: https://www.tes.com/ magazine/teaching-learning/general/ behaviour-management-science-behind-slant.

Morgan, N. and Saxton, J. (2006). *Asking Better Questions*. Ontario: Pembroke Publishers.

Mulcahey, M. (2013). The 100 greatest VHS horror covers: Part I, *Deep Fried Movies* [blog] (4 November). Available at: https://mattmulcahey. wordpress.com/2013/11/04/the-100-greatest-vhs-horror-covers-part-i/.

North Shore Shark Adventures (2019). The shark and the remora fish – a unique relationship! [blog] (15 April). Available at: https://sharktourshawaii.com/blog/ shark-remora-fish-unique-relationship/.

Ohio State University (2021). Meaningful movies help people cope with life's difficulties: study examined response to films like 'Hotel Rwanda' and 'Up'. *ScienceDaily* (10 May). Available at: https://www.sciencedaily.com/ releases/2021/05/210510104345.htm.

O'Neill, C. (ed.) (2015). *Dorothy Heathcote on Education and Drama*. London: David Fulton Books.

O'Toole, G. (2014). If you don't stand for something, you'll fall for anything, *Quote Investigator* (18 February). Available at: https:// quoteinvestigator.com/tag/alexander-hamilton/.

Pilcher, H. (2020). Do lions purr? *BBC Science Focus* (25 November). Available at: https:// www.sciencefocus.com/nature/do-lions-purr/.

Roberts, H. (2012). *Oops! Helping Children Learn Accidentally*. Carmarthen: Independent Thinking Press.

Roberts, H. (2017a). What to do about the ghost child? The kid who does everything right but stays in the shadows, *TES Magazine* (15

February). Available at: https://www.tes.com/magazine/archive/what-do-about-ghost-child-kid-who-does-everything-right-stays-shadows.

Roberts, H. (2017b). Remembering the inset day that resulted in four rap-based lessons – and the pupil who begged it to end, *TES Magazine* (7 April). Available at: https://www.tes.com/magazine/archive/remembering-inset-day-resulted-four-rap-based-lessons-and-pupil-who-begged-it-end.

Roberts, H. (2018). Meet Becky, my 7-year-old ghost of Christmas past, *TES Magazine* (23 December). Available at: https://www.tes.com/magazine/archive/meet-becky-my-7-year-old-ghost-christmas-past.

Roberts, H. (2019a). Even Queen's copyright team can't stop us now, *TES Magazine* (26 January). Available at: https://www.tes.com/magazine/archive/even-queens-copyright-team-cant-stop-us-now.

Roberts, H. (2019b). Teaching primary was animal magic, compared with secondary, *TES Magazine* (20 May). Available at: https://www.tes.com/magazine/archive/teaching-primary-was-animal-magic-compared-secondary.

Roberts, H. (2020). Hywel Roberts classroom storytelling [video], YouTube (2 April). Available at: https://www.youtube.com/watch?v=mnI1gSN1ki0.

Roberts, H. (2021). Storytelling, teacher talk, pedagogy and investment in learning [video], Facebook (3 March). Available at: https://www.facebook.com/243051666257160/videos/3885805924866355.

Roberts, H. and Kidd, D. (2018). *Uncharted Territories*. Carmarthen: Independent Thinking Press.

RSA (2013). Brené Brown on empathy [video], YouTube (10 December). Available at: https://www.youtube.com/watch?v=1Evwgu369Jw.

Schön, D. A. (1983). *The Reflective Practitioner*. London: Basic Books.

Shepard, B. (2006). Affect, Chicago School of Media Theory (16 October). Available at: https://lucian.uchicago.edu/blogs/mediatheory/keywords/affect/.

Smith, E. (2022). Social imagineering, *Tedium* (20 May). Available at: https://tedium.co/2022/05/20/disney-imagineering-word-history/.

StudioBinder (2020). The best movie taglines – 75 examples and why they work, [blog] (22 March). Available at: https://www.studiobinder.com/blog/best-movie-taglines/.

Tanko, G. (2015). 'Reading and writing the world' with mathematics in a Middle Eastern context, *Learning and Teaching in Higher Education: Gulf Perspectives* 12(2): 51–73. DOI:10.18538/lthe.v12.n2.181.

Taylor, T. (2016). *A Beginner's Guide to Mantle of the Expert: A Transformative Approach to Education*. Norwich: Singular Publishing.

TED (2013). How to escape education's death valley | Sir Ken Robinson [video], YouTube (10 May). Available at: https://www.youtube.com/watch?v=wX78iKhInsc.

Thomas, G. (2011). The case: generalisation, theory and phronesis in case study, *Oxford Review of Education* 37(1): 21–35. DOI.10.1080/03054985.2010.521622.

Tolkien, J. R. R. (1954). *The Fellowship of the Ring*. London: Allen & Unwin.

Welsh Government (2022a). Curriculum design and the four purposes, Curriculum for Wales (10 January). Available at: https://hwb.gov.wales/curriculum-for-wales/designing-your-curriculum/developing-a-vision-for-curriculum-design/#curriculum-design-and-the-four-purposes.

Welsh Government (2022b). Pedagogy, Curriculum for Wales (10 January). Available at:

https://hwb.gov.wales/curriculum-for-wales/designing-your-curriculum/implementation-and-practical-considerations#pedagogy.

Wiliam, D. (2011). *Embedded Formative Assessment*. Bloomington, IN: Solution Tree Press.

Wiliam, D. (2013). Is our school model fit for 21st century schooling? *Redesigning Schooling*. Available at: https://assets.markallengroup.com//article-images/87439/Supp-SSAT-2013.pdf.

Willingham, D. T. (2004). The privileged status of story, *American Educator* (Summer). Available at: https://www.aft.org/periodical/american-educator/summer-2004/ask-cognitive-scientist.

Wisecrack (2013). To Kill a Mockingbird – Thug Notes summary and analysis [video], *YouTube* (18 June). Available at: https://www.youtube.com/watch?v=IntI62LWSJA.

Wragg, E. C. and Brown. G. (2001). *Questioning in the Primary School*. London: RoutledgeFalmer.

Ysgol Bro Gwaun (2020a). Languages, literature and communication policy.

Ysgol Bro Gwaun (2020b). Science and technology policy.

Ysgol Harri Tudur (2019). Expressive arts policy.

Farewell and adieu to you, fair Spanish ladies. Farewell and adieu, you ladies of Spain. For we've received orders for to sail back to Boston. And so nevermore shall we see you again.

Quint, *Jaws*[1]

---

1 *Jaws*, dir. Steven Spielberg [film] (Zanuck/Brown Productions, 1975).

BOTHERED
Silver Wolf 2:
The Beast
Inside
DKN

ABOUT THE AUTHOR

Hywel Roberts got taken to the cleaners by 14-year-olds as a novice English teacher in 1992. He's learned a lot since then.

His award-winning book *Oops! Helping Children Learn Accidentally* (2012) has proved very popular with educators around the world and now is a feature on the reading lists of many teacher training courses. His book *Uncharted Territories* (2018) is written with Dr Debra Kidd. Hywel has also contributed fiction to a prison-based literacy reading programme developed by the Shannon Trust. Hywel is also a fellow of the Royal Society of Arts, his favourite film is *Jaws* and he plays double bass in a beat combo called Vest and Pants.

Connect with Hywel here:

Twitter – @Hywel_Roberts   Facebook – @Createlearninspire

Instagram – @hyweleilianwyn

If you'd like to book Hywel for your event, go here:

Independent Thinking –
https://www.independentthinking.co.uk/associates/hywel-roberts/

Create Learn Inspire – www.createlearninspire.co.uk

Mr Roberts

Oops!

Helping children learn accidentally

ISBN: 978-178135009-6

Whether you're new to teaching or have vast experience, you will find in this book inspiration to raise achievement, improve behaviour and enhance creativity in the classroom; and you will change the way you approach lesson planning forever.

This book is about engaging learners in great learning. It's about the dance that happens behind positive engagement – the cool moves and steps a teacher needs to choreograph in order to create a context where great learning can happen – and about the importance of relationships in engagement and how rapport can be learned. The book also shines a spotlight on the role of the teacher and how he or she can do the right things to get the absolute best from students.

Some of the best learning takes place when, rather than imposing on young people a pre-determined curriculum, you find the stimulus that is relevant and engaging for them and build from there. Then the curriculum starts to emerge in a way that simply hooks students into learning almost despite themselves. There is nothing for them to push against ('What's the point?!', 'This is boring …!') as they have helped shape the direction of the lesson in a way that makes it real and useful to them. All this without them even realising what is going on!

They have been 'lured into learning' and the process is shared with teachers in this book, with examples as to how it can be done and how the author has done it. Reading this book will support teachers in developing ideas that motivate everybody in the classroom, from infants to secondary and beyond.